CAMBRIDGE LIBRARY COLLECTION

Books of enduring scholarly value

Linguistics

From the earliest surviving glossaries and translations to nineteenth-century academic philology and the growth of linguistics during the twentieth century, language has been the subject both of scholarly investigation and of practical handbooks produced for the upwardly mobile, as well as for travellers, traders, soldiers, missionaries and explorers. This collection will reissue a wide range of texts pertaining to language, including the work of Latin grammarians, groundbreaking early publications in Indo-European studies, accounts of indigenous languages, many of them now extinct, and texts by pioneering figures such as Jacob Grimm, Wilhelm von Humboldt and Ferdinand de Saussure.

A Grammar of the Somali Language

Somali is one of the Cushitic family of languages spoken in the horn of Africa and the official language of Somalia. This practical grammar, published in 1905, was prepared by J. W. C. Kirk, who first leant to speak the language during his service with Somali troops during the British Empire's failed attempt in 1902–4 to wrest control of the region from the Dervish state under Muhammad Abdullah Hassan. His unique knowledge of the interior of the country and the different tribes making up the population meant that Kirk's insights were invaluable in advancing scholarly knowledge in the West. Perhaps as importantly, Kirk also records a number of literary examples with his translations of Somali stories and songs. Another appendix explores the dialects of the Midgan (or Madhiban) and Yibir, both minority tribes who kept their languages secret from mainstream Somali society.

Cambridge University Press has long been a pioneer in the reissuing of out-of-print titles from its own backlist, producing digital reprints of books that are still sought after by scholars and students but could not be reprinted economically using traditional technology. The Cambridge Library Collection extends this activity to a wider range of books which are still of importance to researchers and professionals, either for the source material they contain, or as landmarks in the history of their academic discipline.

Drawing from the world-renowned collections in the Cambridge University Library, and guided by the advice of experts in each subject area, Cambridge University Press is using state-of-the-art scanning machines in its own Printing House to capture the content of each book selected for inclusion. The files are processed to give a consistently clear, crisp image, and the books finished to the high quality standard for which the Press is recognised around the world. The latest print-on-demand technology ensures that the books will remain available indefinitely, and that orders for single or multiple copies can quickly be supplied.

The Cambridge Library Collection will bring back to life books of enduring scholarly value (including out-of-copyright works originally issued by other publishers) across a wide range of disciplines in the humanities and social sciences and in science and technology.

A Grammar of the Somali Language

With Examples in Prose and Verse, and an Account of the Yibir and Midgan Dialects

J.W.C. KIRK

CAMBRIDGE UNIVERSITY PRESS

Cambridge, New York, Melbourne, Madrid, Cape Town, Singapore,
São Paolo, Delhi, Dubai, Tokyo, Mexico City

Published in the United States of America by Cambridge University Press, New York

www.cambridge.org
Information on this title: www.cambridge.org/9781108013260

© in this compilation Cambridge University Press 2010

This edition first published 1905
This digitally printed version 2010

ISBN 978-1-108-01326-0 Paperback

A GRAMMAR

OF THE

SOMALI LANGUAGE

CAMBRIDGE UNIVERSITY PRESS WAREHOUSE,

C. F. CLAY, Manager.

London: AVE MARIA LANE, E.C.

Glasgow: 50, WELLINGTON STREET.

Leipzig: F. A. BROCKHAUS.

New York: THE MACMILLAN COMPANY.

Bombay and Calcutta: MACMILLAN AND CO., Ltd.

A GRAMMAR

OF THE

SOMALI LANGUAGE

WITH EXAMPLES
IN
PROSE AND VERSE

AND AN ACCOUNT OF THE
YIBIR AND MIDGAN DIALECTS

BY

J. W. C. KIRK, B.A.,

KING'S COLLEGE, CAMBRIDGE,
LIEUTENANT, DUKE OF CORNWALL'S LIGHT INFANTRY,
AND 6TH (SOMALILAND) BATTALION, KING'S AFRICAN RIFLES

CAMBRIDGE
AT THE UNIVERSITY PRESS
1905

Cambridge:

PRINTED BY JOHN CLAY, M.A.

AT THE UNIVERSITY PRESS.

PREFACE.

THERE are but few people who have made any serious study of the many and interesting tongues of that part of the African Continent in which the Somali race has grown up. Our knowledge of the Somali language is due to the labours of Rigby, Hunter, and Larajasse and Sampont. As this is not a written language, great praise is due to those who first grappled with the difficulty of reducing the speech to writing This has now been done so satisfactorily that I myself have lately carried on a successful correspondence with an educated Somali in his native tongue, using the spelling and orthography of the present book. Schleicher's work is rather a philological treatise on the language, gathered largely from isolated individuals of the people, and not from practical acquaintance with the race in their own country ; but he is to be congratulated on having collected a number of stories which are a useful and important foundation to a Somali literature. Paulitschke's work is a purely comparative treatise on the three dialects, Somali, Gala, and Danakil, written from an ethnological point of view.

While serving with Somali troops during the campaigns of 1902 –1904 against the Mullah, Mohammed Abdallah, I had the most favourable opportunities for a practical and wholesale study of the colloquial dialect of this people ; and it seemed only right that results obtained from so intimate an acquaintance should not be left unrecorded, in spite of the many imperfections which must still exist in the record. The work done by others hitherto has been largely confined to the coast and to the mixed population which assembles at the sea-port towns; and it is but recently that any strangers except a few sportsmen have been able to dwell in the interior, and so to know and converse with the natives in their own homes and natural surroundings. The result is that it has now been possible to correct and add to our knowledge, hitherto incomplete, on certain grammatical points, and to give their proper value to certain variations of speech. I refer especially to such peculiarities of the language as the Syntax of the Suffixes, Particles, Verbs, Concord of Nouns, and Compound Sentences. It is generally found to follow very clear and defined, though unwritten, rules, which are disturbed by very few exceptions.

In regard to Orthography, where I have differed from Schleicher and from Larajasse and Sampont, I have given the latters' corresponding signs in the Alphabet. In the spelling of words I have in most cases (subject to the orthographical variations) followed that used by Larajasse in his Dictionary, which leaves little room for improvement or addition. This book is indispensable to the student of Somali, or to anyone who wishes to examine the stories and songs given by Schleicher or myself. I have therefore not included a vocabulary, as such are necessarily deficient and frequently misleading.

In 1903 I published a small practical hand-book, *Notes on the Somali Language*, but this was written on lines totally different from those of the present *Grammar*. It was a compilation of notes which I had found useful to myself, and was intended to serve as an elementary guide to beginners, who had not the time to digest a more lengthy work. The orthography, the spelling, and the few grammatical rules, have since been entirely revised and corrected.

I desire to express my grateful appreciation of the assistance rendered me by Mr H. J. Edwards, Fellow and Assistant Tutor of Peterhouse, Cambridge, and by Mr R. R. Marett, Fellow and Tutor of Exeter College, Oxford, in revising the whole of the present work, in manuscript and proof: Professor E. G. Browne kindly suggested some improvements in the Introduction. I acknowledge with gratitude and admiration the promptness shown by the officials and staff of the Cambridge University Press, in completing against time a work involving unusual difficulties of composition and proof-reading.

J. W. C. K.

SEVENOAKS,
December, 1904.

CONTENTS.

PART I. ORTHOGRAPHY.

PART II. ACCIDENCE.

PART III. SYNTAX OF SIMPLE SENTENCES.

PART IV. SYNTAX OF COMPOUND SENTENCES.

EXAMPLES OF PROSE AND VERSE.

THE DIALECTS OF THE OUTCAST TRIBES, MIDGAN AND YIBIR.

BIBLIOGRAPHY.

RIGBY, Lieut. C. P., "On the Somauli Language"; Transactions of the Bombay Geographical Society, Vol. IX, 1849.

HUNTER, Capt. F. M., A Grammar of the Somali Language; Bombay, 1880.

CUST, R., The Modern Languages of Africa; London, Trübner & Co., 1883.

SCHLEICHER, A. W., Die Somali-Sprache; Berlin, 1892.

PAULITSCHKE, Dr Philipp, Ethnographie Nordost-Afrikas; Berlin, 1896.

LARAJASSE and SAMPONT, Practical Grammar of the Somali Language; London, Kegan Paul, Trench, Trübner & Co., 1897.

LARAJASSE, Somali-English and English-Somali Dictionary; London, Kegan Paul, Trench, Trübner & Co., 1897.

SCHLEICHER, Dr A. W., Somali-Texte (edited by Leo Reinisch); Vienna and Leipzig, 1900.

These are the most important works upon the language, though other writers are also quoted by Paulitschke.

ERRATUM.

§ 15 (*b*). *for* warm, warming *read* warn, warning.

INTRODUCTION.

SOMALI is the language spoken by the inhabitants of the square tract of country, known as the Horn of Africa (*Regio Aromatifera* of the ancients), which lies between the French port of Djibouti, Cape Guardafui and the river Juba. This country was formerly inhabited by a people, now known as Gala[1], who have been steadily driven inland by Mohammedan propagandists, who call themselves Somali. The neighbours of the Somali are the Danakil on the north, the Abyssinians, speaking Amharic, on the north-west, and the retreating Gala on the west and south-west. The languages of the Somali and the Gala are quite distinct, and mutually unintelligible, but possess so many fundamental characteristics in common, that there is ample evidence of their close relationship, even if it can not be proved that modern Somali is actually derived from Gala. There has always been considerable trade between the inhabitants of Aden and Southern Arabia and those of the Somali coast, and the Semitic element in Somali is sufficient proof of the local tradition that the present Somali race had its origin in a Mohammedan colonisation from Southern Arabia.

If we compare the vocabularies of the three languages, Arabic, Gala and Somali, we find many words having a root common to all three, such as the Somali words, **aba** father, **wil** boy, **faras** horse.

The majority of words common to Arabic and Somali are found to be technical or legal terms, or names of utensils or articles of commerce not native to the country. These are obviously borrowed

---

[1] **Gàl** (of which the plural is **Gàlo**) is the name used generally to denote infidels, i.e. those who are not Mohammedans, and may be used by Somalis, without any disrespect, to include English, Abyssinians or others as well as those former inhabitants who would not embrace the faith preached by the Mohammedan missionaries, and to whom the name is now specially applied.

direct from the Arabic and have no bearing on the relationship of the languages. But in a few Somali verbs the Arabic root can be recognised, such as, **ghad** take, carry; **akhri** read; **ibi** sell, buy; **gajo** be hungry.

On the other hand a large number of words in ordinary use are common to Gala and Somali, but are not of Arabic origin. These have simple and elementary meanings, and include many verbs.

Such are,

arag	see	**nin**	man
eg	look	**dig**	blood
jir	be	**if**	light
gal	enter	**af**	month
dùl	attack	**arrab**	tongue
	der	long	

The Somali numerals are common to Gala, except *one, six, ten* and *a hundred*, and are all quite different from the Arabic.

In regard to the structure of the language, the most striking features are the *Suffixes*, with their generic linking consonants, the use of the *Definite Article* and its concord with noun and adjective (the latter is comparable with the declension of the German adjective), the *Negative Conjugation* of verbs, and the *Particles*. In all these points Somali resembles Gala, but apparently has little or no resemblance to Arabic, except in the particles.

All three languages employ similar inflexions in the persons of the verb conjugation, but in the two former, as in Arabic, prefixes are not used, except in the five irregular Somali verbs.

Example,

wan imi	I came
wad timi	thou camest
wu yimi	he came
wei timi	she came
weinu nimi	we came

The regular forms being as follows :

wan shega	I tell
wad shegta	thou tellest
wu shega	he tells
wei shegta	she tells
weinu shegna	we tell

The Semitic element is also exemplified in the guttural and aspirate sounds, which correspond to the Arabic letters Ghain, 'Ain, and Ḥa; and in the form and concord of plural nouns, which largely resemble the Arabic broken plurals.

The Bantu languages, which are prefix languages, seem to have nothing in common with Somali, either in construction or vocabulary.

There are certain slight variations in the speech of different tribes, which almost constitute different dialects. The most notable are the Ishhak, Dolbohanta, Mijjertein and the Esa and Gadabursi.

For instance :

	Ishhak	Dolbohanta
camel	aur	rati
road	dau	jid
go	tag	ad
the saddles	koryashi	koryalki

A Dolbohanta will say **wa dònahaya** (I want), pronounced by the Ishhak as **wa dòneya** or **wa dònaya**. "I want" is translated by **wa dòneya** in Bari, **wa dònaya** in Galbed

Practically all the men I have served with have belonged to the Ishhak section, and in this book it is the everyday speech of these people which is presented, while words and forms which are not familiar to them, but are used by Dolbohanta and others, have been avoided. The Ishhak almost entirely inhabit the British Protectorate, and their speech may therefore be taken by Englishmen as the standard form of the language.

Within the Ishhak there are slight variations again in accent, phrases and idioms, of no great importance. These depend chiefly on geographical distribution.

In the East (*Bari*) the common forms for the personal pronoun are **ban, bad, bu**, etc., while in the West (*Galbed*) they are represented by **yan, yad, yu**, etc.

The *Midgan* and *Yibir* dialects are quite apart. These are dialects spoken by two outcast and homeless tribes living among the Somalis, and are now published for the first time, having hitherto been kept a secret even from the Somalis themselves. They are discussed in full at the end of this book.

Finally, with regard to speaking the language, the mode of speech is that of all Eastern people, like the language of the Bible. Sentences are split up into strings of short simple remarks, with numerous copulative particles, and expressions meaning, "and so," "and then," "he said," etc. In a narrative, after each remark the speaker pauses, when the listener is expected to answer with some suitable expression of assent, such as **Kôdi**, or **Haiye**.

Correct pronunciation is most important, and as there are no definite rules for the accentuation of syllables I have had to use accents freely all through the book. The Somali is not a polite person, and though extremely good-natured he is quite outspoken, and has no hesitation in ridiculing one's false quantities or concords, that is to say, if one's efforts are at all recognisable to him. He expects a high standard of accuracy, chiefly because he is unaccustomed to hearing a European endeavour to grapple with his language, but this has the advantage of not allowing the stranger to form too favourable an idea of his own skill.

PART I. ORTHOGRAPHY.

1. In reducing the Somali language to writing, we are faced by the fact that there is no written language. Many educated Somalis write Arabic, but, so far as the writer is aware, they have never attempted to write their own language either in Arabic or any other characters. Nor would it be possible to employ the Arabic characters to represent Somali sounds. The list of Arabic consonants is too elaborate, whilst the three vowel-signs are insufficient, a great variety of vowel sounds being an important peculiarity of the Somali language.

According to Hunter the alphabetical signs for Urdu contain all the necessary elements, but he and all others have agreed to adopt the Roman characters, for obvious reasons.

The alphabet that is used here, so far as it is applicable, is that recommended by the Royal Geographical Society in "Hints to Travellers," with the addition of two extra signs for the Arabic Aine (ع) and the cerebral d (Sanskrit ड), which are represented respectively by the inverted comma ', and đ, as in the grammar published by Larajasse and Sampont. The double hh is employed to represent the Arabic Ha (ح). Accents are also employed freely to express the different values of the vowels.

2. The Alphabet.

ă, a, ā	= Arabic "fatha," or ا	g	= Arabic	ق
b	,, ب	gh	,,	غ (L. & S. ḫ)
d	,, د, ذ	h	,,	ﻫ
đ	Sanskrit ड	hh	,,	ح
	(half d, half r)		(L. & S. ḥ)	
e, ē	as in Latin languages	i, ī	,,	ـِ
f	= Arabic ف	j	,,	ج

k	= Arabic	ك		*u, ù* = Arabic	'
kh	„	خ		*w*	„	و
l	„	ل		*y*	„	ي
m	„	م		'	„	ع
n	„	ن				
o, ò, ó	„	'		*Diphthongs.*	
r	„	ر		*ai*	
s	„	س		*ei*	
sh	„	ش (Schl. š)		*au*	
t	„	ت		*oi*	

There is no doubt a double *l* (according to Hunter, the Sanskrit ॡ), but it is so seldom used (as in lehh = six) that it is not necessary to have a separate sign. The same remark applies to the Arabic ذ, which occurs in some Somali words, and is commonly used in Yibir.

Vowels.

3. The following accents are used to represent the different values of vowels :—

˘ and ^ are only used with special forms of *a* and *o* respectively.

The grave accent, ` , is used to express the long drawn sounds of each vowel.

The acute accent, ´ , is only used to denote the syllable upon which the accentuation should fall, and may therefore vary in the same word in different contexts or forms ; it is to be understood that this accent does not alter the length or value of the vowel in any way.

4. a corresponds to the Arabic "fatha" and has a nondescript sound, as the *u* in "bun," "sun," or the *a* in "balloon" :

badan	many
ban	plain
dab	fire

ă is pronounced like *a* in "rat," "ham," but is not a common sound :

wanăksan	good
răg	men
kăleh	other
shălei	yesterday

à is long as in "father," "mast" :

> sàn   skin
> dàr   stone building

e is pronounced like *e* in "pen," "fell" :

> hebel   a certain man
> sheg   tell

Before cerebral d *this has almost the value of* u, *as in English* "*fur.*" *Example,* hed *tie.*

è is like the vowels of "fate," "weight," "fare" :

> adèr   uncle
> habèn   night
> gènyo   mare
> gèd   tree

i is short as in "pin" :

> mid   one
> illin   entrance

Care must be taken to pronounce i *with exactly this value before* r, *as* y *in* "*tyranny,*" *and not as in English* "*fir*" :

> bir   iron
> jir   be

ì is like *ee* in "feel," "seem" :

> ʿìd   sand
> dìr   trees
> lìn   orange

o is short as in "on," "cot" :

> kol   time
> ʿoll   army
> ghor   write

ò is quite long as in "foal," "sole" :

> dòn   wish
> gòb   a kind of fruit
> gòl   lioness

ò This is represented by Larajasse and Sampont by *ow*, which, however, seems liable to confusion with the English diphthong

ou. It has a very long drawn out hollow sound like a gasping
" Ohh ! "

đô	near
ilô	forget
madô	black

u is pronounced as in "full," "put" :

Before r *it must retain the same value and* not *be pronounced like
the English "fur."*

gur	pick up
kun	thousand
kulul	warm

ù is long and full as *oo* in "fool," "rule" :

gùr	start to march
fùd	soup
fùl	ride

5. DIPHTHONGS.

ai is pronounced as in "aisle," or "fire" :

ain	sort, kind

ei is pronounced like "feign," but in this case the *i* is sometimes
almost heard :

weidi	ask
samei	make

Note. In many words it is hard to distinguish whether the diphthong
is the one or the other of these, the common *a*, or "fatha," and *e* being so
much alike when preceding another vowel. Thus this work differs from
that of other writers in that the past terminations of verbs, and the
Continuative tense inflexions are spelt with an *e*, instead of *a*, the former
being to the writer's ear distinctly the sound produced by the tribes he
has been in contact with.

au is like the English diphthong in "how," "hour," but with a
round full sound almost like "ao" :

aur	camel

oi very seldom occurs, but where it does it is exactly the same
as in English :

hoi!	an exclamation

Note. The above diphthongs may occur before another vowel, in which case *i* becomes *y*, and *u* becomes *w*:

laya	slay ye (**lai-a**)
wa tégeya	I am going (**tegei-a**)
wa samèya	I make (**samei-a**)
biláwa	dagger (**bilau-a**)
goya	cut ye (**goi-a**)

6. VOWEL CHANGES.

When two vowels occur in succession they may both be pronounced separately and distinctly, in which case the second vowel is marked with the diæresis, ":

aï	curse
baän	badtempered
eï	dog

More commonly the hiatus is avoided (*a*) by elision, (*b*) by the use of the semi-vowels **y, w,** (*c*) by the insertion of some consonant.

(*a*) Elision is the suppression of one of the vowels, and takes place especially before the pronouns which are attached as suffixes to the preceding word.

Examples,	**gorti-u**	becomes	**gortu**	when he
	hadi-an	„	**hadan**	if I

(*b*) **y** is used instead of **i**, or after **ì**, when preceding a vowel.

Examples,	**wa samèi-a**	becomes	**wa samèya**	I make
	wa sì-a	„	**wa sìya**	I give

(*c*) Consonants are inserted in the case of certain inflexions.

Examples,	**abi-hi**	for	**abi-i**	the father
	madô-ba	„	**madô-a**	the black
	wa ilô-ba	„	**ilô-a**	I forget

When **a** is followed by **i**, it is very frequently changed into **e**, whether a consonant is between or not.

Examples,   **ka'** wake,   awaken **ke'i**
             la i becomes **lei.**

sa' cow,	**si'i**, or **su'u** (for **sa'i, sa'u**) the cow
wan taga I go,	**wan tegeya** I am going
aba father,	**abihi**, or **abuhu** (for **abahi, abahu**)
	the father

7. Consonants.

The consonants are sounded as follows :

Faucals (‘, h, hh).

‘ (aine) is an Arabic sound caused by a sudden contraction of the glottis in place of a hiatus. It is treated like a consonant in all rules as to inflexions, etc. :

‘ab	drink
maga‘	name
la‘ag	money
b‘e‘id	oryx
‘id	sand
lo‘	cows
‘oll	army
‘ur‘ur	forearm

In order to learn the correct pronunciation compare the above with

aba	father
nàg	woman
baan	badtempered
beid	egg
idlad	end, completion
lohh	plank
urur	assembly
ulul	growl

Note. The Aine is a hard letter, and must be followed by the hard form of any other class of consonant in inflexion :

wa ka‘da she gets up
for ka‘ta

h is like the English *h* in "hit," but is scarcely sounded when at the end of a word :

harag sheep-skin
gesiah brave

hh is the long drawn Arabic consonant ; in the middle, or end, of a word it is sounded almost as a whole syllable, but is hardly different from *h* at the beginning of a word :

dehh	middle	(dehh(e))
libahh	lion	(libahh(a))
lehhda	the six	(lehh(e)da)
hhun	bad	

Gutturals (g, gh, k, kh).

g is always hard as in "go."

It most nearly resembles the Arabic ﻕ :

ga'an	hand
gèl	camels

gh is the Arabic "ghain," ﻉ, and must be learned by ear :

ghad	carry
ghor	write
ghànso	bow

k is like the English *k* :

kàli	come here
hakama	bridle

kh is a softer guttural-aspirate than the ghain or gh, and more nearly corresponds to the Scotch *ch*, as in "loch," but is harder than this :

sandukh	box
akhal	house

Note. It is often difficult to distinguish between *gh* and *kh*, the former being softer, and the latter harder than in the true Arabic forms.

Palatals[1] (j, sh, y).

j is a hard *j*, as in English "journey," "John[2]" :

ja'al	like
jòg	stand

sh is like the English, as in "shoot" :

shimbir	bird
sheg	tell

---

[1] These are not found at the end of a word in Somali.

[2] There is no sound *ch*, as in "church," in Somali; the English sound is reproduced by the native as *j*.

y is like the English, as in " you " :

yer small
bìyo water

Dentals (**t, d, ḍ, r, s, l, n**).

t as in English :

tuka crow
tehh shower of rain

d as in English :

wadàn skin pail
durug move

Note. At the end of a word *d* is sounded nearly like *t* :

mid one.

ḍ is a cerebral letter, and, as mentioned above, is of Sanskrit origin.

In the middle of a word it has almost the sound of *r*, but at the beginning, or end, of a word it more nearly approaches *d*.

It is formed by curling the tongue back and bringing it forward along the roof of the mouth :

áḍi sheep
faḍí sit
heḍ tie
ḍan all, complete

r is always pronounced distinctly, like the *r* of Latin languages, as in " arrow " :

ra' accompany
bir iron
shimbirtu the bird

s as in English :

sàn skin
so'o go on
hes song

l as in English :

libahh lion
lìn orange
filfil pepper

n as in English :

> **nàg** woman
> **mindi** knife

Note. **l** and **t**, where they occur in inflexions or suffixes, become **sh**.

> **hashi** the camel, for **hal-ti**
> **wa yesha** thou doest, for **yel-ta**

Labials (**b, m, f, w**).

b as in English :

> **barbar** youth
> **biláwa** dagger
> **albab** door

m as in English :

> **mòd** think
> **dambe** behind

f as in English :

> **af** mouth.
> **iftin** light
> **áfar** four

w as in English :

> **wìyil** rhinoceros
> **walàl** brother

PART II. ACCIDENCE.

THE PARTS OF SPEECH.

8. All languages cannot be arranged on exactly the same system, and, in the Somali Language, the arrangement and definitions which are applicable to the grammar of well-known tongues, such as English or Arabic, will not altogether hold good.

Somali is undoubtedly a simple and elementary language, in which the only true and fundamental parts of speech are

Substantive, Verb, Adjective, Particle,

and it is by various combinations or forms of these that the other generally recognised parts of speech are formed.

9. A *Substantive* is a word describing, or referring to, something which exists, or some object of thought, either material or immaterial.

A *Verb* is a word expressing thought, being, action, or the suffering of action, and affirms or predicates something of some person or thing.

These two parts of speech are complementary and essential one to the other, and in any form of speech both these elements must necessarily occur, unless it is tacitly agreed, to save unnecessary verbiage, that one or the other may be obviously understood from the context, and may be omitted from actual expression.

An *Adjective* is a word which describes or qualifies the object or thought represented by a substantive, according to any known idea of quality, such as colour, size, nature, etc.

A *Particle* is a word which has no meaning in itself and can only occur in conjunction with other parts of speech. It may qualify the meaning of a verb, or it may be "Conjunctive," that is, it may connect, or act as a link between, two expressions or parts of speech.

10. Other parts of speech that occur in more advanced languages are, in Somali, all derived from substantives, or are represented by suffixes.

Substantives may be qualified

　(i)　according to place, context, possessor, etc., by

Suffixes, known as
$\begin{cases} \text{Definite Article,} \\ \text{Demonstrative Adjective,} \\ \text{Possessive Pronominal Adjective,} \\ \text{Interrogative Adjective;} \end{cases}$

　(ii)　according to number, by

　Inflexions.

They include,

　(i)　Nouns (actually descriptive of an object or idea).

　(ii)　Numerals[1] (expressing the abstract idea of a number).

　(iii)　Pronouns (words used to refer to a noun or numeral already expressed, or understood, to avoid lengthy and unnecessary repetition).

Note a. All substantives are recognisable by the fact that they are able to have attached to them the suffixes mentioned above, and may stand alone as Subject or Object to a Verb.

Note b. Nouns and numerals have no declension, nouns alone being inflected in the plural. Personal pronouns have an Objective (or Accusative) form as well as the Subjective (or Nominative).

In addition to the above, there are formed, by the use of a noun alone, or a noun combined with any of the other substantives, with or without suffixes or inflexions, and with or without an adjective,

　(iv)　Adverbs (words expressing time, place or manner, relative to the action of a verb).

　(v)　Relative Conjunctions (words introducing expressions of the same value as the above).

　(vi)　Prepositions (words expressing the relationship of one substantive to another).

　　　　[1] These are undoubtedly treated as Substantives in Somali.

A. Substantives.

11. These will be dealt with in the order given in the classification above, but it is necessary first to describe the Noun itself, its Forms, and Gender, after which will follow the Suffixes, to be followed again by the Plural Inflexions.

The reason of this order will be seen on a perusal of the following pages, as the questions of gender and number are inextricably mixed with those concerning the form of the Suffixes.

1. *Classes of Nouns.*

12. Nouns are classified into Proper and Common.

'Proper' nouns are names of people or places.

The commoner and typical Somali men's names are, **Jàma, Fàrah, Hassan, Hussein, Mohammed, Mahhmud, Ahhmed, Àli, Omar, Nur, Liban, Egal, Duàleh, Abdallah, Abdi, Robleh.**

Nicknames are very common ; in fact nearly everyone, whether Somali or English, is always known by his friends by some nickname, such as, **Gurreh** left-handed, **Farùrah** hare-lipped, **Dunjog** active or "cute," **Bulàli** fair, **Timo-wein** long hair, **Awarah** one-eyed, **Galòs, Dèlowein,** etc., always referring to some feature or eccentricity, but without any idea of disrespect.

13. Common nouns are classed in various ways : according to their Nature they are *Concrete,* or *Abstract,*

according to their Derivation they are Radical, Derivative, or Borrowed,

according to their Gender they are Masculine, Feminine, or Common.

14. *Concrete* Nouns include the names of all animate or inanimate objects, or parts of them.

Nearly all of these are Radical words, or else are borrowed entirely from another language.

(i) *Animate* : **nin** man, **nàg** woman, **wil** boy, **gabad** girl, **libahh** lion, **faras** horse, **aur** camel, **shimbir** bird.

They include collective words, as :

dad people, **răg** men, **dumar** women, **arùr** children, **gèl** camels, **hòlo** flocks, **ghalab, alabo** baggage, kit.

Names of relations :

aba father, **hoyo** mother, **walál** brother or sister, **ínan** son, or daughter, **adèr** uncle.

(ii) *Inanimate* objects are :

wahh thing, **bir** iron, **ghori** wood, **dagahh** stone, **bùr** hill, **mìyi** jungle, **akhal** house.

15. *Abstract* Nouns.

(*a*) Many abstract nouns of action and sense are radical, in which case they are also used as intransitive verbs.

hadal talk, **yab** wonder, **dagàl** fight, **'ur** smell, **hàrad** thirst, **hanòn** pain, **aï** curse, **gabei** chant, **ado** rage.

(*b*) *Verb-nouns*, describing the action of a verb, are formed from the verb-root by the addition of certain terminations :

1st Class (ending in a consonant) add **-nin,** or **-in.**
2nd Class (,, ,, **-o**) ,, **-d.**
3rd Class (,, ,, **-i**) ,, **-s,** or **-n.**

1st Class.

dig	warm	**dignin**	warming
tòl	sew	**tòlin**	sewing, seam
ghor	write	**ghorin**	writing
bòd	jump	**bòdin**	jumping
sug	wait	**sugnin**	waiting
	(*Note* : **fùl** ride	**fùlan**	riding.)

2nd Class.

so'o	walk	**so'od**	walking
nokho	return	**nokhod**	return
garo	understand	**garad**	sense
bahso	escape	**bahsad**	escape
idlo	come to an end	**idlad**	end, completion

3rd Class.

weidi	ask	weidis	question
goi	cut	goïs	cutting, cleft
sì	give	sìn	present
samei	make	samein	construction
safei	clean	safein	cleaning

(c) Abstract Nouns of *Quality* are derived from adjectives, or nouns, and have the following forms :

'ulusnímo	heaviness	from	'ulus	heavy
'ajisnímo	laziness	„	'ajis	lazy
fùlanímo	cowardice	„	fùlei	coward
nàgnímo	womanliness	„	nàg	woman
hoyonímo	motherliness	„	hoyo	mother
'adan	whiteness	„	'ad	white
'asan	redness	„	'as	red
weinan	largeness	„	wein	large
adkan	hardness	„	adag	hard
derer	length	„	der	long
fudeid	lightness	„	fudud	light
'uleis	weight	„	'ulus	heavy
adeig	strength	„	adag	hard, strong

(d) Other radical abstract nouns are those of *Quantity, Time,* and *Place,* some of which are used as Indefinite Pronouns.

in some (quantity)   **ghar** some (number)
gidi, kulli, daman all, whole   **gor, kol** time
màlin, 'asho day   **mel, hag** place

16. *Borrowed* words are chiefly Arabic, many being common to all East African languages.

mes table,   **sa'ad** hour,   **kùrsi** chair,   **sandukh** box,   **bandukh** gun,   **hukum** order,   **askàri** soldier

In **albab** (door), the Somali has taken the Arabic definite article as well, but adds his own article to it :

albabki the door.

Verbs are very seldom borrowed, such as **safei** (clean).

English words are now becoming familiar and naturalised over the whole of our Protectorate, as, kôd (coat), tèbel (table), **sord** (sword), **drabel** (trouble), **ketli** (kettle), **kob** (cup).

2. *Gender of Nouns.*

17. There are no rules determining the gender of a Radical Noun, either according to its meaning or form. It must therefore be learned by practice in the case of each word. This however is not so difficult as it would appear, as the definite article is so much a part of the noun, and the gender is so clearly marked by it, that it is best to learn the definite article with the noun in each case. I shall, therefore, when quoting a noun, give the definite article, separated by a hyphen, as in

nin-ki   man

nàg-ti   woman.

This will imply that

    nin = a man   **nàg** = a woman

    ninki = the man   **nàgti** = the woman.

It will suffice here to say that all Feminine nouns are those which take the dental article, i.e. **-ti** or **-di** ;

While all Masculine nouns are those which take a guttural article, i.e. **-ki**, **-gi**, **-hi**, or in some cases the vowel **-i**, alone.

In both cases the Suffix consists of two parts. The final vowel is the Article Suffix, the consonant is the Linking Consonant.

18. The Derivative and Borrowed Nouns do follow certain determinate rules in respect of gender.

Borrowed words are masculine :

    mes-ki, kùrsi-gi, hukum-ki, sandukh-i, albab-ki, tèbel-ki, kôd-ki, etc.

    Exceptions,   **sa'ad-di**   hour   } are feminine.
               warkhád-di   letter   }

19. Of Derivative Nouns,

    Verbal Nouns in -**in** (1st and 3rd Classes) are Feminine :

       dignin-ti, sugnin-ti, samein-ti, etc.

    Verbal Nouns in -**d**, -**s** (2nd and 3rd Classes) are Masculine :

       so'od-ki, idlad-ki, goïs-ki, etc.

Adjectival Nouns in **-nimo -an** are Feminine.
ʽajisnímo-di, weinan-ti.

Adjectival Nouns of other forms are Masculine.
đerer-ki, ʽuleis-ki, etc.

20.   Names of men and animals may have special forms for each gender :

Examples,

nin-ki	man, husband	**nàg-ti**	woman, wife
aba-hi	father	**hoyo-di**	mother
aur-ki	male camel	**hal-shi**[1]	female camel
sanga-hi	stallion	**gènyo-di**	mare
wan-ki	ram	**sabein-ti**	ewe
orgi-gi	he-goat	**ri-di**	she-goat
àr-ki	lion	**gol-shi**[1]	lioness

21.   Some nouns are of common gender, and vary only in the form of the definite article.

ínan-ki	son	**ínan-ti**	daughter
walál-ki	brother	**walál-shi**[1]	sister

3.   *The Suffixes.*

22.   The Suffixes consist of two parts, namely (1) a vowel termination, or syllable beginning with a vowel, and (2) a linking consonant, connecting the termination to the substantive, and denoting the gender of the word.

23.   The following parts of speech are represented by Suffixes in Somali :

viz.

Definite Article (*the*)	**-i**	**-a**	or	**-u.**
Demonstrative Adjective (*this; that*)	**-an;**	**-as**	or	**-à.**
Possessive Pronominal Adjective.				
(*my, thy, his, her*)	**-ai**	**-à**	**-ìs**	**-èd.**
(*our* (1 and 3), *our* (1, 2 and 3)				
your, their)	**-aya**	**-èn**	**-ìn**	**-òd.**
Interrogative Adjective (*what ?*) ...	**-e P**			

---

[1] In Feminine nouns ending in *-l*, the final *l* and the *t* of the Article are transformed into *sh* ; thus **hashi** the she-camel, for **halti, walàshi** for **walàlti.**

ninki, ninka, or ninku	the man
ninkan	this man
ninkas or ninkà	that man
ninkai, ninkà, ninkìs, &c.	my, thy, his, etc. man
ninke ?	what man ?

The above forms are constant, whether the noun qualified is in the Singular or Plural.

(a) Linking Consonants.

24. The Linking Consonants are peculiar to each noun, and conform to its gender and the final letter of the word.

25. *Masculine* words take the gutturals, **k, g, h.**

Nouns ending in any consonant, except **g**, or a gutt. aspirate, take **k**

„ „ -i or **g** .... „ **g**

„ „ -a .... „ **h**

Note i. Nouns ending in -**h, hh,** or a guttural aspirate, would logically be followed by **h,** but this additional aspirate is hardly to be detected by the ear, and need not therefore be written.

Note ii. With nouns ending in ' no linking consonant is required, unless it be another ', but this again the ear cannot detect.

Note iii. Where the noun ends in **a**, -**ah,** the -**a** is assimilated to the form of suffix vowel which follows, i.e. if the suffix is -i, the a becomes i, if **u,** it becomes **u.**

Examples,

(The suffix is here separated by a hyphen, but it must be remembered that it is not spoken as a separate word, and will not be so written in examples later.)

albab-ki	the door	harag-gi	the sheep-skin.
shabèl-ki	the leopard	ilig-gi	the tooth
sul-ki	the thumb	libahh-i	the lion (i)
san-ki	the nose	sandukh-i	the box (i)
af-ki	the mouth	maga'-i	the name (ii)
mìyi-gi	the jungle	muda'-i	the fork (ii)
askàri-gi	the soldier		

| kòra | a saddle | the saddle | kòri-hi, kòra-ha, or kòru-hu (iii) |
| dayah | a moon | the moon | dayi-hi, daya-ha, or dayu-hu (iii) |

and

(**wáranleh**	a spearman	the s.	**wáranlihi, wáranlahá, wáranluhú**
fardòleh	a horseman	the h.	**fardòlihi, fardálaha, fardòluhu**)

26. *Feminine* words take the dentals **-t** or **-d.**

Nouns ending in any consonant except **d,** or **'**, take **-t.**
" " **-d, -i, -o, '**, or an aspirate, " **-d.**

Examples,

nàg-ti	the woman	**laf-ti**	the bone
làn-ti	the branch	**miyid-di**	the corpse
far-ti	the finger	**sàlo-di**	the dung
ga'an-ti	the hand	**ghorahh-di**	the sun
hal-shi	the she-camel	**warákh-di**	the letter
ri-di	the goat	**Nogàl-shi**	the Nogal

27. In many cases the linking consonant may be omitted, as has been noticed after aspirates, and **'**.

It is also omitted in certain words,

rǎg-i the men
gèl-i the camels

with the simple Personal Pronouns,

an-i, an-a I
ad-i, ad-a thou, etc.

after some of the Possessive Pronominal suffixes,

akhal-kìs-i his house
has-kèd-a her family
dad-kèn-i our people

or after the Demonstrative suffix,

nin-kan-a this man
aur-kas-i that camel

(*b*) *The Definite Article.*

28. It is seen in § 23 that the Definite Article has three alternative forms, the use of which depends entirely on the context of the noun defined.

A short general rule is given here, but the question will be more fully dealt with under Syntax (§ 150, etc.).

"The horse" may be, **fáraski, fáraska,** or **fárasku.**
"The place" „ **meshi, mesha,** or **meshu.**

29. (i) **-i** is the most general form, and is used when **-a,** or **-u,** are not required.

(ii) **-a** is used in the following cases :

(1) when referring to a person or thing actually present in front of the speaker, and is very nearly equivalent to the demonstrative adjective (this), but must not be confounded with the demonstrative suffix **-à** (that) ;

(2) when the noun is used possessively, adjectivally or adverbially.

Examples,
(1)	**sandukha ghad**	take the box (which you see)
	ninka ba òg	the man (i.e. he that is present) knows
	ninka ad árkesa	the man thou seest
(but,	**ninki ad áraktei**	the man thou sawest)
(2)	**ákhalki sirkálka**	the house of the officer
	nin magàloda	a man of the town
	galábta	this evening

(iii) **-u** is used when referring to a well-known, or already mentioned, object or person.

Any definition is supposed to be unnecessary, and therefore **-u** is not employed if the noun is qualified by an adjective, nor is it used with the object of a sentence.

It may be represented in English by the use of "The" or capital letters.

Examples,
Sirkálku	The Officer (as a soldier would refer to his company officer or Commandant)
Wadádku	The Mullah (i.e. Mohammed Abdallah Hassan)
ghorahhdu	the sun
dayuhu	the moon
ròbku	the rain

(c) *The Demonstrative Adjective.*

30. The suffixes are,

-an	this
-as, or -à	that

Examples,

fáras-kan	this horse
fáras-kas	that horse
nàg-tan	this woman
gèd-kas	that tree
sandukh-an	this box
busta-has	that blanket
ha-shan	this camel
magàlo-dan	this town

31. The Demonstrative may be intensified by the addition of the definite article in two ways (cf. § 198):

(i) The definite article **-a** and demonstrative adjective both require linking consonants.

In this case the linking consonant used with the Demonstrative Suffix is always **k** for masculine words, and **t** for feminine words.

Examples,

nínkakan	this man	nàgtatà	that woman
ghórigakan	this wood	mèshatas	that place
dágahhakan	this stone	sanadùkhdatan	these boxes

(ii) The definite article is suffixed to the demonstrative without any linking consonant.

Examples,

ninkàsa	that man	gabaddàsu	that girl
nimánkani	these men	gèdkasa	that tree
ròbkanu	this rain	ínantasi	that daughter

(d) *Possessive Pronominal Adjectives.*

32.

my	-ai- (-gi, or -di)
thy	-à- (-gi, or -di)
his	-ìs- (-i)
her	-èd- (-i)
our	-èn- (-i) (including "you")
our	-aya- (-gi, or -di) (excluding "you")
your	-ìn- (-i)
their	-òd- (-i)

Except when qualifying terms of relationship, as "father," "mother," "husband," etc., the above suffixes require the definite article as well, as given in brackets after each person. Only **-ai, -à, -aya,** however, require the linking consonant, the remainder taking the article without any link.

The linking consonant to the article, when used, is always -g- for masculine words, -d- for feminine words.

	Example, **aur-ki**	camel	
aurkaigi	**aurkaiga**	**aurkaigu**	my camel
aurkàgi	**aurkàga**	**aurkàgu**	thy camel
aurkìsi	**aurkìsa**	**aurkìsu**	his camel
aurkèdi	**aurkèda**	**aurkèdu**	her camel
aurkèni	**aurkèna**	**aurkènu**	our camel
aurkayági	**aurkayága**	**aurkayágu**	our camel
aurkìni	**aurkìna**	**aurkìnu**	your camel
aurkòdi	**aurkòda**	**aurkòdu**	their camel

	aur-ti	camels	
aurtaidi	**aurtaida**	**aurtaidu**	my camels
aurtàdi	**aurtàda**	**aurtàdu**	thy camels
aurtìsi	**aurtìsa**	**aurtìsu**	his camels
aurtèdi	**aurtèda**	**aurtèdu**	her camels
aurtèni	**aurtèna**	**aurtènu**	our camels
aurtayádi	**aurtayáda**	**aurtayádu**	our camels
aurtìni	**aurtìna**	**aurtìnu**	your camels
aurtòdi	**aurtòda**	**aurtòdu**	their camels

With terms of relationship, the definite article is not used after the possessive.

Examples,	**abahai**	my father
	hoyodà	thy mother
	nàgtìs	his wife
	ninkèd	her husband
	adèrkèn	our uncle
	tolkaya	our tribe
	awòwigìn	your grandfather
	walálkòd	their brother

(e) The Interrogative Adjective.

33. "Which?" "What?" are expressed often by the suffix -e ? This suffix is sounded distinctly at the end of the noun, like English "eh?", but must not be pronounced as ei or è.

ninke ?	what man?
sandukhe ?	what box?
gabadde ?	what girl?

This form is most commonly used alone, or with the word **wa** (is), and usually repeats some noun already mentioned.

Examples,   **ninki yimi**   the man has come
        ninke ? or **wa ninke ?**   what man?

4. *The Plural of Nouns.*

34. The only inflexion which nouns undergo occurs in the formation of the Plural.

There are six methods of forming the Plural, and in all except the first (Masculine Monosyllables) the gender is reversed in the process, and the linking consonant, required with the suffixes, is altered from guttural to dental, or *vice versá*.

35. (i) Masculine Monosyllables repeat the last two letters. The masculine, or guttural, linking consonant is retained. In words ending in **-n**, the **-n** becomes **-m**, while the inflexion is always **-an**.

Examples,

dab-ki	fire	plural	**dabab-ki**
fas-ki	axe	,,	**fasas-ki**
ràd-ki	track	,,	**ràdad-ki**
kob-ki	cup	,,	**kobob-ki**
'oll-ki	army	,,	**'oll'oll-ki**
nin-ki	man	,,	**niman-ki**
tin-ki	tin	,,	**timan-ki**
'aïn-ki	belly-band	,,	**'aïman-ki**
sun-ki	strap	,,	**suman-ki**

Exceptions,

rèr-ki	family, household	plural	**rèro-hi**
na's-ki	fool	,,	**na'syo-di**
gès-ki	horn	,,	**gèsas-ki**, or **gèso-hi**
'el-ki	well	,,	**'elal-shi**
bàl-ki	feather	,,	**bàlal-shi**
aur-ki	camel	,,	**aur-ti**
sais-ki	groom	,,	**saisis-ki**, or **saisin-ti**

36. (ii) Nouns ending in **-a,** or **-ei** (all Masculine) change **-a,** or **-ei** into **-yal**, and take the feminine, or dental, linking consonant.

Examples,

kòra-hi	saddle	plural	**kòryal, kòryashi**
busta-hi	blanket	,,	**bustyal-shi**
aba-hi	father	,,	**abyal-shi**

tuka-hi	crow	plural	tukyal-shi
bilawa-hi	dagger	,,	bilawyal-shi
hákama-hi	bridle	,,	hákamyal-shi
odei-gi	old man	,,	odyal-shi
fùlei-gi	coward	,,	fùlyal-shi

Exceptions:

These plurals are used with the masculine, or guttural, linking consonant, by Dolbohanta, and other eastern tribes :

bustyalki, kòryalki, hákamyalki, etc.

37. (iii) Nouns ending in -o (all Feminine) add -in, and take the masculine, or guttural, linking consonant.

Examples,

'asho-di	day	plural	'ashoïn-ki
hoyo-di	mother	,,	hoyoïn-ki
¹gudimo-di	native axe	,,	gudimoïn-ki
dèro-di	gazelle	,,	dèroïn-ki
ghànso-di	bow	,,	ghànsoïn-ki

38. (iv) Masculine Polysyllables (except those under ii) add -o. If the final letter is an aspirate or ', -yo is added.

These plurals take the feminine, or dental linking consonant, the -o being then usually changed to -à.

Examples,

fandal-ki	spoon	plural	fandalo, fandaladi
libahh-i	lion	,,	libahhyo-di
kùrsi-gi	chair	,,	kùrsyo-di
muda'-i	fork	,,	muda'yo-di
muftah-i	key	,,	muftahyo-di
maga'-i	name	,,	maga'yo-di

Exceptions,

dagahh-i	stone	,,	dagahhan-ti
ugahh-i	egg	,,	ugahhan-ti
sibaihh-i	sepoy	,,	sibaihhin-ti
àghil-ki	chief	,,	àghilin-ti, or oghàl-shi
fáras-ki	horse	,,	fardo-hi
ilig-gi	tooth	,,	ilko-di
askàri-gi	soldier	,,	askàrr-ti

¹ The common word now used. But it is originally the plural of an older word **gudin**, which is also used.

gùri-gi	enclosure	plural	gùrio-hi
Yibir-ki	Yibir	„	Yibro-hi
Midgàn-ki	Midgan	„	Midgo-hi

Foreign words often add -yo in other cases than those given in the rule above:

| rakàb-ki | stirrup | plural | rakàbyo-di |
| kitàb-ki | book | „ | kitàbyo-di |

39. (v) Words borrowed from the Arabic usually form their plurals after the fashion of the broken plurals of that language, and take the feminine linking consonant.

Examples,

sandukh-i	box	plural	sanadukh-di
bandukh-i	gun	„	banadukh-di, or banadikh-di
sirkál-ki	officer	„	sirakìl-shi
kùrsi-gi	chair	„	kurási-di
warkhád-di	paper	„	warákh-di
moskhìn-ki	beggar	„	mosakhìn-ti
musmar-ki	nail	„	musamar-ti

40. (vi) All Feminine Nouns, except those in (iii), add o, and take the masculine linking consonant, h.

When the noun is defined the o is assimilated to the form of the article vowel, as in the case of masculine nouns in a.

Examples,

nàg-ti	woman	plural	nàgo, nàgihi, nàgaha, nàguhu
hal-shi	she-camel	„	halo, halihi, halaha, haluhu
mel-shi	place	„	melo-hi
lug-ti	leg	„	lugo-hi
ɖeg-ti	ear	„	ɖego-hi
làn-ti	branch	„	làmo-hi
'alen-ti	leaf	„	'alemo-hi
jòniaɖ-di	bag	„	jòniado-hi
ga'an-ti	hand	„	ga'amo-hi
ri-di	goat	„	riyo-hi
kab-ti	shoe	„	kabo-hi

Exception,

| il-shi | eye | „ | indo-hi |

There exist the following plural nouns, all of which end in **o** and take the masculine article **hi**, and therefore belong to this class.

bìyo-hi	water
'àno-hi	milk
gèdo-hi	grass
timo-hi	hair
hòlo-hi	flocks, property

41. An Intensive Plural, ending in -al, -yal, is used in poetic phraseology.

Example, **Idinku baneyal...dùlan ma bulaten ?**
Have ye over plains and plains gone to war ?
Gerar wa bogholal. Songs are in hundreds.

42. After Numerals the plural form of a noun is not used except in the case of Feminine Nouns of class (vi). In this case **d** is added to the inflexion.

Examples,	2 men	**lába nin**
	4 boxes	**áfar sandukh**
	3 blankets	**sádehh busta**
	7 days	**todòba 'asho**
but,	5 she-camels	**shan halod**
	2 places	**lába melod**
	4 bags	**áfar joniadod**
	9 months	**sagàl bilod**

5. *Cases of Nouns.*

43. There are no inflexions of the noun to represent the Declension ; the cases must therefore be distinguished by position and context. This is not an easy matter, and requires a knowledge of other parts of speech not yet described : it will therefore be left to be discussed under Syntax (cf. § 155).

44. The usual order of a simple sentence is,

(i) Subject, (ii) Object, (iii) Verb.

An Adverb may be placed first of all, or before the Verb.

Examples,

	Subject	Object	Verb
		sandukh	la kàli
		a box	bring
	sirkálku	fáraska	fùleya
	the officer	the horse	is riding
Adv.			
galábta	an	Burao	ghobon dòna
this evening	I	Burao	am going to reach
	harùdki	fáraska	sì
	the jowaree	(to) the horse	give

45. The *Possessive Case* may be expressed in two ways.

(i) The common method is by the use of the Possessive suffix.

Examples,

nin akhalkìsu	a man his house
sirkálku faraskìsa	the Officer his horse
nàgti bokhorkèda	the woman her sash

(ii) The Noun in the possessive case is placed after the noun possessed.

This can only be done where the Possessor is defined by the definite article. The Possessor always takes the suffix **a.**

Example,

ákhalki ninka	the house of the man
not ákhalki ninki	

(nor is it possible to say,   ákhalki nin

for "the house of a man ").

The following are the typical forms :

The horse of the officer	fáraski sirkálka
or	sirkálka faraskìsu
The horse of an officer	nin sirkál faraskìsu
A horse of the officer	fáras sirkálka
A horse of the officer has died	fardaha sirkálka mid ba dintei

(literally, of the horses of the officer one has died).

A horse of an officer	sirkál faraskìsi

6. *Numerals.*

46. *Cardinals,*

1.	(kô-di), mid-ki	16.	léhhyo-tòban-ki
2.	lába-di	17.	todòbyo-tòban-ki
3.	sádehh-di	18.	sidèdyo-tòban-ki
4.	áfar-ti	19.	sagàlyo-tòban-ki
5.	shan-ti	20.	labàton-ki
6.	lehh-di	21.	kôbyo-labàton-ki
7.	todòba-di	22.	lábyo-labàton-ki
8.	sidèd-di		etc. etc.
9.	sagàl-ki	30.	sóddon-ki
10.	tòban-ki	40.	afárton-ki
11.	kôbyo-tòban-ki	50.	kónton-ki
12.	lábyo-tòban-ki	60.	léhhdon-ki
13.	sádehhyo-tòban-ki	70.	todobàton-ki
14.	áfaryo-tòban-ki	80.	sidèton-ki
15.	shányo-tòban-ki	90.	sagàshon-ki
	100.	bóghol-ki	
	1,000.	kun-ki	

47. *Rules for the use of the Numerals.*

(i) The Numerals are placed before the noun they qualify.

(ii) Masculine nouns, and Feminine nouns ending in o are used in the singular.

Feminine Nouns (except those ending in o) add od.

(iii) If the Noun qualified by a numeral is defined by the Definite Article, Demonstrative, or Possessive, the suffix is attached to the numeral and not to the noun, numerals 1—8 taking the dental linking consonant, the remainder the guttural linking consonant, irrespectively of the gender of the noun.

Examples,

lába nin	2 men	sádehh 'asho	3 days
áfar fáras	4 horses	shan kòra	5 saddles
lehh halod	6 camels	todòba jòniadod	7 bags
tobánki askàri		the ten soldiers	
áfarti nin		the four men	
lábadà halod		those two camels	
bógholkaigi adi		my hundred sheep.	

48. (i) **Kô** is only used in counting, and is never used with a noun :

mid is not used to qualify a noun, but is used as an Indefinite Impersonal Pronoun.

one man	**nin**
one (thing) is bad	**mid ba hhun**
one (man) is bad	**nin ba hhun**

(ii) The numerals 19, 29, 39, etc., are usually translated by,

labàton midla	20 minus one = 19
sóddon midla	30 minus one = 29
bóghol midla	100 minus one = 99

(iii) The numerals over 100 are translated as follows :

(iyo = and)

101	**boghól-iyo mid**
102	**boghól-iyo lába**
130	**boghól-iyo sóddon**
146	**boghól-iyo léhhyo-afárton**

(iv) Time in hours is translated by the Cardinal numerals with the Definite Article. (**sa'adod** = hours, may be used.)

3 o'clock	**sádehhda (sa'adod)**
1 o'clock	**kôdi**
half-past 2	**lábada iyo badki**

49. *Fractions,*

a portion	**mel-shi**		
$\frac{1}{2}$	**bad-ki**	$\frac{1}{8}$	**fallad-di**
$\frac{1}{3}$	**dalòl-ki**	$\frac{1}{16}$	**rima-di**
$\frac{1}{4}$	**wahh-di**		

50. *Ordinals,*

first	**kôwad, hòre**	eighth	**sidèdad**
second	**lábad**	ninth	**sagàlad**
third	**sádehhad**	tenth	**tòbnad**
fourth	**áfrad**	eleventh	**kôbyo-tòbnad**
fifth	**shánad**		etc.
sixth	**léhhad**	twentieth	**labàtonad**
seventh	**todòbad**		

These are used like adjectives and follow the nouns they qualify,
but are not inflected.

nin lábad	a second man
nàgti áfrad	the fourth woman
ki léhhad	the sixth

51. *Distributive Numbers.* No special forms are used for
these,

each = **kasta**   every = **walba** (see § 68) ;

but distributive numbers are usually expressed by the particle **ba**
(§ 143 (*e*)).

give 10 each	**nin ba tòban sì**
one by one	**mid mid**
in tens	**tòban tòban**

52. *Periodical Numbers,*

(time	**mar, kol, gor**)
once	**kol, mar**
three times	**sádehh gor**

7. *Pronouns.*

(*a*) *Simple Personal Pronouns.*

(1) *Subjective.*

53. The simple, or Enclitic, forms are :

-an	I
-ad	thou
-u	he
-ai ⎱ **-ei** ⎰	she
-ainu ⎱ **-einu** ⎰	we (inclusive)
-annu	we (exclusive)
-aidin ⎱ **-eidin** ⎰	ye
-ai ⎱ **-ei** ⎰	they

These cannot stand alone in a sentence, but must follow, and be
attached to, some preceding word, which may be any part of speech.

Examples,

gortas-u yiđi	then-he said
¹had'-an imàdo	if-I come
Burao-einu nil	at Burao-we lived
¹ìmis'-ad dònesa ?	how-many-do-you want ?
ninki-an dòneya	the man-(whom)-I want

54. Very often, however, these simple forms are combined with the letters **w-**, **b-**, or **y-** (which represent certain particles, **wa**, **ba**, **ya**) and are then used as separate words.

wan, wad, wu, etc. are forms which may be used at the beginning of a sentence, but are never used in any other position.

ban, bad, bu, etc.⎫
yan, yad, yu, etc.⎭ are synonymous forms, and are interchangeable.

b- is preferred by Eastern and Southern Somalis.

y- is preferred by the Coast, Western and Central tribes.

These forms usually occur immediately before the verb or its particles, but never at the beginning of a sentence (cf. § 236).

55. There are two ways of emphasising the Personal Pronouns, which may be used disjunctively, like the French " moi," " toi," etc. This is done by the addition of the Definite Article.

In both cases the simple form for the third person singular masculine is **is**.

(i) The article suffix is added to the simple form without any linking consonant, thus:

ani	I	adi	Thou	(isi)	He
ana		ada		(isa)	
anu		adu		isu	

These are the only persons which are found in this form.

(ii) The article suffix and linking consonant is added to the last or to the Enclitic forms of the plural.

The **-a** and **-u** suffixes only are used in this case, thus :

ánigu, ániga	I
ádigu, ádiga	Thou
ísagu, ísaga	He
íyadu, íyada	She

---

¹ A final vowel is usually dropped before the personal pronoun, as is shown here by an apostrophe '.

ínnagu,	ínnaga	We
ánnagu,	ánnaga	We (exclusive)
ídinku,	ídinka	Ye
íyagu,	íyaga	They

To translate "I myself" cf. § 190.

56. Another form is produced by the suffix **-na** (and).

anna	and I
adna	and you
isna	and he
iyana	and she
innuna	and we
annuna	and we
idinna	and ye
iyana	and they

57. A compound, "Indicative," form is made by the addition of **wahh** (thing).

wahhan has the meaning of "this is what I..."

These forms are especially used with the verbs "want," "say," "think," "do," but may be used with any verb.

wahhan	this is what I...
wahhad	,, ,, ,, thou...
wuhhu	,, ,, ,, he...
wahhai	,, ,, ,, she...
wahhainu	,, ,, ,, we...
wahhannu	,, ,, ,, we...
wahhaidin	,, ,, ,, ye...
wahhai	,, ,, ,, they...

58. An interrogative form of the same is made with **mahha ?** (what ?)

mahhan... ?	what... I...?
mahhad...?	what... thou...?
muhhu...?	what... he...?
mahhai...?	what... she...?
mahhainu...?	what... we...?
mahhannu...?	what... we...?
mahhaidin...?	what... ye...?
mahhai...?	what... they...?

59. These two forms are used very frequently in introducing questions and answers.

Examples,

mahhad dònesa ? ⎫	**wahhan dòneya,** etc. ⎫
what do you want ? ⎭	I want, etc. ⎭
hagg'eidin takten ?⎫	**wahhannu tagnei,** etc.⎫
where did you go ? ⎭	we went to, etc. ⎭
muhhu yiđi ? ⎫	**wuhhu yiđi**... ⎫
what did he say ? ⎭	he said... ⎭

(2) *Objective.*

60. The *objective,* or oblique, case of the Personal Pronouns has special forms, which are used independently as separate words.

	Simple	Emphatic
me	**i**	**ániga**
thee	**ku**	**ádiga**
him	**u**	**iσága**
her	**ku**	**iyáda**
us	**na**	⎧**innága** ⎩**annága**
you	**idin**	**idínka**
them	**u,** or **ku**	**iyága**

The accentuation of these emphatic forms must be noticed, to distinguish them from the Subjective case.

Examples, **iσága** (Obj.) and **íσaga** (Subj.)
　　　　　　iyága ,, and **íyaga** ,,

61. (iii) The *Reflexive Pronoun* is **iss.**

　　　　　　iss dil kill yourself

This is also used reciprocally :

　　　　　　iss laya slay each other

(b) Possessive Pronouns.

62. These have the same forms as the suffixes (§ 32) with a consonant (**k** masc. **t** fem.) prefixed, and the definite article suffixed, to them (cf. § 199).

	Masc.		Fem.	
mine	**kai-gi,**	**-ga, -gu.**	**tai-di,**	**-da, -du.**
thine	**kà-gi,**	**-ga, -gu.**	**tà-di,**	**-da, -du.**
his	**kìs-i,**	**-a, -u.**	**tìs-i,**	**-a, -u.**

hers	kèd-i	-a -u	tèd-i	-a -u
ours	kèn-i	-a -u	tèn-i	-a -u
ours	kayá-gi	-ga -gu	tayá-di	-da -du
yours	kìn-i	-a -u	tìn-i	-a -u
theirs	kòd-i	-a -u	tòd-i	-a -u

In the Plural, the above prefix ku, tu, instead of k, t, to the suffix, as,

kuaigi, tuaidi, kuàgi, tuàdi, etc.

(c) Demonstrative Pronouns.

63. These also have the same forms as the adjectival suffixes (§ 30), and are used with consonants as above.

	Sing.		Plur.	
	Masc.	Fem.	Masc.	Fem.
this	kan, tan		these	kuan, tuan
that	{ kas, tas		those	kuas, tuas
	kà, tà			

They may be intensified by the definite article, as follows:

sing. **kani, kana, kanu, kasa, tasu, etc.**

plur. **kúakan, túatan, kúakas, etc.**

or **kuani, tuani, kuasi, etc.**

Another form is,

kò, tò   that yonder
kuò, tuò   those yonder

The definite article is used independently as a pronoun in the same way.

ki, ka, ku ; ti, ta, tu.
ki kăleh   the other one
ta wein   the big one

The plur. form is

kuer, tuer

Example,   **kuer 'ad'ada**   the white ones

64.   (d) Relative Pronouns.

None.

65.   (e) Interrogative Pronouns.

(i) Subjective :

who ? what ? **ya** P (sing.)
            kue P (plur.)

ke ? te ? are also used disjunctively in this sense, as the other suffixes.

(ii)   Objective:

whom ?	**ya** ?
what?	**mahha** ? (§ 58)

66. The suffix -ma is used as an interrogative pronominal adjective, but is not included among the other suffixes, as it has not the typical form, but is really the interrogative particle (cf. § 94).

ninma ?	what man ?
gorma ?	when ?
wa sa'adma ?	what hour is it ?

-ma is also used suffixed to the simple personal pronouns, and definite article, meaning " which of ? "

kuma ? **tuma** ?	which one ? (indefinite)
innama ?	which of us ?
annama ?	„
idinma ?	which of you two ?
iyama ?	which of them ?

These are used both subjectively and objectively.

The possessive case is,

yàleh ? **kumàleh** ?   whose ?

(*f*)   *Indefinite Pronouns.*

67.   **la**   one, they, people

(similar to the French pronoun "*on*," in meaning and construction).

This pronoun is used in construction like any simple personal pronoun.

The following euphonic alterations take place when any simple pronoun or particle follows :

la i	becomes	**lei**
la u	„	**lo**
la ku	„	**lagu**
la idin	„	**leidin**
la ka	„	**laga**

68. The following are substantival and are used with the definite article suffix when necessary.

wahh-i	something, anything	ǧidi-gi	
mid-ki	one, an, a	kulli-gi	all, whole
'id-di	someone, anyone	damán-ti	
ǧhof-ki	person	hebel-ki	a certain man
ǧhar-ki	some, several	keli-gi	alone
daur-ki	some, a few	gòni-gi	solitary, apart
in-ti	some, a quantity		

The following are treated as adjectives and follow the noun qualified, but are not inflected for number or gender.

badan	many	walba, waliba	every
yer	few	kasta	each
hoǧa	little	o dan	all
un	any, soever	keliah	only
kăleh	other	gòniah	separate, special

B. ADJECTIVES.

69. Adjectives follow the noun they qualify, and agree in Number and Definition.

1. *Classes of Adjectives.*

70. They are divided into :

   a. Radical.
   b. Derivative.
   c. Compound.

(a) *Radical Adjectives.*

71. These are not numerous, and express some simple, natural, or inherent, quality, such as size, shape, colour, or nature. They are radical words and are not derived from other roots.

A complete list is given, with their inflexions, in the Table, § 76.

(b) *Derivative Adjectives.*

(i) *Verbal Adjectives.*

72. Verbal Adjectives are the Passive Past Participles of verbs, ending in **-an**, or **-san**.

They express the result of the action of the verb.

Examples,

'adeisan	clean	from	'adei	clean
hagáksan	straight	„	hagáji	straighten
furan	open	„	fur	open
heđan	closed	„	heđ	close
wanăksan	good	„	wanáji	make good
đameyan	finished	,,	đamei	finish

(ii)   *Noun Adjectives.*

73.   These are formed in four ways.

(1) by the suffix **-leh** (possessing, containing).

Examples,

garadleh	sensible	from	garad	sense
uskagleh	dirty	„	uskag	dirt
arleh	speckled	„	ar	spot
bìyoleh	containing water	,,	bìyo	water

(2) by the suffix **-la** (deprived of).

garadla	foolish	from	garad	sense
indála	blind	„	indo	eyes
đegála	deaf	„	đego	ears

(3) by the suffix **-ah** (being, made of).

ghoriah	wooden	from	ghori	wood
birah	of iron .	„	bir	iron
farìdah	clever	,,	farìd	cleverness

Adjectives may be formed at will like the above from any noun as required.

(4) by the suffix **-ed** (expressing origin).

Somàlied	Somali			
Arabed	Arab			
Àdmed	of Aden			
bađed	of the sea	from	bađ	sea
'ano wìyiled	rhinoceros milk,	„	wìyil	rhinoceros

(c)   *Compound Adjectives.*

74.   Formed from two separate words :

(i) Noun and Adjective.

hòg-wein	strong (hòg strength, wein great)
hunguri-wein	greedy (hunguri throat)

didid-badan	sweaty (**didid** sweat, **badan** plenty)
af-badan	sharp (**af** edge)
adeig-run	hardy (**adeig** hardness, **run** right)

(ii) The 3rd person singular Present Perfect Indicative of a verb, being really an adjectival Relative Clause.

nin ghora	clerk, lit. a man who writes
fùli yaghán	knowing how to ride
af yaghán	interpreter, eloquent
la arka	visible
an la arkin	invisible

2. *Inflexions of Adjectives.*

75. Adjectives are inflected to agree with the nouns they qualify in the following cases :

(i) in the plural number,

(ii) when the noun is defined by the article suffix -**i** (and in certain cases -**a**),

(iii) in case (ii) the inflexion is different for masc. (*guttural*), and fem. (*dental*) *linking consonants* (cf. § 34).

(a) *Radical Adjectives.*

76. The following general rules are followed :

(i)   Plural.   Reduplicate the first syllable.

(ii)⎫ ⎰Article -**ki**, -**gi**, -**hi**.   Add -**a**.

(iii)⎭ ⎱Article -**ti**, -**di**.   Add -**eid**.

(iv)   If the noun is defined with article, -**a**, the adjective only agrees with it in number.

Note. The rule for the inflexions -**a**, -**eid**, (ii and iii) is invariable.

But when qualifying plural nouns with the definite article (other than the Reduplicated Plurals, as **niman**), adjectives may or may not take the plural inflexion (cf. § 164).   Thus,

nàgihi waweina, or **nàgihi weina** the big women,

askàrrti hhunhhumeid, or **askàrrti hhumeid** the bad soldiers.

When qualifying the Reduplicated Plurals, and all indefinite plurals, the plural inflexion of the adjective is always required.

Examples,   **nimánki waweina**
          nàgo wawein
          askàrr hhunhhun

Table of the Inflexions of all known Radical Adjectives.

Number	Sing.			Plur.		
Link. Cons.	Both	Masc. (Gutt.)	Fem. (Dent.)	Both	Masc. (Gutt.)	Fem. (Dent.)
Definition	Indefinite or Suffix -a	Suffix -i	Suffix -i	Indefinite or Suffix -a	Suffix -i	Suffix -i
Exs. of Nouns Qualified	nin nág ninka nágta	ninki (and nágihi)	nágti (and askárrti the soldiers)	niman nimánka nágo nágaha askárr askárrta	nimánki (and nágihi)	askárrti
white	'ad	'ada	'adeid	'ad'ad	'ad'ada	'ad'adeid
hard	adag	adka	adkeid	adadag	adadka	adadkeid
red	'as	'asa	'aseid	'as'as	'as'asa	'as'aseid
yellow	aul	aula	auleid	aulaul	aulaula	aulauleid
ripe	bisil	bisla	bisleid	bisbisil	bisbisla	bisbisleid
long	der	dera	dereid	derder (dader)	derdera (dadera)	derdereid (dadereid)
unripe	'edin	'edna	'edneid	'e'tedin	'ed'edna	'ed'edneid
clever	feyig	feyiga	feyigeid	feyig	feyiga	feyigeid
;;	fi'an	fi'ana	fi'aneid	fi'i'an	fi'i'ana	fi'i'aneid
light	fudud	fududa	fududeid	fudfudud	fudfududa	fudfududeid
cold	ghabô	ghabôba	ghabôbeid	ghabghabô	ghabghabôba	ghabghabôbeid
bad	hhun	hhuma	hhumeid	hhunhhun	hhunhhuma	hhunhhumeid
hot	kulul	kulula	kululeid	kulkulul	kulkulula	kulkululeid
black	madô	madôba	madôbeid	madmadô	madmadôba	madmadôbeid
fat	shilis	shishla	shishleid	shishilis	shishishla	shishishleid
heavy	'ulus	'usla	'usleid	'ul'ulus	'us'usla	'us'usleid
fresh	'usub	'usba	'usbeid	'us'usub	'us'usba	'us'usbeid
large	wein	weina	weineid	wawein	waweina	waweineid
small	yer	yera	yereid	yeryer	yeryera	yeryereid

(b) *Derivative Adjectives.*

77. These are not usually inflected (except some Verbal adjectives) when qualifying a plural noun, the inflexion entirely depending on the definite article, suffix, and linking consonant.

(i) *Verbal Adjectives.*

78. The Inflexions are the same as for Radical Adjectives, except that only some are reduplicated in the plural:

		Indefinite, or Def. Art. -**ka**, -**ta**	Def. Art. -**ki**	Def. Art. -**ti**
good	*sing.* *plur.*	wanăksan	wanăksana	wanăksaneid
broad	*sing.*	baladan	baladna	baladneid
	plur.	balbaladan	balbaladna	balbaladneid
stout	*sing.*	buran	burra	burreid
	plur.	burburan	burburra	burburreid
empty	*sing.*	madan	madana	madaneid
	plur.	madmadan	madmadana	madmadaneid
absent	*sing.* *plur.*	maghan	maghana	maghaneid
tied	*sing.*	hedan	hedna	hedneid
	plur.	hedhedan	hedhedna	hedhedneid
clean	*sing.* *plur.*	safeisan	safeisana	safeisaneid

(ii) *Noun Adjectives.*

79. These are not altered in the Plural.

Classes (i), (ii), and (iii) (adjectives in -**leh**, -**la**, -**ah**), obey the following rules:

1. If the qualified noun is defined by -**a**, or -**i**, the noun portion of the adjective takes its proper article suffix -**a**.

2. After Article -**a** (guttural or dental) there is no further inflexion.

3. After Article -**i** the terminal portion of the adjective is also inflected:

    (a) After Masc. (Gutt.) Link. Cons.

        -**ki**, -**gi**, -**hi**............-**a** is added

    (b) After Fem. (Dent.) Link. Cons.

        -**ti**, -**di** ....-**aid** is added

Inflexions of Noun Adjectives.

	Indefinite	Art. -ka, -ta	Art. -ki	Art. -ti
(i)	garadleh sensible	garadkáleh	garadkálaha	garadkálahaid
	akhlileh sensible	akhligáleh	akhligálaha	akhligálahaid
	oghònleh knowing	oghòntáleh	oghòntálaha	oghòntálahaid
	uskagleh dirty	uskaggáleh	uskaggálaha	uskaggálahaid
	baraleh spotted	barasháleh	barahálaha	barahálahaid
	bìyoleh containing water	bìyasháleh	bìyahálaha	bìyahálahaid
(ii)	garadla senseless	garadkala	garadkálaä	garadkálaäid
	indála blind	indahala	indahálaä	indahálaäid
	lugla legless	lugtala	lugtálaä	lugtálaäid
	haulla unemployed	haushala	haushálaä	haushálaäid
(iii)	farìdah clever	farìdkaäh	farìdkaäha	farìdkaähaid
	birah of iron	birtaäh	birtaäha	birtaähaid
	ghoriah wooden	ghorigaäh	ghorigaäha	ghorigaähaid

The following have special plural forms :

ʻajisah lazy	{ sing.	ʻajiskaäh	ʻajiskaäha	ʻajiskaähaid
	plur.	ʻajisintaäh	ʻajisintaäha	ʻajisintaähaid
gesiah brave	{ sing.	gesigaäh	gesigaäha	gesigaähaid
	plur.	gesiyintaäh	gesiyintaäha	gesiyintaähaid

80. The last class of Noun Adjectives, in **-ed**, have only one inflexion.

When qualifying a noun with article suffix **-i** of any gender or number they take **-a**.

The **e** is usually dropped.

Examples, **Somàlied   Somàlida**
Arabed   Arabta
bilàdki Somàlida the Somali country
afki Arabta the Arab language

(c) *Compound Adjectives.*

81. It is impossible to give rules for the inflexions of these, since as far as possible the necessity is avoided, by a separation into the component parts, and the natives themselves are by no means unanimous on the question.

The following examples, however, are given, being the few types that I have satisfied myself about :

af badan sharp :

mindi af badan a sharp knife ; **mindida afka badan** the sharp knife ; or, **mindidi afka badneid**

mindiyo afaf badbadan sharp knives

mindiyaha afafka badbadan, or, **mindiyihi afafka badbadna** the sharp knives

hog wein strong :

nin, ninka, nag, nagta, hog wein a, or the, strong man, or woman

ninki or **nimanki, hog weina** the strong man, or men ; **nagti hog weineid** the strong women ; **nagihi hog weina** the strong women.

af yaghan eloquent :

In adjectives like this the verb is conjugated and therefore agrees in number and gender.

nin af yaghán	an eloquent man
nàg af taghán	,, woman
ninki / **ninka** } **afka yaghán**	the eloquent man
nàgti / **nàgta** } **afka taghán**	,, woman
niman af yaghánin	eloquent men
nàgo af yaghánin	,, women
nimánki / **nimánka** } **afka yaghánin**	the eloquent men
nàgihi / **nàgaha** } **afka yaghán**	,, women

This adjective may be treated as one word, and take the termination **-ah**, in which case it is inflected regularly like such derivative adjectives :

afyaghánah, afyaghánkaäh, afyaghánkaäha, afyaghánkaähaid.

(3) *Comparison of Adjectives.*

82. There is no inflexion for the comparison of Adjectives. This want is supplied by the use of the particles **ka** more, more than ; **u, ugu** most.

Examples,	**ákhalkan ákhalkas ka wein**
	This house is bigger than that house
	mid ka wein la kàli bring a bigger one
	ki u wanáksana The best
	ya ugu horèya? Which is first of all ?

"is most," is usually translated by **ba, sà.**

kas sà wanáksan	that is best
sádehhdas kán ba wein	of those three this is the biggest

C. Verbs.

1. *Conjugation.*

(a) *Moods and Tenses.*

83. The Verb has four moods :

Imperative,	Indicative,
Infinitive,	Subjunctive.

Also, Verbal Adjective, or Past Participle, and Verbal Noun.

84. There are three Regular Conjugations, distinguished by the form of the Verb root, and the formation of the Infinitive.

The Verb root is the 2nd person singular of the Imperative.

	1st Conjugation.	Root ends in a consonant.
	2nd „ „ „	**-o.**
	3rd „ „ „	**-i.**

The Infinitive is formed

in   1,   by adding **-i** to the root.
2 and 3, by adding **-n** to the root.

85. The following is a paradigm of the verb **sheg** (tell), a regular verb of the 1st Conjugation.

There are four terminations for the Tense inflexions.

-a	is used in the Present Indicative tenses.			
-ei	,,	,,	Past	,,	,,
-e	,,	,,	Potential tense.	
-o	,,	,,	Subjunctive mood.	

Imperative	**sheg**	tell thou.
Verb Adjective	**shègan**	told.
Verb Noun	**shegnin**	telling.
Infinitive	**shègi**	to tell

Indicative :

Aorist	[1]**wa shèga**	I (usually) tell, I am to tell.
Preterite	**wa shègei**	I told, have told, had told.
Continuative Present	**wa shègeya**	I am telling, intend to tell.
Continuative Past	**wa shègeyei**	I was telling.
Future Definite	**wa shègi dòna**	I am going to tell.
Habitual Present	**wa shegí jira**	I am in the habit of telling.
Habitual Past	**wa shegí jirei**	I used to tell.
Conditional	**wa shègi laha**	I would, or should tell, I would have, or should have told.
Potential	**an shège**	I may, might tell.

Subjunctive :

Aorist	(**hadi**)**an shègo**	(If) I tell, told, had told.
Continuative	(**hadi**)**an shègeyo**	(If) I were to tell, were telling.
Future	(**hadi**)**an shègi dòno**	(If) I were, had been, about to tell.
Habitual	(**hadi**)**an shegí jiro**	(If) I were, had been, accustomed to tell.

86. The tenses fall into three classes.

(i) The Aorist, Preterite, and Potential Indicative, and the Aorist Subjunctive, are simple or radical, and the terminations are added directly to the root.

---

[1] **wa** is a particle used frequently with the verb, and may take the place of a personal pronoun.

(ii) In the Continuative tenses the terminations are,

-eya (or -aya, or -ahaya),
-eyei (or -ayei, or -ahayei),
-eyo (or -ayo, or -ahayo).

These are suffixed, in the 1st Conjugation apparently to the root, but in the 2nd and 3rd Conjugations to the Infinitive.

The syllable ey is short and is not accented.

(iii) The third class consists of Auxiliary tenses, formed by the Infinitive with an auxiliary verb.

87. In the 2nd Conjugation (verbs ending in -o), the -o is often changed to -a in the Infinitive and other moods.

In the Simple tenses of this Conjugation, d is inserted between the root and tense termination.

Examples, **baro** learn   Infinitive **baran**
        jògso stop   **wan jògsoda** I stop

88. There are three persons in the Singular and Plural, and two genders in the 3rd person singular.

The following are the variations in the four tense terminations for the different persons.

	Present Indicative	Past Indicative	Potential Indicative	Subjunctive
Sing. 1.	-a	-ei	-e	-o
2.	⌠-ta ⌡-sa	⌠-tei ⌡-sei	⌠-te, -tide ⌡-se, -side	⌠-to, -tid ⌡-so, -sid
3 m.	-a	-ei	-e	-o
3 f.	⌠-ta ⌡-sa	⌠-tei ⌡-sei	⌠-te ⌡-se	⌠-to ⌡-so
Plur. 1.	-na	-nei	-ne	-no
2.	⌠-tan ⌡-san	⌠-ten ⌡-sen	⌠-tène ⌡-sène	⌠-tán ⌡-sán
3.	-an	-en	-ène	-án

In the 2nd person singular and plural, and 3rd person fem. singular, t is used after a consonant,

s is used after i, e.g. in the 3rd Conjugation,
and in Continuative tenses of all Conjugations.

89.   (*b*) *Affirmative Conjugation.*

I. **sheg** tell.   II. **gùrso** marry.   III. **samèi** make.

Infinitive.

shègi   **gùrsan**   **samèin.**

Imperative.

		Let me tell	Let me marry	Let me make
Sing.	1.	an shègo	an gùrsado	an samèyo
	2.	sheg	gùrso	samèi
	3 m.	ha shègo	ha gùrsado	ha samèyo
	3 f.	ha shegto	ha gùrsato	ha samèiso
Plur.	1.	an shegno	an gùrsano	an samèino
	2.	shèga	gùrsada	samèya
	3.	ha shègan	ha gùrsadan	ha samèyan

Indicative.

Aorist.

		I tell	I marry	I make
Sing.	1.	shèga	gùrsada	samèya
	2.	shegta	gùrsata	samèisa
	3 m.	shèga	gùrsada	samèya
	3 f.	shegta	gùrsata	samèisa
Plur.	1.	shegna	gùrsana	samèina
	2.	shegtan	gùrsatan	samèisan
	3.	shègan	gùrsadan	samèyan

Preterite.

		I told	I married	I made
Sing.	1.	shègei	gùrsadei	samèyei
	2.	shegtei	gùrsatei	samèisei
	3 m.	shègei	gùrsadei	samèyei
	3 f.	shegtei	gùrsatei	samèisei
Plur.	1.	shegnei	gùrsanei	samèinei
	2.	shegten	gùrsaten	samèisen
	3.	shègen	gùrsaden	samèyen

Continuative Present.

		I am telling	I am marrying	I am making
Sing.	1.	shègeya	gùrsáneya	samèineya
	2.	shègesa	gùrsánesa	samèinesa
	3 m.	shègeya	gùrsáneya	samèineya
	3 f.	shègesa	gùrsánesa	samèinesa
Plur.	1.	shègena	gùrsánena	samèinena
	2.	shègesan	gùrsánesan	samèinesan
	3.	shègeyan	gùrsáneyan	samèineyan

Continuative Past.

		I was telling	I was marrying	I was making
Sing.	1.	shègeyei	gùrsáneyei	samèineyei
	2.	shègesei	gùrsánesei	samèinesei
	3 m.	shègeyei	gùrsáneyei	samèineyei
	3 f.	shègesei	gùrsánesei	samèinesei
Plur.	1.	shègenei	gùrsánenei	samèinenei
	2.	shègesen	gùrsánesen	samèinesen
	3.	shègeyen	gùrsáneyen	samèineyen

Future Definite.

		I am going to tell	I am going to marry	I am going to make
Sing.	1.	shègi dòna	gùrsan dona	samèin dòna
	2.	„ dònta	„ dònta	„ dònta
	3 m.	„ dòna	etc.	etc.
	3 f.	„ dònta		
Plur.	1.	„ dònna		
	2.	„ dòntan		
	3.	„ dònan		

Habitual Present.

I am accustomed to tell	I am accustomed to marry	I am accustomed to make
shegí jira	gùrsán jira	samèin jira

declined like "dòna" above.

Habitual Past.

		I used to tell	I used to marry	I used to make
Sing.	1.	shegí jirei	gùrsán jirei	samèin jirei
	2.	shegí jirtei	etc.	etc.
	3 m.	shegí jirei		
	3 f.	shegí jirtei		
Plur.	1.	shegí jirnei		
	2.	shegí jirten		
	3.	shegí jiren		

Conditional.

		I should tell	I should marry	I should make
Sing.	1.	shègi laha	gùrsán laha	samèin laha
	2.	shègi lahaid	etc.	etc.
	3 m.	shègi laha		
	3 f.	shègi lahaid		
Plur.	1.	shègi lahain		
	2.	shègi lahaiden		
	3.	shègi lahaiyen		

Potential.

		I may tell	I may marry	I may make
Sing.	1.	an shège	an gùrsade	an samèye
	2.	ad shegtide	ad gùrsátide	ad samèiside
	3 m.	ha shège	ha gùrsade	ha samèye
	3 f.	ha shegte	ha gùrsate	ha samèise
Plur.	1.	an shegne	an gùrsane	an samèine
	2.	ad shegtène	ad gùrsatène	ad samèisène
	3.	ha shegène	ha gùrsadène	ha samèyène

Subjunctive.
(Only found in Subordinate Clauses.)

Aorist.

Sing.	1.	shègo	gùrsado	samèyo
	2.	shegto, shegtid	gùrsato, gùrsatid	samèiso, samèisid
	3 m.	shègo	gùrsado	samèyo
	3 f.	shegto	gùrsato	samèiso
Plur.	1.	shegno	gùrsano	samèino
	2.	shegtán	gùrsatán	samèisán
	3.	shègán	gùrsadán	samèyán

Continuative.

Sing.	1.	shègeyo	gùrsáneyo	samèineyo
	2.	shègeso, shègesid	gùrsáneso, -id	samèineso, -id
	3 m.	shègeyo	gùrsáneyo	samèineyo
	3 f.	shègeso	gùrsáneso	samèineso
Plur.	1.	shègeno	gùrsáneno	samèineno
	2.	shègesán	gùrsánesán	samèinesán
	3.	shègeyán	gùrsáneyán	samèineyán

Future.

Sing.	1.	shègi dòno	gùrsan dòno	samèin dòno
	2.	shègi dònto	etc.	etc.
		etc. as "shègo."		

Habitual.

shegí jiro	gùrsán jiro	samèin jiro
etc.	etc.	etc.

90. The following table gives all the types necessary for the formation of the tenses of a regular verb :

Conjugation	Root	Engl.	Inf.	Aorist	Continuative Pres.
I	hel	get	heli	hela	héleya
II	so'o	walk	so'on	so'oda	so'óneya
III	sì	give	sìn	sìya	sìneya

The other Indicative, and the Subjunctive, tenses are formed by changing final -a into -ei, -e, or -o.

91.   (*c*)   *Negative Conjugation.*

The Negative Particles are :

> Imperative Mood,   ha, or yan.
> Indicative Mood,   ma.
> Subjunctive Mood,   an.

Imperative*	ha shègin	ha gùrsan	ha samèin

Indicative :

Aorist*	ma shègo	ma gùrsado	ma samèyo
Preterite	maan shègin	maan gùrsan	maan samèin
Contin. Pres.*	shègi mayo	gùrsan mayo	samèin mayo
Contin. Past	ma shèginin	ma gùrsáninin	ma samèininin
Fut. Def.*	ma shègi dòno	ma gùrsan dòno	ma samèin dono
Habit. Pres.*	ma shegí jiro	ma gùrsán jiro	ma samèin jiro
Habit. Past	ma shegí jirin	ma gùrsán jirin	ma samèin jirin
Conditional*⎫ Potential ⎭	maan shègen	maan gùrsaden	maan samèyen

Subjunctive :

Aorist	-anan shègin	-anan gùrsan	-anan samèin
Continuative	-anan shèg- inin	-anan gùrsán- inin	-anan samèin- inin
Future	-anan shègi dònin	-anan gùrsan dònin	-anan samèin dònin
Habitual	-anan shegí jirin	-anan gùrsán jirin	-anan samèin jirin

Notes,

(i) Only the tenses marked * are conjugated, the remainder having one form of the verb for all persons.

(ii) The Personal Pronouns are only used with the following negative tenses :

Imperative, Preterite and Conditional tenses of the Indicative Mood, and the Subjunctive tenses.

In other tenses of the Negative Conjugation no pronouns are used.

(iii) In the Present Continuative tense, **mayo** (am not) is conjugated like an auxiliary verb.

(iv) In the Subjunctive tenses, the negative particle, -**an,** and the pronouns are added as suffixes to the conjunction, or conjunctive particle.

Imperative.

		Let me not tell	Let me not marry	Let me not make
Sing.	1.	yanan shègin	yanan gùrsan	yanan samèin
	2.	ha shègin	ha gùrsan	ha samèin
	3 m.	yanu (or yu) shègin	yanu (or yu) gùrsan	yanu (or yu) samèin
	3 f.	yanei (or yai) shègin	yanei (or yai) gùrsan	yanei (or yai) samèin
Plur.	1.	yanan shègin	yanan gùrsan	yanan samèin
	2.	ha shègina	ha gùrsánina	ha samèinina
	3.	yanei (or yai) shègin	yanei (or yai) gùrsan	yanei (or yai) samèin

Indicative.

Aorist.

(Conjugated like Aorist Subj. Affirmative.)

		I do not tell	I do not marry	I do not make
Sing.	1.	ma shègo	ma gùrsado	ma samèyo
	2.	ma shegto	ma gùrsato	ma samèiso
	3 m.	ma shègo	ma gùrsado	ma samèyo
	3 f.	ma shegto	ma gùrsato	ma samèiso
Plur.	1.	ma shegno	ma gùrsano	ma samèino
	2.	ma shegtán	ma gùrsatán	ma samèisán
	3.	ma shègán	ma gùrsadán	ma samèyán

Continuative Present.

		I am not telling	I am not marrying	I am not making
Sing.	1.	shègi mayo	gùrsan mayo	samèin mayo
	2.	shègi mayso (or maysid)	etc.	etc.
	3 m.	shègi mayo		
	3 f.	shègi mayso		
Plur.	1.	shègi mayno		
	2.	shègi maysan		
	3.	shègi mayan		

Future Definite.

(The Auxiliary verb is declined as the Negative Aorist tense of 1st Conjugation.)

		I am not going to tell	I am not going to marry	I am not going to make
Sing.	1.	ma shègi dòno	ma gùrsan dòno	ma samèin dòno
	2.	ma shègi dònto (dòntid)	etc.	etc.
	3 m.	ma shègi dòno		
	3 f.	ma shègi dònto		
Plur.	1.	ma shègi dònno		
	2.	ma shègi dòntan		
	3.	ma shègi dònan		

Habitual Present.

		I am not accustomed to tell	I am not accustomed to marry	I am not accustomed to make
Sing.	1.	ma shegí jiro	ma gùrsán jiro	ma samèin jiro
	2.	ma shegí jirto	ma gùrsán jirto	ma samèin jirto
		(jirtid)	(jirtid)	(jirtid)
		etc.	etc.	etc.

Conditional.

		I should not tell	I should not marry	I should not make
Sing.	1.	maan shègen	maan gùrsaden	maan samèyen
	2.	maad shegten	maad gùrsaten	maad samèisen
	3 m.	mau shègen	mau gùrsaden	mau samèyen
	3 f.	maai shegten	maai gùrsaten	maai samèisen
Plur.	1.	maainu shegnen	maainu gùrsanen	maainu samèinen
	2.	maaidin shegten	maaidin gùrsaten	maaidin samèisen
	3.	maai shègen	maai gùrsaden	maai samèyen

92. *The Derivation of the Continuative tenses.*

In § 86, three alternative types were given for the Continuative tense terminations,

-eya,   -aya,   -ahaya.

These are added to the Infinitive of the verb, but in the 1st Conjugation the final -i of the Infinitive is lost.

-aháya is the form used among *Dolbohanta*:

wa tegaháya	I am going
wa so'onaháya	I am walking
wa sìnaháya	I am giving

-aya is the form used by the tribes of the North Coast and Western Somaliland:

wa tegaya,   wa so'onaya,   wa sìnaya.

-eya, which is pronounced quite short, and nearly like **-ya**, is used by the Central tribes, such as *Habr Yunis* and Western *Habr Toljàla*:

wa tégeya,   wa so'óneya,   wa sìneya.

The last two are contracted forms of the first, which is really a compound tense, in which the auxiliary verb, **ahai** be (modern **aho,**

4—2

q.v.) is used, with the Infinitive of the principal verb, as in the case
of compound tenses.

In the Negative tenses this is more clearly seen, and here the
1st Conjugation retains the -i of the Infinitive.

The negative tenses of **ahai** are used as a separate word with
the particles **ma,** or **an** :

> **shègi maháyo,** or **shègi mayo** I am not telling
> (for **ma-aháyo**)

In the past tenses the **ma** may be separated :

> **yèli mahain** (for **ma-ahain**)⎫   I was not doing,
> or, **ma yèli ahain**   ⎭ or, I would not do

These are contracted by *Ishhàk* tribes into

> **yèli maïn,** or **ma yèlinin**

The Subjunctive Mood is similarly formed :

> **hadánu yèli ahain**⎫
> or, **hadánu yèlinin** ⎭ if he will not do.

93.   (*d*) *Interrogative Conjugation.*

The Interrogative particle is **ma,** which, when combined with
Personal Pronouns, becomes **mi.**

The Conjugation is otherwise the same as the Affirmative.

Indicative :

Aorist	**mian shèga** ?	**mian gùrsada** ?	**mian samèya** ?
Preterite	**mian shègei** ?	etc.	etc.
Contin. Pres.	**mian shègeya** ?		
„ Past	**mian shègeyei** ?		
Future Def.	**mian shègi dòna** ?		
Habit. Pres.	**mian shegí jira** ?		
„ Past	**mian shegí jirei** ?		
Conditional	·**mian shègi laha** ?		

(*e*) *Negative-Interrogative Conjugation.*

94. Here the negative particle used is **an.**

No tense is declined except the Conditional, which is the same
as in the simple Negative form.

Indicative :

Aorist	mianan shègin ?⎫	mianan	mianan
Preterite	mianan shègin ?⎭	gùrsan ?	samèin ?
Contin. Pres.	mianan shèginin ?⎫	mianan	mianan
Contin. Past	mianan shèginin ?⎭	gùrsáninin ?	samèininin ?
Fut. Def.	mianan shègi dònin ?	mianan gùrsan dònin ?	mianan samèin dònin ?
Habit. Pres.	mianan shegí jirin ?⎫	mianan gùrsán jirin ?	mianan samèin jirin ?
„ Past	mianan shegí jirin ?⎭		
Conditional	mianan shègen ?	mianan gùrsaden ?	mianan samèyen ?

2. Peculiarities and Irregular Verbs of the Three Conjugations.

(a) 1st Conjugation.

95. These verbs have the root ending in any consonant, aspirate, guttural aspirate (**gh** or **kh**), or "*aine*," or ô.

The following changes take place in certain letters when they occur together:

l followed by **t** become **sh.**

n, after **l** or **r,** is often assimilated to either of the latter.

t, after **',** **gh, kh, hh,** ô, and **i,** becomes **d.**

Examples,

	dil kill,	hel get,	yel do,	dagàl fight

Aorist.

Sing. 1.	dila	hela	yèla	dagàla
„ 2.	disha	hesha	yesha	dagàsha
Plur. 1.	dilla	hella	yella	dagàlla
„ 2.	dishan	heshan	yeshan	dagàshan

dir	send...1st Plur. Aorist	dirra, or dirna
dírir	fight... „ „	dírirra, or dírirna
jir	be ... „ „	jirra, or jirna.

ra'	accompany	...2nd sing. Aorist	**wad** ra'da
da'	fall	... ,, ,,	,, da'da
dagh	graze	... ,, ,,	,, daghda
bagh	fear	... ,, ,,	,, baghda
bahh	go	... ,, ,,	,, bahhda
jehh	tear	... ,, ,,	,, jehhda
ilô	forget	... ,, ,,	,, ilôda
fadì	sit (cf. § 109)	,, ,,	,, fadída

Verbs ending in **n**, change **n** to **m** when it is preceded by two short syllables and the inflexions begin with a vowel.

| | **warran** | give the news | **dagàlan** | fight |
| Infin. | **warrami** | | **dagàlami** | |

	Aorist.	*Aorist.*
Sing. 1.	**wan warrama**	**wan dagàlama**
,, 2.	**wad warranta**	**wad dagàlanta**

96. In the case of Polysyllabic verbs, of which the last syllable is short and contains the vowels **a, o, u**, these vowels are dropped in the Continuative Tenses, and in those persons of all Simple Tenses in which the inflexion does not begin with a consonant, i.e. in 1st and 3rd masc. sing. and 3rd plur.

g becomes **k** before a vowel or **t**.

Examples,

Root		Infin.	Aorist	Contin. Pres.
arag	see	**arki**	**arka**	**arkeya**
dulun	cheat	**dulmi**	**dulma**	**dulmeya**
durug	move	**durki**	**durka**	**durkeya**
gògol	make the bed	**gògli**	**gògla**	**gògleya**
hadal	talk	**hadli**	**hadla**	**hadleya**
húrud	sleep	**hurdi**	**hurda**	**hurdeya**
khatalan	err	**khatalmi**	**khatalma**	**khatalmeya**
ghosol	laugh	**ghosli**	**ghosla**	**ghosleya**
jèdal	whip	**jèdli**	**jèdla**	**jèdleya**
makhal	hear	**makhli**	**makhla**	**makhleya**
orod	run	**ordi**	**orda**	**ordeya**
rehan	pledge (pawn)	**rehmi**	**rehma**	**rehmeya**

Examples of Conjugations of the above,

arag see   **hadal** talk   **dulun** cheat   **makhal** hear

Aorist Indicative.

Sing. 1.	arka	hadla	dulma	makhla
„ 2.	árakta	hádasha	dulunta	mákhasha
Plur. 1.	áragna	hádalla	dulunna	mákhalla
„ 2.	áraktan	hádashan	duluntan	mákhashan

Present Continuative Indicative.

Sing. 1.	árkeya	hádleya	dúlmeya	mákhleya
„ 2.	árkesa	hádlesa	dúlmesa	¹mákhalesa
Plur. 1.	árkena	hádlena	dúlmena	mákhalena
„ 2.	árkesan	hádlesan	dúlmesan	mákhalesan

97. The following verbs (all containing the vowel a) change a into e or i in the Infinitive and the Continuative Tenses :

Root.		Infin.	Aorist Indic.	Contin. Pres. Indic.
tag	go	tegi	taga	tégeya
gal	enter	geli	gala	géleya
ka'	get up	ke'i	ka'a	ké'eya
da'	fall, or rob	di'i	da'a	dí'eya
na'	hate	ni'i	na'a	ní'eya
²gama'	sleep	gam'i	gama'a	gam'eya
bahh	go	bihhi	bahha	³bahháya
dahh	travel	dihhi	dahha	³dahháya
nahh	be astounded	nihhi	nahha	níhheya
tahh	put in line	tihhi	tahha	tíhheya
Exc. nàhh	be fat	nàhhi	nàhha	nàhheya
dagh	save	dighi	dagha	digheya
daba'	imprint	dabi'i	daba'a	dabi'eya

The following make Infinitives like the 3rd Conjugation :

da	leave	dein	daya	deineya
la̅	slay	lein	laya	leineya

98. Verbs ending in ô, require b after the root in all inflexions, except those beginning with a consonant.

d is used for t in the inflexions.

		Infin.	Aorist.	Continuative.
'atô	be tired	'atôbi	'atôba	'atôbeya
gabô	be old	gabôbi	gabôba	gabôbeya
ghabô	be cold	ghabôbi	ghabôba	ghabôbeya
hallô	be lost	hallàbi	hallàba	hallàbeya

¹ makhal retains the a in these persons.
² Participle gama'san asleep.
³ The forms of the Contin. tenses of these verbs must be noticed. Cf. § 92.

		Infin.	Aorist	Continuative
hasô	converse	{ **hasôbi**	**hasôba**	**hasôbeya**
		hasàwi	**hasàwa**	**hasàweya**
ilô	forget	**ilôbi**	**ilôba**	**ilôbeya**
karô	defend	**karèbi**	**karèba**	**karèbeya**
ʻollô	be hostile	**ʻollôbi**	**ʻollôba**	**ʻollôbeya**
hambarô	fall heavily	**hamba-rôbi**	**hamba-rôba**	**hambarô-beya**
madô	be black	**madôbi**	**madôba**	**madôbeya**
weidô	be lean	**weidôbi**	**weidôba**	**weidôbeya**
màlô	get possession of	**màlôbi**	**màlôba**	**màlôbeya**

Aorist Indic.

Sing. 1. **wan ilôba** I forget
2. **wad ilôda**
Plur. 1. **weinu ilôna**
2. **weidin ilôdan**

99. **tag** (go), is irregular in the Preterite Indicative.

Sing. 1. **wan tegei** I went
2. **wad taktei**
3 m. **wu tegei**
3 f. **wei taktei**
Plur. 1. **weinu tagnei**
2. **weidin takten**
3. **wei tegen**

daʻ (fall, rob) forms either

deʻei, or **daʻei**, in the Preterite.

Its Aorist Subjunctive is

inan dʻo.

Verbs in **-ahh** conjugate the Preterite as follows.

Example,

bahh go
Sing. 1. **wan bahhái** I went
2. **wad báhhdei**
3 m. **wu bahhái**
3 f. **wei báhhdei**
Plur. 1. **weinu báhhnei**
2. **weidin báhhden**
3. **wei behhén**

100. The verb **oll** (lie, be in, dwell), is irregular in the Present and Past Perfect Indicative.

Imperative	oll	dwell
Infinitive	olli	

Indicative :

Aorist	al	I dwell (Neg. **ma al**)
Preterite	il	I dwelt (Neg. **ma ollin**)
Contin. Pres.	ólleya	I am dwelling, I intend to dwell
,, Past	ólleyei	I was dwelling
Fut. Def.	olli dòna	I am going to dwell
Habit. Pres.	ollí jira	I am accustomed to dwell
,, Past	ollí jirei	I used to dwell
Conditional	ólli laha	I would dwell, or would have dwelt

Subjunctive :

Aorist	inan ollo	that I may dwell
Continuative	inan ólleyo	that I may dwell

		Aorist Indic.	Preterite Indic.
Sing.	1.	al	il
	2.	tal	til
	3 m.	yal	yil
	3 f.	tal	til
Plur.	1.	nal	nil
	2.	tàlin	tillen
	3.	yàlin	yillen

Note that the consonants denoting the persons are *prefixed* to the verb, and that there are no personal endings in these tenses (except in 2nd and 3rd plur.).

The Negative form of the Present is the same as the Affirmative.

ma al	I do not dwell
ma tal	
etc.	etc.

(b) 2nd Conjugation.

101. In this Conjugation the root ends in **o**, and the Infinitive is formed by adding **n**, but in a great many cases the **o** is changed to **a**.

This change may also take place in both Simple and Continuative tenses.

In the Simple tenses **d** is added to the root, before adding the tense terminations, but in the 2nd pers. and 3rd pers. fem. sing. the **d** is lost, being assimilated into the **t** of the termination, and in the 1st pers. plur. the **d** is dropped before the **n.**

Table I.

102. The **o** in the Simple tenses is long, or at least as accentuated as the preceding syllable.

The consonant before the **o** is, **h, sh, k, g, j,** or **ʻ,** or **y.**

		Infin.	Aorist	Continuative
amahho	borrow	amahhòn	amahhòda	amahhóneya
ashtako	complain	asktakòn	ashtakòda	ashtakóneya
gajo	be hungry	gajòn	gajòda	gajóneya
gasho	put on	gashòn	gashòda	gashóneya
harrago	swagger	harragòn	harragòda	harrogóneya
riyo	dream	riyòn	riyòda	riyóneya
soʻo	walk	soʻon	sóʻoda	soʻóneya
tasho	consider	tashòn	tashòda	tashóneya
tuko	pray	tukòn	túkoda	tukóneya

Table II.

103. These are Attributive Verbs formed by adding **o** to an adjective.

In conjugation **o** is changed to **a,** which is long in the Simple tenses.

		Infin.	Aorist	Continuative
ado	grow angry	adan	adàda	adáneya
bislo	become ripe	bislan	bislàda	bisláneya
damo	be completed	daman	damàda	damáneya
dôwo	approach	dôwan	dôwàda	dôwáneya
fogo	go far	fogan	fogàda	fogáneya
hhumo	become bad	hhuman	hhumàda	hhumáneya
idlo	come to an end	idlan	idlàda	idláneya
mergo	be entangled	mergan	mergàda	mergáneya
shishlo	grow fat	shishlan	shishlàda	shishláneya
weino	grow big	weinan	weinàda	weináneya

Table III.

104. Verbs ending in **so,** which is preceded by a consonant, or in **hho,** have the vowel of the Simple tenses short, but it may or may not be changed to **a.**

	Infin.	Aorist	Continuative
badso be plentiful	**badson**	**bádsoda**	**badsóneya**
bahhso escape	**bahhson**	**báhhsoda**	**bahhsóneya**
buhso be full	**buhsan**	**búhsada**	**buhsámeya**
bukso be cured	**buksan**	**búksada**	**buksáneya**
dafso exchange	**dafson**	**dáfsoda**	**dafsóneya**
'ehho be partial	**'ehhon**	**'éhhoda**	**'ehhóneya**
gùrso marry	**gùrsan**	**gùrsada**	**gùrsáneya**
hubso ascertain	**hubson**	**húbsoda**	**hubsóneya**
ghaibso take your share	**ghaibson**	**gháibsoda**	**ghaibsóneya**
ghállohho be bent	**ghállohhon**	**ghállohhoda**	**ghallohhóneya**
ghobso seize	**ghobson**	**ghóbsoda**	**ghobsóneya**
ìbso buy for yourself	**ìbson**	**ìbsoda**	**ìbsóneya**
jògso shop	**jògson**	**jògsoda**	**jògsóneya**
sehho sleep	**sehhan**	**séhhada**	**sehháneya**
tirso count for yourself	**tirson**	**tírsoda**	**tirsóneya**

In the verbs of this class the Aorist and Preterite tenses are found very frequently in a contracted form, in the 1st and 3rd masc. sing. and 3rd plural, the terminations being **-sha, -shan,** or **-sa, -san,** etc.

Example,   ìbso buy

Aorist Indicative.

Sing.	1.	**wa ìbsha**	I buy	Plur.	1.	**wa ìbsona**
	2.	,, ìbsota			2.	,, ìbsotan
	3 m.	,, ìbsha			3.	,, ìbshan
	3 f.	,, ìbsota				

			Aorist.	*Preterite.*
Similarly,	**badso**	makes	**badsha,**	**badshei**
,,	**ghaibso**	,,	**ghaibsha,**	**ghaibshei**
,,	**bahhso**	,,	**bahhsa,**	**bahhsei**
,,	**gùrso**	,,	**gùrsa,**	**gùrsei**
,,	**bukso**	,,	**buksa,**	**buksei**

Table IV.

105. In the following verbs **o** is preceded by, **b, d, ɖ, f, gh, kh, l, n, r, s.** These drop the **o** in the Simple tenses, except in 2nd pers. and 3rd fem. sing. and 1st plur., in which the vowel usually appears as short **a** in 2nd and 3rd fem., and as **o** in 1st plur.

In all persons the **d** of the Simple tenses becomes **t**, except after **gh, kh.**

lt, as usual, becomes **sh.**

Example,   **haïso** have got

Aorist Indicative.

wa haïsta I have got	**wa haïsona**
,, haïsata	,, haïsatan
,, haïsta	,, haïstan
,, haïsata	

	Infin.	Aorist	Continuative
bagho be afraid	**baghan**	**baghda**	**bagháneya**
baro learn	**baran**	**barta**	**baranéya**
ɖalo be born	**ɖalan**	**ɖasha**	**(ɖalóneya)**
damìno be surety	**damìnon**	**damìnta**	**(damìnóneya)**
degeiso listen	**degeison**	**degeista**	**degeisóneya**
difo strike	**difon**	**difta**	**difóneya**

	Infin.	Aorist	Continuative
ɗimo die	ɗiman	ɗinta	ɗimáneya
ɗiso build for yourself	ɗison	ɗista	ɗisóneya
dòno look for	dònon	dònta	dònóneya
doro choose	doron	dorta	doróneya
ɗumo hide yourself	ɗuman	ɗunta	ɗumáneya
dabbalo swim	dabbalan	dabbasha	dabbaláneya
faɗìso sit down	faɗìson	faɗìsta	fadisóneya
farahhalo wash your hands	farahhalan	farahhasha	farahhaláneya
garo understand	garan	garta	garanéya
haïso have got	haïson	haïsta	haïsóneya
heɗo tie on yourself	heɗon	heɗta	heɗóneya
hiro shave yourself	hiron	hirta	hiróneya
ghado take for yourself	ghadon	ghata	ghadóneya
ghobo catch	ghobon	ghobta	ghobóneya
jèso turn yourself	jèson	jesta	jèsóneya
jìdo hurry on	jìdan	jìta	jìdáneya
maiɗo be washed	maidon	maiɗta	maiɗóneya
naso take a rest	nason	nasta	nasóneya
nokho return	nokhon	nokhda	nokhóneya
sameiso make for yourself	sameison	sameista	sameisóneya

	Infin	Aorist	Continuative
sido carry, wear	**sidon**	**sita**	**sidóneya**
sìso pay for	**sìson**	**sìsta**	**sìsóneya**
weidìso ask for	**weidìson**	**weidìsta**	**weidìsóneya**
lukho gulp	**lukhon**	**lukhda**	**lukhóneya**

The Irregular Verbs, **imo, odo, ogho.**

106. These verbs are declined irregularly in the Simple tenses, with the same peculiarity as the verb **oll.**

Note. The root from which the Simple tenses of **odo** are formed is related to the regular verb **yeð** call, and also a verb **yað,** found in songs :

Examples, **dabyera tehhdo yaða ba.**
"The little song I sing is like a shower of rain."

Yan sidi dánabka yèdei.
"I spoke like the lightning."

Imperative	**imo** come	**(odo)**[1] say	**ogho** know
Infinitive	**iman**	**odan**	**oghòn**
Adject.	—	—	—
Noun	**imad-ki**	—	**oghòn-ti**
Indic. Aorist	**imàda**	**idahhda** or **idahha**	**aghán**
Preterite	**imi**	**idi,** or **idahhei**	**ighín**
Contin. Pres.	**imáneya**	**odáneya**	**ogháneya**
„ Past	**imáneyei**	**odáneyei**	**ogháneyei**
Fut. Def.	**iman dòna**	**odan dòna**	**oghòn dòna**
Habit. Pres.	**imán jira**	**odán jira**	**oghòn jira**
„ Past	**imán jirei**	**odán jirei**	**oghòn jirei**
Conditional	**imán laha**	**odán laha**	**oghòn laha**
Potential	**imàde**	**idahhde** or **idahhe**	**oghàde**

Subjunctive :

Aorist	**imàdo**	**idahhdo**	**oghàdo**
Continuative	**imáneyo**	**odáneyo**	**ogháneyo**

[1] Instead of the Imperative **odo,** the word **ðeh** is used.

Aorist Indicative.

Sing.	1.	imàda	idahhda, or idahha	aghán
	2.	timàda	tidahhda, or tidahha	taghán
	3 m.	yimàda	yidahhda, or yidahha	yaghán
	3 f.	timàda	tidahhda, or tidahha	taghán
Plur.	1.	nimádna	nidahhna, or nidahha	naghán
	2.	timadan	tidahhdan, or tidahhan	tagánin
	3.	yimàdan	yidahhdan, or yidahhan	yaghánin

Preterite Indicative.

Sing.	1.	ími, or ímid	idi, or idahhei	ighín
	2.	tími, or tímid	tidi, or tidahhdei	tighín
	3 m.	yími, or yímid	yidi, or yidahhei	yighín
	3 f.	tími, or tímid	tidi, or tidahhdei	tighín
Plur.	1.	ními, or nímid	nidi, or nidahhnei	nighín
	2.	tímaden	tidahhden	tighínen
	3.	yímaden	yidahhden, or yidahhen	yighínen

The Aorist Subjunctive of **imo**, and **odo**, is declined like the
Indicative, with the Subjunctive terminations, **o** and **an**.

> inan imàdo   hadan idahhdo
> inad timàdo, etc.   hadad tidahhdo, etc.

The Aorist Subj. of **ogho** is regular : **oghàdo, oghàto,** etc.

The Negatives of the Aorist Indic. and Conditional are regularly
formed, in the former by using the Aorist Subj., and in the latter by
replacing the Aorist terminations by **en**; but in the verb **ogho** the
Pres. Indicative is unaltered.

> I do not come   **ma imàdo**   I would not   **maan ímaden**
> I do not know   **ma aghán**   have come

All other Negative forms are regular.

(c) 3rd Conjugation.

107. These verbs all end in **-i** or **-ei**, and form the Infinitive
by adding **-n.** In the Simple tenses **i** becomes **y** for euphony
before the tense terminations which do not begin with a consonant.

108. Certain Participles are irregular :

ingeji	dry	Part.	ingegan	dried.
wanăji	make good	,,	wanăksan	good
hagaji	make straight	,,	hagáksan	straight.
ghoi	make wet	,,	ghoiyan	wetted

109. Certain verbs in **i** are conjugated like the first Conjugation, adding **-yi** in the Infinitive. These take **-d** instead of **-t** in the 2nd and 3rd fem. persons.

Root		Infin.	Aorist Indicative 1st pers. sing.	2nd pers. sing.	Contin. Pres. Indic.
ʻaffi	pardon	ʻaffìyi	ʻaffìya	ʻaffida	ʻaffìyeya
ahdi	swear	ahdìyi	ahdiya	ahdida	ahdìyeya
akhri	read	akhrìyi	akhriya	akhrida	akhrìyeya
ʻaï	curse	ʻaìyi	ʻaïya	ʻaïda	ʻaìyeya
ʻari	ebb	ʻarìyi	ʻariya	ʻarida	ʻarìyeya
awawi	dream	awawìyi	awawiya	awawida	awawìyeya
bakhti	die	bakhtìyi	bakhtiya	bakhtida	bakhtìyeya
bari	beseech	barìyi	bariya	barida	barìyeya
bari	be safe, well	barìyi	bariya	barida	barìyeya
ɗai	look	ɗaìyi	ɗaiya	ɗaida	ɗaìyeya
ʻei	cry	ʻeìyi	ʻeiya	ʻeida	ʻeìyeya
ʻeri	drive away	ʻerìyi	ʻeriya	ʻerida	ʻerìyeya
faɗì	sit, dwell	faɗìyi	faɗìya	faɗída	faɗìyeya
fòri	whistle	fòrìyi	fòriya	fòrida	fòrìyeya
gábei	sing	gábeyi	gábeya	gábeda	gábeyeya
haji	make a pilgrimage	hajìyi	hajiya	hajida	hajìyeya
oi	cry	oiyi	oiya	oida	oiyeya
sileiʻ	be tortured	silèiʻyi	silèiʻa	silèiʻda	silèiʻyeya

(d) The Irregular Verbs aho, laho, wah.

110. aho (be), is an Irregular Defective Verb of doubtful conjugation. It has the same peculiarity in the Present Indicative as the other Irregular Verbs, inasmuch as it places the Personal consonants **t, n,** at the beginning of the word.

Affirmative Tenses.

Imperative	aho	be
Infin.	ahain	

Indicative :

Present	wan ahai	I am
Past	wan aha	I was
Future	wan ahain dòna	I am going to be

Habit. Pres.	wan aháin jira	I usually am
,, Past	wan aháin jirei	I used to be
Conditional	wan aháin laha	I should be
Potential	an ahàde	I may be
Subjunctive	inan ahàdo	that I may be

111. It is only irregular in the Infinitive and Indicative. There are no Continuative tenses.

		Present		Past.	
Sing.	1.	wan ahai	I am	wan aha	I was
	2.	wad tahai		wad ahaid	
	3 m.	wu yahai		wu aha	
	3 f.	wei tahai		wei ahaid	
Plur.	1.	weinu nahai		weinu ahain	
	2.	weidin tihin		weidin ahaiden	
	3.	wei yihin		wei ahayen	

112. When **aho** is conjugated negatively, it is only irregular in the Present Indicative.

		Neg. Pres. Indic.		Neg. Past. Indic.	
Sing.	1.	miihi	I am not	maan ahain	I was not
	2.	miihid		etc.	
	3 m.	maaha		Neg. Conditional	
	3 f.	maaha		maan ahàden	I should not be
Plur.	1.	miihin		maad ahàten	
	2.	maihidin		etc.	
	3.	maaha		Neg. Subjunctive	

inánan ahain   that I may not be
etc.

113. This verb is used independently as in :

na's bad tahai	you are a fool
nin 'àjis bu aha	he was a lazy man
askàri ban aháin jirei	I used to be a soldier

But it most frequently occurs combined with adjectives, especially participles.

Such adjectives are pluralised in the Plural persons.

hedan	tied	wein	large

Present Indicative Affirmative.

Sing.	1.	wa hédnahai	I am tied	wa weinahai	I am large
	2.	,, hedántahai		,, weintahai	
	3 m.	,, hedányahai		,, weinyahai	
	3 f.	,, hedántahai		,, weintahai	
Plur.	1.	,, hedhedánnahai		,, waweinnahai	
	2.	,, hedhedántihin		,, waweintihin	
	3.	,, hedhedányihin		,, waweinyihin	

Present Indicative Negative.

Sing.	1.	ma hedni	I am not tied	ma weini	I am not large
	2.	ma hednid		ma weinid	
	3 m.	ma hedna		ma weina	
	3 f.	ma hedna		ma weina	
Plur.	1.	ma hednin		ma weinin	
	2.	ma hednidin		ma weinidin	
	3.	ma hedna		ma weina	

Past Indicative Affirmative.

Sing.	1.	wa hedna	I was tied	wa weina	I was big
	2.	,, hednahaid		,, weinahaid	
	3 m.	,, hedna		,, weina	
	3 f.	,, hednahaid		,, weinahaid	
Plur.	1.	,, hedhednahain		,, waweinahain	
	2.	,, hedhednahaiden		,, waweinahaiden	
	3.	,, hedhednahayen		,, waweinahayen	

Past Indicative Negative.

Sing.	1.	maan hednahain	maan weinahain
		I was not tied	I was not big
		etc.	etc.

114. The adjectival roots, **òg** (knowing), **ja'al** (liking), **ogòl** (agreeing), are similarly conjugated with **aho,** in the Present and Past tenses.

Pres. Affirm.		Past Affirm.	
wa ògahai	I know	wa ògaha	I knew
,, ja'alahai	I like	,, ja'alaha	I liked
,, ogòlahai	I agree	,, ogòlaha	I agreed

Pres. Negative		Past Negative	
ma ògi[1]	I do not know	maan ògahain	I did not know
ma ja'alihi	I do not like	maan ja'alahain	I did not like
ma ogòlihi	I do not agree	maan ogòlahain	I did not agree

Other tenses are formed according to the 2nd conjugation from the verbs,

ogho	know (q.v.)
ja'alo	like
ogòlo	agree

After adjectives ending in **a, h, ô,** the **t** of the Personal inflexions is changed to **d.**

wa lugoládahai	she is legless
wa garadléhdahai	she is sensible
wa dôdahai	it is near

115. The verb **laho** (possess), is conjugated like **aho.**

	Affirm.	Negative
Imperative	laho	
Infinitive	lahaín	
Indicative :		
Present	wa lehahai	má lihi
Past	„ laha	má lahain
Habit. Pres.	„ lahaín jira	má lahaín jiro
„ Past	„ lahaín jirei	má lahaín jirin
Future	„ lahaín dòna	má lahaín dòno
Conditional	„ lahaín laha ⎱	maan lahàden
Potential	an lahàde ⎰	
Subjunctive	inan lahàdo	inanan lahain

Affirmative.

	Present		Past	
Sing. 1.	wa lehahai	I possess	wa laha	I possessed
2.	„ lehdahai		„ lahaid	
3 m.	„ lehyahai		„ laha	
3 f.	„ lehdahai		„ lahaid	
Plur. 1.	„ lehnahai		„ lahain	
2.	„ lehdihin		„ lahaiden	
3.	„ lehyihin		„ lahayen	

[1] The 1st Sing. Present Negative is contracted into **mòji,** or **mòyi.**

Negative.

	Present		Past	
Sing. 1.	málihi	I do not possess	ma(an) laháin	I did not possess
2.	málihid		etc.	
3 m.	málaha			
3 f.	málaha			
Plur. 1.	málihin			
2.	málihidin			
3.	málaha			

116.   *Uses of* **laho.**

This verb is made up of the root **leh** (possessing), and **aho** (be).

In the Indicative the tenses of **aho** are conjugated in full, preceded by **leh**; but other tenses are contracted, as if from the root **laho.**

laho literally means "have possession of," "own."

> **gèl badan ma lehdahai ?** have you many camels ?
> **nàg ma lehdahai ?** have you a wife ?

[**hai** (have, hold), could not be used in these examples.]

The root alone is used in the following expressions :

> **anigà leh, adigà leh**   it is mine, it is yours
> etc.   etc.

> **dáktarkà leh,** }
> or **dáktarki bu lehyahai** } it belongs to the doctor
> **nin bà leh**   it belongs to someone

Other idiomatic meanings :

> **mahhád lehdahai ?** what have you to say ? what do you mean ? what is the matter with you ?

> **wuhhu lehyahai, dòni mayo,** he means, he does not want to.

> **lába rubod ban ugu lehahai,** I am owed two rupees by you.

The Past Indicative is used as an auxiliary with an Infinitive, to form the Conditional tense of verbs.

> **wa tégi laha** I should go

It may also govern substantival sentences, introduced by **in**:

málihi inan ku ra'o,   it is not my business to go with you.

inad berrì takto bad lehdahai,   you ought (have) to go to-morrow.

117.   **wah.**

The verb root **wah** is conjugated as an irregular defective verb, and is used as an auxiliary verb, meaning, "fail," "be unable," "cannot find."

It is only conjugated in the Present and Past Indicative, and in one tense of the Subjunctive.

Indicative.

		Present		Past
Sing.	1.	wahya, waiya, wai	I fail	wahyei, waiyei, wai
	2.	weida		weidei, wei
	3 m.	wahya, waiya, wai		wahyei, waiyei, wai
	3 f.	weida		weidei
Plur.	1.	weina		weinei
	2.	weidan		weiden
	3.	wahyan, waiyan, wai		wahyen, waiyen, wai

Subjunctive.

Sing.	1.	waiyo
	2.	weido
	3 m.	waiyo
	3 f.	weido
Plur.	1.	weino
	2.	weidan
	3.	waiyan

Examples (cf. §§ 146, 195, 274 note),

iman waiya	I, or he, cannot (or will not) come
so'on wai	I, he, or they cannot (fail to) walk
shakhèin waiyen	they would not (failed to) work
hadad tegi weido	if you fail to go
hadeinu gàdi weino	if we fail to reach it
bìyo meshà ka weina	we cannot find water there
ghori ka wein wa wai	I cannot find larger wood
mahhad u iman weida	why don't you come?
wa wai	I, he, or they cannot find it
la wah	one cannot find it, it cannot be found

118.   (*e*)   *The Passive Voice.*

There is no Passive Voice in the conjugation of the Somali verb.

It is translated in two ways :

(i) by the Past Participle and the verb **aho,** cf. § 113 ;

(ii) by the Indefinite pronoun **la,** with the 3rd pers. masc. sing. of the Active voice of the verb.

Here **la** is identical in meaning and construction with the French pronoun *on,* and means "they," "people," "one."

Examples,

wahha la yiđi	it is said
wahhba lagu má falo	nothing is done with it
lei shègei	I was told
la na ghobsóneya	we shall be caught

In neither case can the Instrument be expressed.   If required, the Instrument must be expressed as the Subject :
ninkan igu diftei I was struck by this man (this man struck me).

3.   *Derivative Verbs.*

119. These are, Intensive, Reflexive, Attributive, Causative, and may be formed from either nouns, adjectives, or verbs.

120. (*a*) *Intensive verbs* express an emphatic, intensified or repeated action, and are formed by reduplication of the simple radical verb.   These all belong to the 1st Conjugation.

Examples,

lab	fold	lablab	fold up ⎫ i.e.
fur	open	furfur	unfold ⎭ many folds
goi	cut	gogoi	cut up in pieces
dòn	want	dòndòn	look around for
gur	pick up	gurgur	pick up all
heđ	tie	heđheđ	tie up, pack up
jehh	tear	jehhjehh	tear up
sheg	tell	shegsheg	repeat word by word

121. (*b*) *Reflexive verbs* imply doing something to or for oneself, or may be passive in meaning. They are formed by adding -o or -so to a noun or verb (words ending in i always take -so).

These are all of the 2nd Conjugation.

Examples,

fadì	sit	fadìso	seat yourself, sit down
jòg	wait, be	jògso	halt, stop
jed	turn	jèso	turn yourself
hub	be sure	hubso	ascertain, assure yourself
bar	teach	baro	learn
gar-ti	justice	garo	understand
amahh-di	loan	amahho	borrow
dòn	want	dòno	find for yourself
bagh	fear	baghho	be afraid
dor-ki	choice	doro	choose
jìd	pull	jìdo	hurry on
maid	wash	maido	be washed, wash yourself
sid	carry	sido	carry for yourself, wear
ghad	take away	ghado	take for yourself
hir	shave	hiro	shave yourself
hed	tie	hedo	tie on to yourself
ghob	take	ghobo	catch, take hold of
		ghobso	,, ,,
haï	have, keep	haïso	have got, keep for yourself
ghaib-ki	share	ghaibso	take your share
ìb-ki	price	ìbso	buy, sell
samèi	make	samèiso	make for yourself
gùr-ki	marriage	gùrso	marry
kahhai	take, lead	kahhaiso	take to yourself
sì	give	sìso	pay for
weidì	ask	weidìso	ask for yourself

122. (*c*) *Attributive verbs* are formed by adding -o to an adjective or participle, and are conjugated according to the 2nd Conjugation, the o being changed to a in all tenses and moods. This o gives the meaning of "become," and not "be," the latter being translated by **aho.**

Examples,

'ad	white	'ado	become white

bisil	ripe, cooked	bislo	become ripe, cooked
dô	near	dôwo	approach
gab	short	gabo	become short
hhun	bad	humo	become bad
fòg	far	fògo	go to a distance
shilis	fat	shishlo	become fat

Distinguish between the following tenses :

　　　　wa hhúnyahai　　it is bad
　　　　wa hhumàda　　it becomes bad
　　　　wa hhumáneya　　it will become bad

fardahaiga ma shishla, my ponies are not fat.
farduhu meshatan ma shishlàdo, ponies do not get fat here.
hadi mìyi lo kahháyo wa shishlàneya, if they are taken to the
　　　　　　　　　　　　　　　　　jungle, they will get fat.

123. (*d*) *Causative verbs* imply the causing of an action or production of a state or attribute in some object. They are formed (i) by adding -i, or -si (-si always to a word ending in -i) to any noun or verb, (ii) by adding -ei to an adjective. They are all transitive verbs of the 3rd Conjugation.

Examples,

shakhei	work	shakheisi	make to work
dambei	be behind	dambeisi	put behind
'ab	drink	'absi	cause to drink
ghaib	share	ghaibsi	divide in shares
gab	be short	gabi	shorten
amùs	be silent	amùsi	make silent
dalòl-shi	hole	dalòli	perforate
habàb	loss	habàbi	cause to lose
ràd-ki	track	ràdi	follow the track
bad	be plentiful	badi	increase
durug	move	durki	remove, cause to move

Where the last letter of the radical is a guttural it is usually altered to **j**.

Examples,

dagh	graze	daji	cause to graze
bagh	fear	baji	frighten
jòg	wait	jòji	stop (*transitive*)
ingeg	be dry	ingeji	cause to be dry

hagag	be straight	hagaji	make straight
wanag	goodness	wanaji	make good
wereg	go round	wereji	cause to go round
also			
ghabô	be cold	ghabôji	make cold

Verbs formed from adjectives:

'ad	white	'adei	whiten
bisil	cooked	bislei	cook
kulul	hot	kululei	make hot
adag	hard	adkei	harden
fòg	far	fògei	put afar off
dan	all, complete	damei	finish

The Verbs mentioned in § 97 alter **a** to **e**:

| gal | enter | geli | insert |
| ka' | awake | ke'i | awaken, arouse |

D. THE PARTICLES.

124. Particles are used in Somali to correspond to various English parts of speech, but cannot be actually translated, except by reference to the context of the sentence in which they occur. They cannot stand by themselves, but only in conjunction with other parts of speech, nor are they subject to any inflexions of any kind.

They may either have reference to a verb (Verbal Particles), or they may correspond to conjunctions (Conjunctive Particles).

The Verbal Particles may correspond to certain adverbs or prepositions.

The Conjunctive Particles may serve to introduce a principal or subordinate sentence, or they may act as links between two co-ordinate sentences or parts of speech.

1. *Verbal Particles.*

125. (*a*) Adverbial Particles.

wada	altogether, completely
kala	apart, separately
si	that way
so	this way

These may be used with any verb.

Examples,

fárdihi wada kéna	bring all the ponies
la wada ghadei	they are all removed
kala durka	move apart, separate
kala dufo	stretch out
kala goi	cut apart
si so'o go on	so so'o come on
si jèso turn that way	so jèso turn this way
si gal go in	so gal come in
so wada kahhai bring all	

Other Adverbial Particles are :

ha, yan, ma, an.   Negative Particles.   Cf. §§ 91, 145.
ma.   Interrogative Particle.   Cf. §§ 94, 145.
wa, ba, ya.   Affirmative Particles.   Cf. §§ 138—144.

Further idiomatic meanings of si and so should be noticed:
si means "continue" an action

si shakhei	continue to work
si baro	continue to learn

so means "begin" to do something, or "go and" do....

so aròri hòlaha	go and water the flocks
so ìbso	go and buy for yourself
so safei	go and clean

126.   (*b*)   Prepositional Particles (ku, u, ka, la).

ku   at, in, by means of, for :

bìyo galáska ku shub	pour some water into the glass
gèd bu ku heđna	he was tied to a tree
'el bu ku da'ei	he fell into a well
ga'anta ku ghobo	hold with your hand
hađig ku heđ	tie with a rope
gèl bannu ku dírirra	we fight for camels

u   on account of :

mahhad u taktei P	what did you go for?

to (a person) :

sirkálki u tag	go to the officer
Fàrah u gei	take to Farah

ka   from, across, concerning:

mèsha ka kàli	come from that place
mèsha ka tága	go away from there
ka ghob	pour away
ka goi	cut off
dehhda ka taláb	go across the nullah
muska ka bòd	jump over the fence
wahhas wahhba ka gáran mayo	I understand nothing about that

la   together with:

na la ra'	come with us
wa ku la hádleya	I am talking with you

2.   Conjunctive Particles.

127.   (a)   Introductory Particles.

sô, or shô   perhaps:

sô magàladu jòga	perhaps he is in the town
sô gáran maysid P	don't you understand?

mala, malaha (lit. thought)   probably:

mala wa árarei	he has probably run away

bal.   The meaning of this is impossible to express.   It is used in the following constructions,

(i)   With Imperative: **bal káli**   well, come

bal an ègo   let me look, then

(ii)   With the particle **in**, introducing an indirect question:
weidi bal inei fògtahai   ask if it is far

(b)   Conjunctive Particles.

iyo   and (coupling two substantives)

o   and (coupling two clauses).

-na   and, also, (a suffix, usually introducing a fresh sentence)

-se   but (a suffix).

ama, mise,   either, or

in   that ⎱
hadi   if ⎰   these usually require the Subjunctive mood.

Examples,

Fàrah iyo ániga,   Farah and I.

órod o só ghad,   run and fetch it.

wa adágyahai o lagu goïn kari mayo,   it is hard and cannot be cut.

ádiguna mahhad dònesa ? and what do you want?
isna wa tégei, he too has gone.
dabedédna, and afterwards.
wa jògei, ninkuse árarei, I was there, but the man ran away.
ama tag ama jòg, either go or stay.
ma shegtei mise ilôdei ? did you tell or forget?
inad takto ban dòneya, I want you to go.
hadu yimàdo, i kàli, if he comes, come to me.

E. Adverbs, Prepositions, Conjunctions.

128. With the exception of the radical particles given in the last section, these parts of speech are represented in Somali by substantival expressions.

129. Adverbs of Quality and Manner:

ain-ki	kind, sort
ainkan, ainkas	like this, like that
si-di	manner
sida, sidas, or sàs	so, thus

si is also used with an adjective, forming an abstract substantive:

si wanàksan	good manner
si hhun	bad „
si 'ajis	lazy „

Such expressions with the particle **u** become adverbial.

Examples,

si wanàksan u samei	make properly
wa si 'ajis u shakhèineya	he is working lazily

The following nouns are commonly used in this way with **u**:

àd	force, effort	hòs	downwards
mìyir	prudence	dib	backwards
khumàti	straightness	hor	forwards
kor	upwards	ghunyar	slowness
	also the verb root **dakhso** hurry		

Examples,

àd u heji	hold tight
mìyir u fùl	ride carefully
dib u jògso	stand back
dakhso u tag	go quickly

130. Adverbs of Time and Place:

Time: gor-ti, kol-ki, mar-ki, had-di, wà-gi, béri-gi, gélin-ki.

Place: mel-shi, hal-ki, hag-gi.

Time.

this time	gortan, kolkan, markan	another time	mar dambe
now	íminka, áminka	often	gor badan, mar badan
now at once	haddan	sometimes	mar mar
now therefore	haddaba	again	mar kăleh
then	gortas, kolkas, markas	at no time	kolla
soon	gor dô	first	horta
later on	haddô, haddôtò	once	kol, gor
before	kolki hòre, marki hòre	twice	lába gor
afterwards	kolki dambe, marki dambe, dabadéd	yet, still	wèli
formerly	kol hòre, wàgi hòre, bérigi hòre	never	wèligi
		always	gor walba

Place.

here	halkan, mèshan	above	dùsha
this way	haggan	beneath	hòsta
there	halkas, halkà, mèshas	in front	hòre, horti, ka hòre
that way	haggas	behind	dambe, ka dambe, ka daba
yonder	halkò, haggò	inside	gudaha
near	mel dô	outside	dibadda
far	mel fòg	aside	ges
somewhere	mel, melun	on that side	gestà
everywhere	mel walba	around	harèro
nowhere	mella	in the middle	dehhda

(For hours, days, months, etc., see Appendix.)

78

ACCIDENCE

131. INTERROGATIVE ADVERBS.

of what sort ?	ainma ?
how ?	side ?
how much ?	inte ?
why ?	mahha u ? (cf. § 195)
when ?	gorma ?
at what time ?	hadma ?
how often ?	ìmisa gor ?
how long	halkyo gorma ?
where ?	halke? hagge ? melma ? me ? meyei ? medei ?
how far ?	inte ?

132. PREPOSITIONS.

The simple prepositions (to, for, from, with, etc.) are represented by the Particles (cf. § 126).

Other prepositions are represented by Adverbial Nouns, the word governed being placed in the possessive (cf. § 201). This may be done by using the adverb alone, with the governed word following it in the possessive position, as

sidi na's	like a fool
gorti dagàlki	at the time of battle

Or the adverb is used with the possessive adjective, as

ákhalka hortìsi	in front of the house
jòniad gudahèda	inside a bag

as, like	sidi	outside	dibaddìsi
at the time of	gorti, kolki, marki	beside	gestìsi
before	hortìsi	around	harèrodìsi
after	dabadìsi	between, among	dehhdìsi
until	hadyo inti	opposite	hortìst
since	halkyo gorti	beyond	ka shishéi
near to	agtìsi	on this side of	ka sòkei
far from	fògtìsi	instead of	meshìsi
over, on	dushìsi	for the sake of	awadìsi
under	hòstìsi	behind	dambìsi
in front of	hortìsi	within	gudahìsi
and,			
except	mahai	without laän	

133. RELATIVE CONJUNCTIONS.

when	**gorti, kolki, marki**
until	**haḍyo inti, inti**
while	**inti**
since	**halkyo gorti**
before	**intan** (= **inti-an**, negative)
where	**mèshi, halki, haggi**
as much as	**inti**
as	**sidi**

F. INTERJECTIONS AND SALUTATIONS.

134. *Interjections.*

war	man, sir
na	woman, miss, madam

Examples,

war, 'ss ká tag! go away, man!
na, ayà tahai ? who art thou, woman?

warya! is used to draw attention.

-ô is added as a suffix to Proper Names in calling out to persons.

warya, Libanô! Hi! Liban!

ha	yes
maya	no
hoi hoi!	a shout to attract attention
jog!	an exclamation of astonishment
Wallahh!	by God!
èga, Wallahh!	lit. means "look, by God!"
dèga!	lit. means "listen!"
Wallàhhi, iyo Billàhhi, iyo Tallàhhi.	An Arabic oath
hauràrsan	all right
ha ahàto	so be it
wàtahai	very well (lit. it is)
yelkìs	that's his business, never mind
'ss ka da	let be
'ss kà eg	look out
Illàhhi maháddi	thank God
Illàhhi ba òg	God knows
kô, kôdi, haiye	yes, well?

135.   *Salutations.*

Nábad   Peace

Greeting		Reply	
[1]**ma nábad ba ?**		**wa nábad**	
or	is it peace ?	or	it is peace
sô nábad mìya ?		**nábad weiye**	
ma nábad ghóbota ?	have you peace ?	**wa nábad ghobta**	I have peace
[2]**mahhád shégta ?**	what do you tell ?	**nábad ban shèga**	I tell peace
[3]**ma báriden ?**	are you safe ?	**ha, bárinei**	yes, we are safe
sidè tahai ?	how are you ?		
'ss ka wárran	give news of yourself		
mèsha ka wárran	give news of the place		
ma bukta ?	are you sick ?		
ma buksánesa ?	are you getting better ?		
ma ladántahai ?	are you well ?		
wa ka sì dara	I am worse		

[1] The formal salutation.
[2] The colloquial, informal greeting, "How do you do?"
[3] Corresponds to "Good morning."

PART III. SYNTAX OF SIMPLE SENTENCES.

A. The Structure of a Simple Sentence.

1. *Order of Words.*

136. The usual order of a simple sentence, such as a command or statement, is

1. Subject.   2. Object.   3. Verb.

Examples,

o.   v.
sor na si,   give us food.

o.   v.
fáraska kòrei,   saddle the horse.

s.   o.   v.
nin ba libahh dilei,   a man has killed a lion.

137. Adverbs may be placed anywhere except last. Adverbs of Time are usually placed first.

a.   o.   v.
háddatan aurta rèra,   load the camels at once.

o.   a.   v.
fáraska dakhso u sò kahhai,   fetch the horse quickly.

a.   s.   v.
markàsa ninki yiđi,   then the man said.

s.   a.   o.   v.
habàrti ba habènki dambe àkhalki Suldànka so ag martei,
the old woman on the following night passed near the Sultan's house.

a.   s.   o.   v.
'ashodi dambe ya habàrti barìyo dònatei,
on the following day the old woman begged alms.

s.   o.   a.   v.
ninka hòlihìsi Burao bu gèineya,
the man is taking his flocks to Burao.

138.   2. *The Particles* **wa, ba, ya.**

These particles are of such universal occurrence, and so essential to idiomatic speech, that a correct understanding of their use is necessary at the outset. No one meaning can be assigned to them, as each may represent at one time a pronoun, at another a definite or indefinite article, at another the verb " is," " are," and at yet another time an adverb.

Their meanings may be divided into two classes :

(i) All three, **wa, ba, ya,** are Particles of Affirmation, just as **ma** is a Particle of Negation or Interrogation.

> **wa** draws attention to, and precedes, the verb.
> **ba,** and **ya** (especially **ba**), draw attention to, and follow, the subject.

(ii) **ba,** and **ya** (especially **ya**), may be conjunctive or adverbial particles, often to be translated by " and so," " and then."

> This usage is found in narratives.

139.   (i) *As Particles of Affirmation.*

If used without either a personal pronoun or a particle, a verb is considered abrupt.

Compare **ba** and **wa** in the following examples :

(*Note. In these cases* **ba** *and* **ya** *are synonymous, and either form may be used equally, but* **ba** *is preferred by Eastern and Central tribes.*)

1.	**nin ba yimi**	a man has come
2.	**nin wa yimi**	a man has arrived
3.	**Fàrah ba yimi**	Farah has come
4.	**Fàrah wa yimi**	Farah has arrived

1, 3 mean respectively that " it is a man that has come," and that " it is Farah that has come."

2, 4 mean respectively that " a man (as expected, or ordered) has arrived," and that " Farah (as expected, or ordered) has arrived."

In the first case the information relates to the individual who has come ; in the second case it relates to the arrival of some known person.

In short, **ba** emphasizes the identity of the subject, while **wa** emphasizes the meaning of the verb.

140. This explains the fact that **wa** may be used with a verb
when no subject is expressed, and **ba** may be used when no verb is
expressed.

Examples,

wa imáneya	he is coming
wa wanăksányahai	it is good
sádehhdas ba wanăksan	those three are the best
ma Árab ba ?	is he an Arab ?
nin ba la dilei	a man has been killed
hòlihi wa la da'ei	the flocks have been looted
hòlihi răg Musa Ismail ba ka da'ei	
	Musa Ismail's men looted the flocks

141. ba thus distinguishes the subject from the object where
otherwise it would be doubtful.

Examples,

nin libahh ba ghobtei	a lion caught a man
nin ba libahh ghobtei	a man caught a lion

142. Special uses of **wa**.

(*a*) **wa** assists or emphasizes the meaning of the verb, but
especially emphasizes an affirmation in reply to a question, expressed or understood.

ma imáneya ? ha, wa imáneya.
Is he coming ? Yes, he is coming.

ma garanésa ? ha, wa garanéya.
Do you understand ? Yes, I understand.

(*b*) **wa** means "is," "are," where the complement is a noun or
numeral, and not an adjective.

wa nin hhun	he is a bad man
wa shabèl	it is a leopard
wa áfar	they are four
wà kan	here he is
wà ke ?	which is it ?
wa kúma ?	who are you ?
wa inte ?	how much is it ?
wà mahai ?	what is it ?

(*c*)   Where the complement of "is," "are," is an adjective, **wa** is used, but the verb **aho** (be) is also used, suffixed to the adjective.

hádalkas wa hhúnyahai	that arrangement is bad
la'agti wa 'ulùstahai	the money is heavy
sirkálka wa ògyahai	the officer knows
wàyahai, wàtahai	all right, so be it

(*d*)   When the Preterite tense is used with **wa** it becomes a Perfect or Completed tense.

wa yimi	he has come
wa arkei	I have seen

143.   Special uses of **ba** and **ya.**

(*a*)   **ba**, or **ya**, emphasizes the identity of the subject, especially in reply to a question expressed or understood.

ya ku la rá'eya P Fàrah ba i la rá'eya.
who is going with you? Farah is.

'id ma timi P ha, Jàma ba yimi.
has anyone come? Yes, Jama has.

Suldàn ba ínan laha.
(there was) a Sultan (who) had a son.

(*b*)   When the subject of a sentence is a numeral it nearly always requires **ba**, or **ya**.

soddon ba jòga	thirty are present
lába bá maghán	two are absent
ìmisa ba jòga P	how many are present?

(*Note.   In the following cases only* **ba** *is used, and not* **ya.**)

(*c*)   **ba** is used in questions where the complement of "is," "are," is a substantive.

ma áur ba P	is it a camel?
ma Árab ba P	is he an Arab?
ma kaigi ba P	is it mine?
ma ísaga ba P	is it he?
ma lába ba P	is it two?

(*a*)   In affirmative sentences, where the complement is an adjective, **ba** may be used, but the verb **aho**, be, is not then employed.

In this case **ba** may give a superlative sense to the adjective.

Illàhhi ba òg	God knows
nin ba maghán	one man is absent
báhalaha g̈har ba hhun	some animals are bad
sádehhdas kán ba wanăksan	this is the best of those three

(*e*) **ba**, used after the object of a sentence, has a distributive meaning.

nin ba mid sì	give each man one
ain ba mel gòniah ḏiga	put each kind in a separate place
kol ba nin keliah ha yimàdo	let one man come at a time

(*f*) **ba** may give an indefinite meaning to a word of time or place; or is used with a verb, meaning "at all."

mel ba kú jira	it is somewhere or other
wahhba dòni mayo	I don't want anything at all
ha tégin ba	don't go at all
walba	every
lábadabá	both
sádehhdabá	all three
wahhad dòneso ba	whatever you want
mèshi ad tákto ba	wherever you go
kolba ad dòneso	whenever you want

144. (ii) *As Adverbial or Conjunctive Particles.*

ba and **ya**, in this sense, correspond to the English particles "now," "and then," "and so." Their position in the sentence has no relation to the subject, object, or verb, but follows the first phrase in the sentence.

("Phrase" here includes both unqualified nouns, or nouns with their attributes, whether adjective or relative clause, or adverbial expressions.)

ba is apparently not used except when the phrase is an unqualified noun, usually one which has already been referred to in the preceding sentence.

ya is always used after an adverb, or adverbial expression.

The examples illustrating these are taken from the stories, q.v.

  Suldànka nàg bu g̈ùrsadei, suldànki ba hajki g̈hobtei.
            (p. 145, l. 2.)

Kolkàsei tiđi, "Bèrka gènyoda ínankàga." Ínanki ba
suldànki u yèđei.   (p. 146, l. 7.)
"Galábtaän ku so mermero." Galábti ba ínanki gènyodi
fùlei.   (p. 146, l. 9.)
Mas ba lei heđei, maskas ba igu imáneya, o i 'uneya.
                                                   (p. 150, l. 21.)
Daràrti dambe, ya suldànku yimi.   (p. 146, l. 3.)
Dúhurki kolkei ahaid, ya wìyishi timi. (p. 148, l. 11.)
Ísago gèdka hurda, ya shanti ìnan u yímaden.
                                                   (p. 148, l. 16.)

3. *Simple Interrogative and Negative Sentences.*

145. The same particle **ma** is used in both kinds of sentences.
There are certain differences in its several uses.

The Negative **ma** is placed as near to the verb as possible,
while the Interrogative **ma** comes before any pronoun or particle
qualifying the verb (cf. § 236).

Examples,

⌠bìyo ma kú jiran ?	is there any water in ?
⌡bìyo ku má jiran	there is no water in
⌠wahh ma lagu sìyei ?	has anything been given you ?
⌡wahhba lei ma sìn	nothing has been given me

When joined to the personal pronoun the interrogative particle
becomes **mi-**, while the negative particle is unaltered.

⌠miad áraktei ?	did you see ?
⌡maad arkin	you did not see
⌠miu ku shègei ?	did he tell you ?
⌡i mau shègin	he did not tell me

In both cases the pronoun is often omitted when the person
referred to is obvious from the context.

i ma shègin	(he) did not tell me
maärkin, or maärag	(I) did not see
bùrta ma árkesa ?	do you see the hill ?
wahh ma dònesa ?	do you want anything ?

Interrogative **ma** may be separated from the pronoun by another
word. In this case **ban, bad,** etc. are used (see also § 229).

ma hálka bu tégeya ?	is it there he is going ?
ma nínkan bu ku díftei ?	is it this man that struck you ?

Where the subject of an interrogative or negative sentence is a noun, it is placed first in the sentence. Generally, in interrogative sentences the personal pronoun is required as well, but need not be used.

'ollku ma ká bahhai ?	has the army left ?
ninku miu arkei libahha ?	did the man see the lion ?
manta sirkálku Burao ma ghobóneya ?	
	is the officer going to Burao to-day ?

146. Questions expressing surprise are introduced by **sô** or **shô**.

Examples,

la'agta badan sô dòni maysid ?	don't you want all this money?
sô gáran maysid ?	don't you understand ?
sô ma garanésa ?	surely you understand ?

Questions introduced by Interrogative Pronouns and Adverbs :

Examples,

ya ku shègei hádalkas ?	who told you that story ?
wa kúma ? ayà tahai ?	who are you ?
ayad áraktei ?	whom did you see ?
ninmad u dìbtei ?	to whom did you give it ?
mahhá ka da'ei ?	what has happened?
'id ma la dilei ?	is anyone killed ?
adèrkà muhhu aurkas' ka sìsóneya ?	what will your uncle give for that camel ?
abbahà mahhá la yidáhha ?	what do you call your father ?
ídinma warákhdan Burao gèya ?	which of you will take this chit to Burao ?
fárasma buka ? ma aínabka ?	which horse is sick? the black?
mahhán la'ag ugu sìya ?	why should I give you any money ?
mahhád ugu hedántahai meshà ?	what are you tied there for ?
'ollku gormu Kirrit ka bah- háya ?	when does the force leave Kirrit ?
hagge hòlahaiga ka takten ?	where did you leave my animals ?
ninkakan hagge bu ku diftei ?	where did this man hit you ?

gènyadi mèdeiＰ hámarku mèyeiＰ	where is the mare? where is the bay?
hérodi sirakìshu fadída wa hagge Ｐ	where is the officers' camp?
halkiyo Bòhotleh intèi jirtaＰ	how far is Bohotle from here?
intu mághana wa inteＰ	how long was he absent?
ìmisa rubod bu ku bihhìyeiＰ	how many rupees did he pay you?
haggà bùrta ká shishei sidu dulyahaiＰ	how does the country lie beyond that hill?
bùrtà ka sòkei sidèi tahaiＰ	how is it on this side?
jòniadà 'uleiskèda wa inteＰ	how heavy is that bag?
'elka ɗererkìsu wa inte Ｐ (or intu deràda Ｐ)	how deep is the well?
bàhalkan wa ainma Ｐ	what sort of an animal is this?

In Negative questions introduced by "why?" (**mahha u Ｐ**) a special idiom is used with the verb **wah** (§§ 117, 195).

mahhad u dòni weida inad takto Ｐ   why don't you want to go?

4. *The Verbs of existence, and attributive verbs.*

147. These Verbs (be, live, stay, dwell, grow, exist, lie, be found, become) have an equal variety of corresponding Somali expressions, as **aho, oll, jòg, jir, fadi, laho, nokho.**

(i) The Auxiliary verb "be" requires a complement in the form of noun, adjective or pronoun.

(*a*) This may be translated simply by **wa**, or **ba**, as shewn in the examples of those particles.

(*b*) Or it is translated by **aho**, which is used independently when the complement is a noun, or is combined with an adjective when the complement is the latter, and forms an Attributive verb. In the latter case **wa** is required as well, but pronouns are never used.

Examples,

nin wein ban ahai	I am a big man.
na's bad tahai (contracted into **bàt'hai**)	thou art a fool
nin fi'an miu aha Ｐ	was he a clever man?
Somàli mïïhid	thou art not a Somali

askàri maäha	he is not a soldier
tollmà tahai ?	of what tribe are you ?
wa wanăksányahai	he is good
ma wanăksana	he is not good
la'agti ma 'ulústahai ?	is the money heavy ?

148. (ii) It may refer to the presence or existence of an object in a certain place.

(a) **jòg** is used when referring to animate objects.

Examples,

ninki ma jòga ?	is the man here ?
aurti haggàsei jògta	the camels are there
răgu ìmisa ba jòga ?	how many of the men are present ?

(b) **jir** is used of inanimate objects.

Examples,

wahh kăleh má jira ?	is there anything else ?
halkan mahha kú jira ?	what is there here ?
wahhba ku má jiran	there is nothing
bìyo wa kú jiran	there is water in

oll (literally lie) is often used in this sense :

sanadúkhdi halkan tal	the boxes are here
akhalkaiga bu yal	it is in my house
kitábki meska dushìsi yal	the book is on the table
bìyo badan ba yàlin	there is plenty of water

(c) **oll** (dwell, live), also refers to people :

Examples,

tollma halkan yal?	what tribe lives here ?
Burao-einu nil	we lived at Burao
hagge ollí jirten ?	where used you to live ?

fadi is used with same meaning (lit. sit, abide) :

Examples,

magalodaän fadìya	I stay in the town
Berberu fadìya	he stays in Berbera
hagge sirakìshu fadída ?	where do the officers dwell ?

(d) When referring to the existence of animals or plants, **laho** (possess) is used.

Examples,

meshàsa ugad ma lehdahai ?
is there any game in that place ? (lit. does that place possess game?).
gerenùk iyo dèro bei lehdahai,
it possesses gerenuk and dero (or g. and d. are found there).
b'e'id málaha,   there is no oryx there.
mel walba aus bei lehdahai,   there is grass everywhere.
dáreiga Nogàshu bei lehdahai,   the fig grows in the Nogal.

  (vi) **nokho**   become
       'ss ka ɗig   pretend

  Examples,
    suldàn bu nòkhdei   he became Sultan
    nàg bu 'ss ka dígeya he is pretending to be a woman

B. THE PARTS OF SPEECH.

1. *The Article.*

149. A noun, which in English is qualified by the indefinite
pronoun, a, an, or some, any, is used in Somali in its simplest
form in an indefinite sense.

    Suldàn ba ínan laha   a Sultan had a son
    eï ba 'eíyeya   a dog is barking
    kùrsi wein ban dòneya I want a big chair
    fardo ba imáneya   some horses are coming
    gèdo ban haïsta   I have got some grass
    hòlo ma lehdahai ?   have you any flocks ?
    la'ag málihi   I have not any money

150. The Definite article suffix (§ 28) is used to define nouns in
a particular or general sense.

151. -i is always used for the definite article where -u or -a are
not required by the following rules.

152. -a (i) is used primarily in defining nouns, referring to
objects or persons actually present, or in front of the speaker.

sandúkha ghad   remove the box (which is in front of us)
bein bu shègeya ninka the man is telling lies

  Note. Where the noun in this sense is the subject of the sentence, it is
more usual to use the demonstrative adjective -an this.

(ii)   It is also used with a noun in a general sense when in the objective case (§ 153, (vi)).

(iii)   With Definite nouns which are possessive, or adjectival:

ákhalki ninka	the house of the man
ínanki Suldànka	the Sultan's son
nin magàloda	a man of the town

even where the Possessive adjective is used ;

sirkálka ghalabkìsi   the officer's luggage

(iv)   With nouns used adverbially:

galábta   this evening   Isninta   on Monday

153.   u is used in the following cases :

(i)   With well-known persons or objects of nature.

Wadádku	the Mullah (i.e. Mohammed Abdallah)
Sirkálku	the Officer (i.e. as a soldier would say, referring to his own officer)
oghàshu shirka fadída	the headmen sit in council
ghorahhdu wa kulúshahai	the sun is hot
ròbku wa gàdeya	the rain is stopping

(ii)   With persons or things already referred to, and about which one is talking, as in the following example :

A man brings a complaint that another man has stolen his camel ; the judge may ask :

hashu ma jògta ?   is the camel here ?

or the man may say :

ninku wa árarei,   the man has run away.

In this way it is used when referring to a character in a story who has already been mentioned, as :

Suldànku, ínanku, habàrtu, etc.

(iii)   It is also used with the Personal pronouns in the Emphatic forms,

ánigu, ádigu, ádu, etc. (§ 55).

(iv)   When a noun is used in a general sense, referring to all

members of a class, it is used in English with no article, but in
Somali usually takes the article -u.

sirakìshu 'ano halad ma ja'ashahai?   do officers like camel's
milk?

nàguhu wa hádal badányahai   women are great talkers.

(v) -u cannot be used with a noun which is qualified by an
epithet. In such cases -i, or -a, only are found.

        oghàshi Habr Yunis   the H. Y. headmen
        sirkálki hàkinkaäha   the judge-officer

(vi) -u is not used with a noun in the objective case. If a noun
in one of the above senses is objective, -a is used (cf. *supra*).

gorma la ghobóneya Wadádka?   when will the Mullah be
caught?

154.   The Definite Article may be used with any noun, numeral
or pronoun, and is often used together with the Demonstrative
Adjective and Possessive Adjective suffixes, q.v.

.   Where a definite noun is qualified by a numeral, it is the latter
which takes the article, and not the noun:

        lábadi nin   the two men

2. *The Noun.*

(a) *Cases.*

155.   There are no case inflexions in Somali, and the relation
of a noun to the rest of the sentence must be recognised from its
position or the context.

156.   A general rule for subject and object was given in the first
section on syntax, but this is subject to colloquial variation, where
the meaning is obvious from the context.

Generally, the subject may be distinguished from the object by
the gender and number of the verb, and pronoun, if the latter occurs,
but only in cases where both are different.

    ninki nàgti bu dilei   the man killed the woman
    nàgti ninki bei dishei⎫
or **ninki nàgti bei dishei**⎭   the woman killed the man

    Suldànki ba gartei nàgtìsi   and the Sultan recognised his wife.
bérigi dambe ya ínan, Suldàn dalei, ya ínanti arkei   Afterwards
a son of a Sultan saw the girl.

ba, ya (§ 141) help to distinguish the subject.

dabku ya maska iyo hhaska bakhtìyei   the fire destroyed the snake and the fence.

Here the subject is also denoted by the article **-u**.

The special forms of the pronouns, **wuhhu**, etc., following the subject, are used to make it clear.

'ollki Habr Toljàla wuhhu dùlei Ali Nalèyah,   the force of H. T., they attacked the Ali Naleyah.

Dative.

157. Some verbs may have two objects, one being in the dative case, or indirect object.

The usual order is to place the direct object before the indirect.

Fàrah warákhdi sirkálki bu sìyei	Farah gave the letter to the officer
gèdo fáraska sì	give the horse grass
ninba tòban-an dìbei	I gave each man ten

Motion *to a person* is expressed by the particle **u**, but motion to a place requires no particle, the place being translated as an indirect object.

Àli u tag	go to Ali
àghilki igu yimi	the headman came to me
aurti Sirkálki u gèya	take the camels to the Officer
Burao ban tégeya	I am going to Burao
Àli hòlihìsi rerkìsi bu gèineya	Ali is taking his flocks to his family

158. Nouns may be used adverbially, as in the last two examples, with verbs of motion or rest, or expressing duration of time.   But if they are abstract nouns expressing manner or quality, **u** is required before the verb (see § 129).

Burao ban fadìya	I stay at Burao
lába 'asho beinu so'onei	we marched for two days

159. The *Ablative* is expressed by the prepositional particle **ka.**

magàlodan ka imi	I have come from the town

'ollku shăleito meshan ká bahhai,   the army left this place
yesterday.

The *Possessive* Case (cf. § 45).

160. Nouns are used adjectivally, following another noun which
they qualify, expressing origin, quality, value, use, space of time.

nin magàloda	a man of the town
nin dagàl badan	a great man for fighting
dagàlki shălei	yesterday's battle

If the noun expresses material, profession, or nationality, it may
be made into an adjective by the suffix **-ah** (being).

sandukh birah	a box of iron
nin Tomàlah	a Tomal
lába nin o sirkàlah, or lába nin o sirakil	} two officers
ninki askàrigaäha	the soldier man

If it expresses the contents, or features, the suffix **-leh** is used.

balli bìyoleh	a "pan" of water
nin gaḍleh	a bearded man

Features or clothes may be used alone descriptively.

nin san wein	a big nosed man
gholidi gambo 'as	the party in red puggarees
nàgta maro 'as	that woman in a red tobe
bùrta figh ḍer	that high peaked hill

161. The *Partitive* Case. "Some of," "any of," "one of."

The noun expressing the whole is either plaçed first in the
sentence, parenthetically, or follows the noun expressing the portion,
separated by the particle **o.**

răgu in yer ba jògta	a few of the men are here
sádehhdas ki u wanăksana wà ka	of those three that is the best one
aurtaida mid ba ḍintei	one of my camels has died
wahh badan o hòlahaiga	plenty of my animals

(b) *Number.*

162. The plural of nouns is used as in English, wherever it is
desired to express plural number, except after numerals.

nàguhu wa hádal badányahai	women are great talkers
wa askàrr hhunhhun	they are bad soldiers
oghàl bei nòkhdan	they become headmen
aurti timi	the camels have come

163. After numerals the plural number is only used in the case of feminine nouns, except those ending in -o (cf. § 42).

lába nin	two men	áfar 'asho	four days
lehh nàgod	six women	sádehh halod	three camels

(c) Concord of Plural Nouns.

164. In the Accidence (§§ 34, 76) it was noticed that the Guttural, and Dental, definite articles of the singular nouns are changed in the plural to Dental, and Guttural, respectively, except in the case of masculine monosyllables.

fas-ki	axe	plur.	fasas-ki
busta-hi	blanket	,,	bustyal-shi
'asho-di	day	,,	'ashoïn-ki
muda'-i	fork	,,	muda'yo-di
sirkál-ki	officer	,,	sirakìl-shi
làn-ti	branch	,,	làmo-hi

This is more noticeable in irregular plurals, as :

aur-ki	he camel	plur.	aur-ti
àghil-ki	headman	,,	oghàl-shi or àghilin-ti
Árab-ki	Arab-man	,,	Árab-ti
ìl-shi	eye	,,	indo-hi

This is comparable with, and is no doubt related to, the Arabic broken plurals, which are always feminine.

165. The plurals of the 1st class are true plurals, and adjectives and verbs always agree with them in number.

fasaska wa hhunhhúnyihin	those axes are bad
sumanki daḍera wa hallàban	the long straps are lost

In all other plurals, the adjective and verb should agree with the noun according to the form of the linking consonant alone, and not in number.

Compare the following examples :

nàgti wa imánesa (3rd fem. sing.)	the woman is coming
aurki wa imáneya (3rd masc. sing.)	the camel is coming
nimanki wa imáneyan (3rd plur.)	the men are coming
nàgihi wa imáneya (3rd masc. sing.)	the women are coming
aurti wa imánesa (3rd fem. sing.)	the camels are coming
Sirkálki ghalabkìsi (3rd masc. sing.)	the officer's baggage
gabaddi bokhorkèda (3rd fem. sing.)	the girl's sash
Sirakìshi ghalabkèda (3rd fem. sing.)	the officers' baggage
gènyadi wà tan (fem.)	there is the mare
aurki wà kan (masc.)	here is the camel
aurti wà tan (fem.)	here are the camels
sanadúkhdi weineid halkan tal (3rd fem. sing.)	the big boxes lie here
jòniadihi madana wa kú jira (3rd masc. sing.)	the empty bags are in
oghàl ba fadída (3rd fem. sing.)	some headmen are sitting

Note. The following case of false analogy is interesting, as shewing how in the Somali mind the article is the important factor to be considered in the concord of nouns with adjectives and verbs.

fardihi (the horses) is often contracted to **fardi**. In the latter case the feminine concord is most usual, as to the ear it appears that the article suffix is **-di**, the original masculine suffix **-hi** having been lost.

Example,

fardihi wa ka'dleineya (3rd masc. sing.)} the horses are trotting
fardi wa ka'dleinesa (3rd fem. sing.) }

166. The plural nouns, **bìyo, 'ano, gèdo, hòlo, timo,** are treated as true plurals.

bìyo ma yàlin	there is no water
'anihi wa kuan	here is the milk

wahhba (nothing) is usually considered plural :

wahhba ku má jiran	there is nothing there

167. Adjectives qualifying plural nouns, when used indefinitely, usually agree in number (see note to Table in § 76).

nàgo wawein	some big women
Yibruhu wa niman hhunhhun	the Yibirs are bad men

168. When the noun is qualified by a numeral special rules for concord apply.

If the subject is indefinite (the numeral having no article suffix) the verb is used in the singular.

The masculine may always be used, but if the plural is feminine, and would take a dental linking consonant if definite, the feminine form of the verb may be used.

> **shan aur mìyigi ku bakhtìyei,** or **bakhtidei,**
> five camels died in the jungle.

> **lába nin ba yimi,**   two men came.

> **áfar nàgo ba yimi,**   four women came.

If an adjective qualifies the noun as well, it is used in the plural.

> **shan aur o hhunhhun ya bakhtìyei,**   five bad camels died.

If however the noun is definite, the verb may be either singular or plural; if it is singular it may agree in gender as with indefinite nouns.

> **shanti aur mìyigi ku bakhtidei,** or **bakhtiyen,**
> the five camels died in the jungle.

Where the noun refers to persons, the verb is usually used in the plural.

When the subject of the verb is a plural pronoun alone, or when the pronoun **wahhai** is used, the verb is always plural.

The following examples are taken from passages in the stories given in this book, and in Schleicher's *Somali Texte.*

shanti gabdod e kăleh wahhai ku diftan shan ínan o hoḋanah,
the five other girls struck five rich young men.

shanti ínan u yímaden,   the five boys came to him.

lábadas u sarrèyen,   those two were in command.

wahha ugu yimi abahèd iyo walalkèd,
there came to her her father and brother.

lehh aur ka haḋei,   six camels were left.

lehhdi aur, o lehh libahh 'unesa,
the six camels which six lions were eating.

shan iyo labàton nin, o hábsiga kú jirei, wahhai ghàten...
twenty-five men, who were in gaol, took... (Schl. p. 13, l. 12.)

sirkálka wuhhu direi askàro aur ku jogta,
the officer sent soldiers on camels. (Schl. p. 13, l. 18.)

markàsa sagàlki walàlahed tashàden,
Then her nine brothers considered. (Schl. p. 22, l. 18.)
áfarti walàlaäha ya tashàdei,
the four brothers considered. (Schl. p. 29, l. 21.)
lábadi odei ya yiđi, the two old men said. (Schl. p. 30, l. 13.)

3. The Adjective.

(a) Order and Syntax.

169. It has been seen in the Accidence (§ 69) that adjectives follow the substantives they qualify, and are inflected to agree with them in gender and number (§ 75).

170. When a noun is qualified by more than one adjective, the second is coupled by the particle o (and).

kitáb yer o madô	a small black book
răg kăleh o wanăksan	other good men
dagahhánta wawein o 'ul'ulus	the big heavy stones

The adjective is coupled by o, if the noun is also qualified by a numeral.

lehh halod o hhunhhun	six bad camels
áfar bákhalod o wawein	four big mules
lába nin o Habr Yunis	two men of the Habr Yunis

Note. When the word kăleh (other) is one of two epithets qualifying a noun, it is coupled by e instead of o.
o kăleh has a special meaning. Cf. § 177.

Example,

lehh gabđod e kăleh   six other girls,
but, lehh gabđod o kăleh   would mean,   six similar girls

Where nouns are used adjectivally they follow the same rule.

sádehh nin o askàri	three soldiers
todòba nin o sirakil	seven officers

boghol, and kun, are treated adjectively also, and require o following them when more than one hundred or thousand is referred to.

lába boghol o askàri	200 soldiers
sádehh kun o ađi	3,000 sheep

171. Attributive verbs are formed from adjectives, by the particle **wa,** and the verb **aho,** which is suffixed to the adjective (see Conjugations, § 114, and 142 (*c*)).

fáraskan wa wanăksányahai	this horse is good
sandukha wa fudúdyahai	the box is light
ràdadkan wa gabgabôyihin	these tracks are old

ba may be used with the adjective, without **aho,** but gives a superlative sense (§ 143 (*d*)).

kan ba wanăksan	this is the good one
ùshatan ba fudud	this stick is the lightest

Adjectives in -leh, -la may be split up into their component parts, the suffix being represented by the verb **laho.**

garad bu lehyahai	he is sensible
oghòn bu lehyahai } or **wa oghòn lehyahai** }	he is wise
garad málaha, } or **wa garad án lahain** }	he is foolish

(b) Comparison of Adjectives.

172. The particle **ka** is used before the adjective, and means "more than."

The object of comparison is treated adverbially, and is distinguished from the subject by its position, relative to the latter, in the sentence.

The adjective, describing the quality in which the comparison is made, is treated as part of the verb.

. . . . . .

If the Subject of comparison is the subject of the principal verb, it precedes the Object of comparison.

If the Subject of comparison is the object of the principal verb, it follows the Object of comparison.

. . . . . .

Types of simple Comparative Sentences.

S.	Adv.	O.	V.
{**ninkan** {this man	**halkan** here	**ákhal** a house	**bu diseya** he is building
{**ninkas** {that man	**halka** there	**ákhal** a house	**bu diseya** he is building

7—2

S.	Adv.	O.	V.
{ákhalkan	ákhalkas		ka wein
this house	than that house		(is) bigger
{ninkan	ákhalkas	ákhal	ka wein bu diseya
this man	than that house	a house	bigger he is building
{	ákhalkas	ákhal	ka wein so dis
	than that house	a house	bigger build
{ákhalkan	ákhalkas		ma ka wein ?
this house	than that house		(is it) bigger ?
{ma	ákhalkas	ákhal	ka wein disesa ?
	than that house	a house	bigger are you building?

173. In simple statements of comparison, the verb **aho** may be used with the adjective, or omitted.

kas ma kán gabányahai ? is this shorter than that?

răgakan răgas ma ka badányahai ? are these men more numerous than those?

răgas innagu ka badan, we are more than those men.

sanaddi hòre răgi jògei, kana ka badan, there are more people here now than last year.

In three of these examples the usual order is inverted, owing to the subject being a pronoun, which is placed near the verb.

174. Certain words have a comparative meaning without the particle **ka.**

dàma better.

shúkhulka shukhul dàma saméya, do better work than that.

yerei make less   **kordi** }
                       badi } make more, increase.

u yerei, make it less.

mushahàrodaida ma i kordínesa ? will you increase my pay?

175. **ka** may be used with certain attributive verbs, such as **fogo** be far.

inad A. ka fogàdo dòni mayo, I do not wish you to go further than A.

fáraskàgu fáraskaiga ka ma deréyo, your horse is not faster than mine.

176. The superlative may be expressed by **sà** (= **sida**) or the particle **ba**, or most commonly by **u**, or **ugu**.

wa sà wanăksan, it is best.

sà sà wanăksan, that is best.

or **sádehhdas kan sà der,** **kan ba der,** } this is longest of those three.

wárankà ba fudud, that spear is lightest.

ísagu wa ugu wanăksányahai, he is the best of all.

răgakan ki u yera, the smallest of these men.

ínanti ugu yereid, the youngest girl.

bilàdki Somàlida hòlihi laga dofìya mahha u badan P of the things which are exported from Somaliland, what is the chief?

177. *(c) Similarity.*

sida so, in the manner, as :

aurtayáda sida aurti waweineid bìyo badan dòni mayso, our camels do not want so much water as the big ones.

wa wanăksányahai sidàdu o kăleh, he is just as good as you.

Jàma sida Abdi u wanăksányahai, Jama is as good as Abdi.

sida u ma weina, sida kàgi wahh badan ghadi mayo, it is not so big, and will not carry so much as yours.

ó kăleh the same as :

báhalka wein aur ó kăleh weyei, that big animal is just like a camel.

dagahhas mid ó kăleh, another stone like that.

lèheg resembling :

gèdkàsa lehh aur bu lèhegyahai, that tree is as high as six camels.

bákhashi fáraska bei lèhegtahai, the mule is equal to the horse.

kábahan ma iss-lèhega, those shoes are not a pair.

iss ku or **'ss ku** the same (equal to one another) (cf. § 250) :
kala different (cf. § 239).

These qualify adjectives or abstract nouns :

wa 'ss ku ìb, they are the same price.

lábadatan wa 'ss ku der, these two are the same length.

'ss ku mid, the same.

rakabyada wa kala hòs, the stirrups are of different length.

sanadúkhda wa kala 'uleis, the boxes are of different weight.

wa kala wanáksan, they are not as good as one another (are separately good).

Special idioms.

dóliskas 'elka ma gàdeya ? will that rope reach (be long enough for) the well ?

aurkàsa aurkaigi la hòg maäha, that camel is not so strong as mine (literally, that camel is not of strength with my camel).

4. *The Numèrals.*

178. The number of nouns qualified by a numeral and the position of the latter has already been dealt with in the Accidence (§§ 42, 47), and in the Syntax (§ 163).

The concord of adjectives and verbs with numerals is dealt with in Syntax (§ 168).

179. The numeral in Somali is considered as a substantive, and may take any of the suffixes. Nouns which in English are qualified by a numeral are considered in Somali as qualifying that numeral adjectivally (§ 170).

sádehhdas aur o hhunhhun	those three bad camels
áfartan nef	these four animals
afártanka nef	the forty animals
sagàlkaigi aur	my nine camels

180. When a numeral qualifies a pronoun, the possessive adjective is used in Somali suffixed to the numeral.

labadìni	you two
afartayáda	we four
lehhdòdi	they six

181. "One" when qualifying a noun is not translated.

one man	**nin**
one animal	**nef**
101 men	**boghól iyo nin**
101 animals	**boghól iyo nef**

kô is only used in counting consecutively.
mid is an indefinite pronoun, = "one."

182. Fractions. In describing a fraction of anything the Possessive Adjective is used.

half a bag	jôniad badkèd
give me a quarter of the camel	hashi wahhdèda i sì
a third of that belongs to me	inta dalolkèd ban lehahai

5. The Pronouns and Pronominal Adjectives.

(a) Persons.

183. The 2nd persons, singular and plural, are each strictly used according to the number of persons addressed. If only one person is spoken to, the 2nd sing. must be used.

There are two forms of the 1st person plural,

-einu, innagu (possess. -en) (inclusive form) include the 1st and 2nd, or 1st, 2nd, and 3rd persons ;

-annu, annagu (possess. -aya) (exclusive form) refer only to 1st and 3rd persons, and are not used when the 2nd person is included.

Illahhìna, annaguna Illahhayága, innagu Illahhèna bu nòkhda, your God and our God is the God of both of us.

184. The pronoun of the 3rd person singular has masculine and feminine forms. As the 3rd pers. fem. sing. and 3rd pers. plur. are the same, there is no question as to which pronoun is to be used in reference to a feminine plural. Where reference is made to a plural noun with the masculine article, when the pronoun is used in the presence of the noun, either singular or plural form may be used (see § 164 sqq.).

(b) Simple Personal Pronouns.

185. The Subjective Personal Pronouns (§ 53) are usually expressed with the verb, in addition to a nominal subject. They may be in their simplest form -an, -ad, etc., suffixed to any word in the sentence, or may be combined with the particles, wa, ba, ya, in the forms wan, ban, yan, etc.

yan, yad, etc., and ya ᴘ are often lengthened into ayan, ayad, etc., and aya ᴘ or ayo ᴘ, but these seem to have no special meaning or use.

186. When the simple form is attached to a word ending in a vowel, this final vowel is usually dropped in speaking, especially in the conjunctions **gorti, halki, hadi,** etc.

gortasu yiđi	then he said
ínankuse gènyu (gènyo-u) lehyahai	but the boy has a mare
gorm'u (gorma-u) yimàda ?	when does he come?
kolk'annu (kolki-annu) 'ollki áragnei	when we saw the army
nàgti Suldank'u (Suldanka-u) la sahhèbei	he made friends with the Sultan's wife

187. As stated in Accidence (§ 54), **wan,** etc., is only used at the beginning of a sentence, while **ban, yan,** etc., are never used at the beginning but only in the middle, and usually as close to the verb as possible.

wan, ban, yan, are not used in Dependent or Relative clauses, the simple suffixed form only being found, attached to the conjunction, or, in Relative Adjectival clauses, where there is no relative pronoun, to the antecedent.

> **ninkad u yèđei yimi**   the man you called has come

188. The objective pronouns (§ 60) are placed between the subjective and the verb.

> **la'ag ban ku sìneya**   I will give you money
> **gormu idin no (na-u) direi ?**   when did he send you to us?

"it," "him," are usually omitted in Somali.

> **i sì**   give it to me   **u gei fáraska**   take him the horse

(here **u** is the particle and not the pronoun, cf. § 125).

189. When there is more than one verb in a sentence whose subjects are the same person, the pronoun is omitted with the second verb as in English. But if the subjects of the two verbs are different, the forms **anna, adna, isna,** etc., or **aniguna,** etc., are used (§ 56).

> **gortasan ka daba so'odei o so ghobtei,**
> then I followed after him and caught him.

> **kolkasan só marei, isna halkasu si so'odei,**
> then I came this way, and he went on there.

190. The Emphatic forms (§ 55) may be used followed by the simple pronouns or not.

ánigu **wa shakheíneya**   I am working
ánigu **dòlada ban ka sha-**   as for me, I am working for
   kheíneya   the Government

I myself, etc., are translated by certain words meaning "self,"
with the Possessive adjective.

naf-ti life   (**ghud-di** sole, single   **ruhh-hi** spirit)

ánigu **naftaida ku arkei**   I saw you myself
naftaidan ka shakheista   I work for myself
annagu ruhhayaga magàloda   we have seen the town our-
   yannu so áragnei   selves

191. To do a thing for oneself is expressed by the derivative
verbs in **so** (cf. § 121).

samei make   **sameiso** make for yourself
ìbi buy   **ìbso** buy for yourself

192. The compound forms **wahhan, wahhad**, etc., and
mahhan, mahhad, etc., are important (§§ 57, 58).

The Somali likes to be very careful that he has the listener's
attention, before he says what he has to say, and the forms
wahhan, etc., serve to introduce a quotation or statement of an
event, preparing the listener for the nature of the statement to
follow. Thus in quoting a remark, after several interjections,
as **warya! i degeiso! kôdi,** he will proceed with, **ninkasu yidi,
wuhhu yidi,...** that man said, this is what he said,... and then will
follow what he really did say.

These forms may be used with any kind of verb.

gortasannu tagnei, wahhannu tagnei, Olesan,
then we went, this is where we went to, Olesàn.

They are nearly always used with verbs such as **dòn, malei.**

wahhan dòneya, inan manta tago   I want to go to-day
wahhan ù maleineya, inu árari   I think he is going to
   dòno   run away

193. The 2nd person of this compound form is used to
introduce instructions as to what a man is to do, followed by the
Aorist indicative of the verb, as in the common expression to an
interpreter (cf. § 217).

   wahhad tidahhda   this is what you are to say
   wahhad yesha   this is what you are to do

194. mahhan, etc., are interrogative forms.

mahhad dònesa ?	what do you want ?
mahhan yèla ?	what am I to do ?

195. Followed by **u, ku,** these pronouns mean, 'Why ?' 'This is why.'

wahhas mahhad u tidi ?	why did you say that ?
wahhan ku idi	this is why I said it
mahhad u dònesa hadig ?	what do you want rope for ? I
wahhan ku dòneya, inan	want it to tie up the things
ghálabka ku hedhedo	with

If the verb after **wahhan u,** or **mahhan u,** etc., is negative, the verb **wah** is used (see Conjugation, § 117).

mahhad igu sheg weida ?	why do you not tell me ?
not, mahhad igu shegi maysid ?	
wahhan kugu shègi wai	this is why I do not tell you

196. The pronoun **iss** is both Reflexive and Reciprocal.

wu iss dilei	he killed himself
wa iss leineyan	they are fighting together

iss is used with **ku** and **ka** in special idioms (§ 248).

(c) The Suffixes.

197. The Definite Article suffix has already been dealt with in the Accidence and Syntax (§§ 29, 151—154).

The Linking Consonant, which is necessary to all, has also been described in the Accidence (§§ 24—27).

198. The three suffixes, Definite Article, Demonstrative and Possessive Adjectives, may each be used alone, or any two or all three may be attached to one noun.

The following are the possible combinations.

(a) Demonstrative and Definite Article (§ 31 (ii)).

The latter is attached without a linking consonant.

    ninkanu, gèdkasa, kolkasi.

(b) Definite Article and Demonstrative (§ 31 (i)).

The Demonstrative when following the article takes a linking consonant, which however is always **k** for masculine words, and **t** for feminine words. Only the **a** form of article is used.

ninkakan, ghorigakan, gabaddatan.

(c) Possessive and Definite Article (§ 32).

The Possessive adjective always requires a definite article suffix, except with names of relationship. The 1st and 2nd sing. and 1st (exclusive) plur. are the only persons which take the linking consonant.

ghalabkaiga, holahàgu, ninkai, inantìsi, etc.

(d) Possessive and Definite Article and Demonstrative.

The Demonstrative may be added to the above.

aurkaigakan	this camel of mine
shukhulkìsakan	this work of his

(d) *Impersonal Pronouns.*

199. All the suffixes may be used independently as pronouns with the linking consonant **k** or **t** (§§ 62, 63). The Definite Article may be attached to the Demonstrative or Possessive Pronoun.

ki weina	the big one
kan ma aurkaigi ba ?	is this my camel ?
tan kăleh	this other one
tasu wa mid	that is one
kayága ba wawein	ours are the biggest
tìsi wà ta	his is there

"There it is" is translated by **wà ta,** or **wà ka.**

200. All the suffixes have the same form whether attached to a singular or a plural noun, but the Demonstrative and Possessive Pronouns have special forms in the plural :

kuan, tuan; kuer, tuer; kuas, tuas; kuaigi, kuàgi, etc.

The plural form of the Def. Article pronoun is **kuer,** or **kua, kui.**

The latter may take the Demonstrative suffix, as **kuakan, kuakas.**

(e) *The Possessive Adjective.*

201. The Possessive Adjective has certain special functions.

(i) It translates the Possessive case (§ 45).

ninki ákhalkìsi	the man's house
habàrta ninkèd	the old woman's husband

(ii)   It is used with adverbial nouns to form Prepositions (§ 132).

sandukhi dushìsi	on the top of the box
meska hostìsi	underneath the table
jòniada gudahèda	inside the bag

Such possessives, used with adverbs alone, translate a personal pronoun governed by a preposition.

hortìna	in front of you
dehhdòda	between them
sidàda	like you

(iii)   Where in English a personal pronoun is qualified by a numeral, in Somali the numeral takes the possessive adjective.

labadayáda	we two
afartíni	you four

In the same way the possessive adjective is used with indefinite pronouns (§§ 67 and 206).

intìna kăleh	the rest of you

The difference must be noticed between the examples,

labadaidi aur, or lábadi aurtaidi	my two camels
aurtaidi lába	two of my camels·

(iv)   It is used with the following words :

run	right	bein	lie
wà run	it is right	wa bein	it is a lie
wa runtai	I am right	wa beintai	I am lying
wa runtà	thou art right	wa beintà	thou art lying
wa runtìs	he is right	wa beintìs	he is lying
wa runtèd	she is right	wa beintèd	she is lying
wa runtèn	we are right	wa beintèn	we are lying
wa runtaya	we are right	wa beintaya	we are lying
wa runtìn	ye are right	wa beintìn	ye are lying
wa runtòd	they are right	wa beintòd	they are lying

(f)   The Interrogative Pronoun and Adjective.

202.   -e may be used either as a suffix (Interrog. Adj.) or as an Interrogative Pronoun, with the consonants k and t.

akhalke ?	what house ?
ke ?	which one ?

-ma is only used as a suffix (cf. § 65).

ninma P	what man ?
ninma ku shègei P	what man told you ?

ya P aya P ayo P   what ? who ? whom ? (cf. § 185).

ya ku sìyei P	who gave it to you ?
ayad árɑktei P	whom did you see ?

mahha P   what ? (objective).

mahhad dònesa P	what do you want ?
mahhad ku fálesa P	what are you doing it for ?

-ma suffixed to a pronoun, means "which of ?"

idinma P	which of you ?
annama P	which of us ?
kuma P	who ? (impersonally)

203. The Possessive Pronoun and Possessive Interrogative Pronoun may be formed with the verb root **leh** having (cf. § 116).

anigà leh	it is mine (or **anà leh**)
isagà leh	it is his
etc.	

These are more idiomatic than **wa kaigi, wa kìsa.**

yàleh P kumàleh P	whose ?
fáraskan yàleh P	whose is this horse ?

(g) Indefinite Pronouns and Adjectives.

204. (i) **la** is a pure pronoun, and is used to translate the passive voice of the verb (see § 118).

205. (ii) Substantival words, "some," "any," "all," "alone" (§§ 67, 68).

nin ba yimi	someone has come
'id ma ku taghán P	does anyone know you ?
wahh ma dònesa P	do you want anything ?
sadehh ghof ba dintei	three persons have died
'idla	unaccompanied, alone
halkan ghar ba yal	some lie here
daur ba hadei	some are left
daur iyo labàton	twenty odd

in răg ba jògta	some men are here
inti sàka timi	those that came this morning
nin hebel	a certain man
war, hebel O P	you, what's your name?

206. When used with a Personal Pronoun in a descriptive sense, the Possessive adjective is suffixed (cf. § 201 (iii)).

intìna kăleh	the rest of you
gharkòda	those few
ninki kéligi tegei	the man went alone
annagu keligayága sameinei	we did it by ourselves
gidigòd, đamántod	all of them
kulligèni	all of us
ísagu gonigìsi si so'odei	he went on separately

207. wèli-gi never, is used in the same way with possessives.

wèligai maan arag	I have never seen it
wèligìn arki maysan	you will never see it
wèligà hau nokhon	never do it again

208. "Some," "a few," etc., in a partitive sense are translated as follows.

intìna ghar ba hhun	some of you are bad
inta barìska ba hađei, or	thus much of rice is left
inta barìskaäh	

(iii) Indefinite Adjectives.

209. "Many," "little," "few," "other," "every," "all."
These are usually used qualifying an indefinite pronoun (only **badan** and **yer** agree with the Definite Article).

wahh badan o barìs la kàli	bring us plenty of rice
wahh ka yer i sì	give me less
răg badan	many men
răga badan	all those men (i.e. those many men)
răgi badna	the many men
fardo yer	a few horses
nin un, mid un	any man, anything at all
inta kăleh aur gòniah u sàra	put the rest on a separate camel
fardu o đan	all the horses

wahh hoga o răgas	a few of those men
in yer o sanadúkhda	a few of those boxes
nefka gònigaäh	that animal apart

210. The Indefinite Pronouns are made negative by the suffix -na, but the verb is also used in the negative form.

ninna ma iman	no one has come
ʻidna i ma arkin	no one saw me
midna maan tàbin	I did not touch one
wahh is used with ba:	
wahhba dòni mayo	I do not want anything
wahhba heli mayso	you will get nothing

6. *The Verb.*

(a) *The Moods and Tenses.*

211. *The Imperative Mood* has only one tense, and expresses a command, wish, or permission.

The 2nd pers. sing. is the Verb Root, from which are formed all other parts of the verb.

The 2nd pers. plur. is formed by adding -a (2nd conjugation -da) tag, taga; jògso, jògsoda; shakhèi, shakhèya.

For the other persons the Aorist Subjunctive tense is used, with particles an (1st pers.) and ha (3rd pers.) in the Affirmative.

an tagno	let us go
ha yimàdo	let him come

212. The particle bal is very commonly used with the Imperative, but is hardly translatable.

bal en ègo	let me look then
bal kàli	come then

It is not used with the 3rd person.

213. The Negative Imperative may be emphasized by the particle ba:

ha tégin ba	see that you don't go at all
or by wèliga	never
wèliga wahhas ha tàbin	never you touch that

214. The *Infinitive* is only used with auxiliary verbs,

dòn will   **jir** be accustomed to   **laha** would   **kar** be able

wa ku shègi dòna	I am going to tell you
halkas an faðìyí jirei	that is where I used to live

(*Note that the accent is placed on the last syllable of the Infinitive before* **jir**, *and, in the* 2nd *and* 3rd *Conjugations, before* **laha**.)

ainkas ma ghobón lahaid?	would you have done like that?
ma so'on karta?	can you walk?

The auxiliary and principal verbs are treated as one, and are not separated by any particles at any time.

kú ma arki karo	I cannot see you
Somàlidu ainkas ma ghobon karto	Somalis cannot do like that

In the Future Definite, the auxiliary is often dropped.

wa yèli	I am going to do it
u shègi	I will tell him

The Infinitive is the basis from which all Imperfect tenses and most Negative tenses are formed.

215. The *Verb-Adjective* and *Verb-Noun* have been described in Accidence (§§ 15 (*b*), 72).

216. *Aorist Indicative.*

This tense ordinarily expresses a habitual or customary act, without the emphasis on the habit implied in the Present Habitual.

Sirakìshu timir ma 'unta?	do officers eat dates?
Tomàlidu iyo Midgu wa iss gùrsada	Tomals and Midgans intermarry
rèrkayága gù walba 'elashatan ka so ðamín jira	my family is accustomed to draw from these wells every summer

217. It also indicates what is to be done, or can be done:

hagge lò mara Burao?	how (by what way) does one go to Burao?
hilib magàloda malagaìbsoda?	is meat to be bought in the town?
haggeinu tagna? wahhaidin taktan, Bòhotleh.	where are we to go? you are to go to Bohotleh (cf. §§ 192, 193).

wahhad tidahhda	you are to say this, or, do you say this ?
ma tùra ?	am I to throw it away ? or, shall I throw it away ?
ma ku kena ?	shall I bring it to you ?

218. The 3rd person of this tense is used to translate the Present Participle, or relative clause.

nin af yaghán	a man knowing the language
shimbir fórida	a singing bird
ísago gèdka hurda	while he was asleep by the tree

219. *The Preterite* expresses a completed act in past time.

shălei bu yimi	he came yesterday
Fàrah i shègei intanad iman	Farah had told me before you came

220. Or an act just completed at the present time (usually found with **wa**) (§ 142 *d*).

sirkálku wa tegei manta	the officer has gone to-day
shălei sirkálku tegei	the officer went yesterday

221. *The Present Continuative* expresses either a continuous action in present time, or an intention or willingness, as in English.

hagge tégesa ?	where are you going ?
ákhal ban díseya	I am building a house
nàg ban gùrsáneya	I am going to marry a wife
la'ag ban ku sìneya	I will give you money
mahhád iga sìsónesa ?	what will you give me for it ?
ma garanésa ?	do you understand (what I am saying) ?
but, **af Somàli ma gárata ?** *(Aorist)*	do you understand Somali ?

222. *The Past Continuative* expresses a continuous, or incompleted action, in past time.

fáras ban fùleyei	I was riding a horse

223. *The Future Definite* is a deliberate statement of what is about to happen.

wa tégi dòna	I am going to go
mahhád yèli dònta ?	what are you going to do ?

224. *The Present and Past Habitual* express a usual occurrence or habit.

subahh walba Fàrah ba auski so ghadí jira	Farah usually fetches the grass every morning
bérigi hòre Somàlidu fardo badan laháin jirtei	formerly the Somalis used to possess many ponies

225. *The Conditional* is used whenever a condition exists, whether expressed or understood. It refers to all times, and cannot be used except in the Principal sentence.

wa ku sín laha	I should, or should have given you
hadan arko wa gáran laha	if I saw him I should recognise him

226. *The Potential* expresses suggestion, possibility, or probability, and is often used euphemistically for the Future Definite. It is very common in songs.

mala iman dòne	he may probably come
insha Allahh wa la hele	please God, we may find it
an walálka dilne	we might kill your brother
iman dòne iyo iman màyo, war ma hàyo	he may come or not, I don't know
wahha kasta ad áraktide, ha jògson	whatever you may see, do not stop
in kasta há jirte, wa gàdeya	however far it may be, I will reach it

227. *The Subjunctive tenses* are only used in Subordinate or Relative clauses, and will be dealt with in the sections referring to them.

(b) *The Persons.*

228. The 2nd pers. and 3rd fem. sing. are denoted by **t**, or **s**, in the tense termination.

The 1st pers. plur. is denoted by **n**.

The 1st pers. plur. of the verb has only one form for both the inclusive and exclusive pronouns.

The 2nd pers. plur. must always be used in addressing more than one person.

Concord of verbs with nouns has been described already under Syntax of Nouns (§ 165).

229. The Emphatic pronouns **ánigu, ániga,** etc. (§ 55) have different constructions.

After the **-u** form ;

the verb is regularly inflected to agree with the various persons,

the particle **wa** is usually employed in Affirmative Sentences,

the particle **ma,** in Interrogative sentences, follows the pronoun.

ánigu wa tégeya	I am going
ádigu wa tégesa	thou art going
ídinku ma tégesan ?	are you going ?
íyagu tégi mayán	they are not going

After the **-a** form ;

the 3rd pers. sing. is used for all persons except the 1st pers. plur.

the particle **ba** is used in Affirmations,

the Interrogative particle **ma** precedes the pronoun.

ániga ba shakhèineya	it is I who am working
ádiga ba shakhèineya	it is thou who art working
ánnaga keligaya ba hadnei	we alone were left
ma ádiga arkei ?	was it thou who sawest ?
ma íyaga tégeya ?	is it they who are going ?

(c) Formation of Negative Tenses.

230. The Negative particles are,

ha used in 2nd pers. Imperative,
yan „ 1st and 3rd pers. Imperative,
ma „ Indicative mood, in Statements,
an „ Subjunctive mood, Dependent or Relative clauses, and Questions.

Forms of the Verb.

231. (i) *The Aorist Indicative* (statements) is conjugated like the Definite Subjunctive Affirmative, with the particle **ma,** and no Personal Pronouns.

ma jògo he is not here

8—2

232. (ii) *Conditional* ⎱ n is added to the Affirmative Poten-
and *Potential.* ⎰ tial. This is conjugated with **ma**
and the Personal Pronouns.

      maan garten   I should not understand

233. (iii) *Imperative, Preterite* and *Aorist Subjunctive* (statements). **n** is added to the Infinitive (in the 2nd and 3rd Conjugations the Infinitive already ends in **n**, and is therefore unaltered).

This is not conjugated in the persons, except in the Imperative,
in which the 2nd pers. plur. takes **-a** in the 1st conjugation, **-ina** in
the 2nd and 3rd conjugations.

ha shègin (2nd sing.)	do not tell
ha dílina (2nd plur.)	do not kill
ha jògsonina (2nd plur.)	do not stop
yanu (contracted to **yu**) **dilin**	let him not kill
yanai (,, **yai**) **gùrsan**	let them not marry
maan tegin	I did not go
inanad tégin ban dòneya	I want you not to go
maainu soʻon karin	we were unable to walk

234. (iv) The *Continuative* tenses of the *Indicative* and
Subjunctive have already been described in § 92.

235. (v) In all *Negative Interrogative* tenses (except the
Conditional), the particle **an** is used.

Simple tenses (Aorist, Preterite, Aorist Subj.) have the simple,
Infinitive, form as in (iii).

Continuative tenses have the form used in Past Continuative
(statements) and Continuative Subjunctive.

mianan ku shègin ?	do, or, did I not tell you ?
mianad Sirkál la jògin ?	are, or, were you not with an officer ?
mianu imáninin ?	is, or, was he not coming ?
ìmisa nin an téginin ?	how many men are not coming ?
ìmisa nin busta án lahain ?	how many men have no blanket ?

7. *The Particles.*

(a) *Order.*

236. The Verbal Particles and the Personal Pronouns are all placed in front of the verb. Where more than one are found to the same verb, they follow a strict rule as to their relative positions, having, so to speak, separate values, or affinities with the verb, so that the particle or pronoun having the greatest affinity with the verb is placed immediately before the verb, the others preceding it in the order of their affinities, as in the following table.

(A has the greatest affinity, H the least.)

H	G	F	E	D	C	B	A	
ma ? (§ 145) wa	an (Neg.)	Pers. Pron. (subj.)	Pers. Pron. (obj.)	u	ma (Neg.) (§ 145)	so	kala	
ba				ku		si	wada	VERB
ba				ka				
ya				la				

Examples,

H G F   E D B   A
mi-an-ad na la so wada kahain?   did you not bring all
                                          with us?

B   A
so kala diga   put down here separately

  F E C B
lei (la i) ma so dìbin   it has not been handed me

H D
ma kú jira?   is it there?

D C
ku má jiro   it is not there

    F E D
mahhád igu sheg-weidei?   why did you not tell me?

(b) *Uses.*

237. Particles have been divided (§§ 124—127) into Verbal and Conjunctive.

The Syntax of Conjunctive Particles will be found in the section on Coordinate and Subordinate sentences (Part IV).

The Verbal Particles may be Adverbial or Prepositional. Adverbial particles, as the name implies, qualify the verb. (i) They indicate Affirmation, Interrogation or Negation (**ha, ma, an, yan, wa, ba, ya**). These have all their special uses and constructions. (ii) They may correspond to certain simple adverbs or prepositions.

The latter are used in close relation with a verb, and are an essential feature of the language. By suitable combinations a number of changes may be rung, a variety of meanings given to one verb, and expressions which would otherwise require paraphrasing put more concisely.

(c) Adverbial Particles (**wada, kala, si, so**).

238. wada (all, whole) may be used with the verb alone, or in addition to the indefinite parts of speech, **kulli, gidi, ó dan**, etc.

sanadúkhdi ó dan wada kéna	bring all the boxes together
Somàlidu ó dan wa ku wáda taghán	all the Somalis know you

239. kala apart, in different ways

sirakìshi iyo aurti wa kála dahhaísa	the officers are travelling apart from the camels
side la kála garta ?	how does one distinguish them?
ninki hhuma iyo ninki wanǎksana ma kála taghán ?	do you know the difference between a good and a bad man?
wa kála jerèbeya fardaha	I am trying the ponies (for comparison)

It may be used with verbs, adjectives, or nouns (cf. § 177).

kala bihhi	unfold, expand
kala dòro	take your choice
wa kala derèyan	they are not as fast as each other
wa kala der	they are different lengths

240. si, so (§ 125) are used with the Verb Nouns as well as with other parts of the verb.

si so'odki	the march out
so nokhodki	the return

(d) *Prepositional particles* (**ku, u, ka, la**).

241. These cannot be treated as true prepositions, as they do not govern a noun, but only qualify the meaning of a verb in such a way as to render a preposition unnecessary.

tag go

Farah u tag go to (approach) Farah

meshà ka taga go from (leave) that place

u tag go to (him), and **ka tag** depart, may be used alone, without any object being expressed.

These particles are not attached to the noun governed by the English preposition to which they correspond, while on the other hand they cannot be separated from the verb by any part of speech except other particles or a personal pronoun.

Examples,

ka taga meshà	leave that place
sandukha (the box) **ghálabka ká bihhi**	take out the things from the box
mahhád ku fálesa hadigà (rope) **P**	what are you doing with that rope ?
wahhba lagu má falo	nothing is done with (it)

These particles are so much a part of the verb with which they are used that in many cases new meanings may be derived.

Example,

ka tag (leave, depart from) is used in the sense of leaving an object at a place.

lehh nin ba meshà laga tegei, literally, one went from six men there, i.e. six men were left there.

haggu ka tegei gèla P where did he go from the camels ? i.e. where did he leave the camels ?

Other similar cases will be quoted under each particle.

242. ku (i) at, upon, in, into.

magàloda agtèda bu ku arkei	near the town he saw six girls
lehh gabdod o 'el ku maidóneya	washing at a well
gèd bu ku hedna	he was tied to a tree
nin fáras ku jòga	a man on a horse

'anihi yu sibràr ku lissei   the milk he milked into a skin

(ii) with, by means of.

ha mindi ku tàbin   do not touch it with a knife
wahhba laugu má falo   nothing is done with it
banadúkhdi bei ugu dishei   they shot them with the rifles

243. ku, or u   for, on account of, for the sake of.

bìyo bu ku maghányahai   he is gone for water
kolkasei haràd u bakhtìyen   then they died of thirst
gènyoda yan u gháleya ayodà   I am going to kill the mare for
                       your stepmother

lába rubod ban ugu lehahai   I am owed two rupees by you
mahhád u taktei ?   why did you go ?

244. u is used with certain nouns in an adverbial sense.

àd u hádal   speak up
dib u fadìso   sit back
dakhso u tag   go quickly

      u   to (a person).

sirkálka u tag   go to the officer
u dig   teach

245. ka   from, out of, off

hagge ka tími ?   where have you come from ?
ghálabki sandukha ka so ghad   take the thing out of the box
hòlahaigi leiga hàdei   my flocks have been looted
                       from me

     Idiomatic uses of ka.

mel walba an ka dòneyo, ka   wherever I looked, I could not
   wai   find it
kolkei meshà ka ègen, wa ka   when they looked there, they
   waiyen   could not find her
mahhád ka bághatei ?   what are you afraid of ?

ka tag go from, i.e. leave, is also used in the sense of leaving a
    thing at a place.

lehh nin ba mèshà laga tégei   six men were left there
ínanki ba ínanti uga tégei wán   the boy left the girl a ram

    across, over, through.

ka taláb   step across
ka bòd   jump over

hòggi dàrta bei ka so dustei	she came through the hole in the wall

about, concerning, as to.

war ma ka haïsa ninka ?	have you news of the man ?
war ka ma hayo	I have no news (of him).
dôlada ban ka shakhèineya	I am working for the Government
lug ban ka jábei	I have broken my leg
mahhád uga hádlesa ?	what are you grumbling at ?
mahhád iga sìsónesa ?	what will you give me for it ?

246. kaga upon, against

kolkasu mádaha kaga díftei	then he struck it upon the head
wahhai rìyotei íyadu laba shím-birod lábada lugod kaga jògta	she dreamed that two birds sat upon her two legs
kaga rid	shoot
nin sirkál rasàs ba ku da'dei, bòdodi kaga da'dei	a bullet struck an officer, and hit him on the thigh

247. la together with

In addition to having the simple meaning of the preposition, **la** is used in certain euphemistic and other phrases.

la tag ⎫	
la so'o ⎬ steal, loot (literally, go off with)	
la bòb ⎭	
la kàli	bring (a thing)
la sôrod (so órod)	bring (a person)
la jòg	halt, cause to halt
la bahso	escape with, save
la jòg, la fadìso	live with (as a servant)

248. The reflexive pronoun **iss** is used with the particles **ka, ku, u.** It is usually contracted to **'ss ka, 'ss ku** (pronounced **ska, sku**).

249. iss ka, 'ss ka,

used in abrupt commands.

'ss ka tag	go away !
'ss ka bahha	get away with you !
'ss ka eg	look out !
'ss ka da	never mind !

With other tenses it may be translated by "just," "simply."

wa 'ss ka fadìya	I am just sitting down
wa 'ss ka dintei	he simply died (i.e. a natural death)

250.   iss ku, 'ss ku, iss u   with one another, together.

iss ku dowàda!	close together!
'ss ku lablab	fold up together
'ss ku tòl	sew together
iss u gei	bring together
iss u dar, or 'ss ku dar	mix together
tollollki wa iss ú jiran	the tribes are all together (mixed up)

It is the opposite of **kala** (cf. §§ 177 and 239).

sidei iss kú yihin ?	how do they compare?
'ss ku mid	the same
'ss ku toll	of the same tribe
'ss ku aba	(children) of the same father
'ss ku ìb	of the same price

PART IV. SYNTAX OF COMPOUND SENTENCES.

251. Compound Sentences consist of more than one simple sentence, and may be Coordinate or Subordinate.

A. COORDINATE SENTENCES.

252. Coordinate sentences are principal sentences, not dependent on one another, but connected by simple copulative or conjunctive particles, as "and," "or," "but," and having their verbs in the same mood.

Conjunctive Particles.

253. iyo and (used only between two substantives).

Fàrah iyo àniga	Farah and I

or, in the following cases :

làba iyo sadehh	two or three, i.e. a few
hadad takto iyo hadi kăleh	if you go or otherwise
inei fògtahai iyo ín kăleh so hubso	find out if it is far or otherwise

254. o and (not used to connect substantives).

kolkas askàrrti dibadda u bahhdei o 'éridei	then the soldiers turned out and drove them away

It is also used,

(i) between two epithets governing one noun.

niman badan o wawein	many big men
làba fàras o wanăksan	two good horses
làba askàri o fàras ku jògta	two soldiers on horseback

(ii) with the Indicative tenses of the verb to translate the English participles.

wahhai arken ínanti o dìrti fadída	they saw the girl sitting in the trees
rèrkòdi o la da'ei bu arkei	he found his family looted
hòlihìsi an ka ghadno, ísago (isaga o) shirka ku maghán-yahai	let us loot his flocks while he is away at the council

(iii) as meaning because.

wa lo takhsìrei o íyagu shúk-hulki ghobon waiyen	they were punished because they would not do the work

(iv) in the idiom **o mahai** without (Conditional).

ha só nokhon o bándukhi heli mahái	do not come back without finding the rifle
ániga o fásahhi mahái ha ka tégina héroda	do not leave the enclosure without my leave

255. **-na** and, usually introduces a new subject.

ádiguna mahhád dònesa ?	and you, what do you want ?
dabadédna	and afterwards
midna wa wanăksányahai, midna wa hhunyahai	one is good and one is bad

-na followed by a negative verb means " no."

ninna ma jògo	no one is here
midna ma tegin	not one went

256. For other particles, see § 127, and Syntax of Compound Sentences, Final and Conditional.

B. SUBORDINATE SENTENCES.

257. A Subordinate sentence is one which depends on, or represents some part of speech in, the principal sentence, and is connected with it by a conjunction or relative pronoun. It may represent

Substantive, Adjective, or Adverb.

1. *General Rules.*

258. In all Subordinate sentences, if the verb is in Past time, the Indicative mood is used, except in Conditional sentences. In Present or Future time the Indicative or Subjunctive may be used.

The Subjunctive is used to express uncertainty, or what is in the mind of the speaker, while the Indicative is confined to definite facts.

The negative particle in all Subordinate clauses is **an** (cf. § 274, note).

2. *Adjectival Sentences.*

259. In English these sentences are usually introduced by a relative pronoun, "who," "whom," "which," etc., but the Somali has no such pronoun.

The clause therefore follows directly after the Antecedent, as in many cases in English.

Where the English relative pronoun would be the subject of the relative clause, no personal pronoun is used in Somali as subject to the verb in the clause.

nimanka, halkò fadìyan, u yeđ	call those men, who are sitting over there
askàrrti, hujuddas samèisei, takhsìr ʻulus bei lehdahai	the soldiers, who committed that crime, deserve a heavy punishment
ninki, áminkan[1] árkeyei, haggu[2] kaʻei ?	where has the man gone, whom I saw just now ?
fardihi, shălei mèjorku ìbshei[3], wa laʻag badna[4]	the ponies the major bought yesterday cost a lot of money
hòlihi, sàka la kénei, ma la só wada aròriyei ?	have the animals, which were brought this morning, been all watered ?
dadka, gèlìsi la daʻei, wa yimi	the people, whose camels were looted, have come
ninki, ai[5] ákhalkìsa fadídei, yu ku yiđi	he said to the man, whose house she was in

---

[1] áminka an.   [2] hagge u.
[3] Cf. note to Table III. § 105.   [4] Cf. § 114.
[5] Pronounced as one word **ninkyai. ai**=she.

wilki, an wáranki ka ghadei, wa adáneya	the boy I took the spear from is angry
ninki, an hòla lahain, wahhba má taro	the man, who has no property, is of no use
fáraski, an bìyo badan dònin, bilàdkan ku wanăksányahai[1]	the horse, which does not want much water, is good for this country

260. The particle **e**, followed by the Indicative mood, is used apparently as a relative pronoun, where the latter is the subject of the verb in the clause, usually when the antecedent is also qualified by another epithet, such as an adjective or numeral.

shanti ínan, e gábdihi gùrsadei, u yímaden	the five boys, who married the girls, came
ínanka H. B., e gábaddaidi yereid gùrsadei, yan u dìbei húkumka	I have given authority to the boy H. B., who married my young daughter

261. The Conjunction **o** is used with the Indicative mood to translate the English participles, or an adjectival clause, when it is literally only a coordinate sentence.

wahhan arkei lehh gabdod o 'el ku maidóneya	I saw six girls washing at a well
wahhai árakta lábadi shimbirod, o lábadi lugod kaga jòga	she sees the two birds sitting upon her two legs
rèrkòdi o la da'ei bu arkei, o 'oll da'ei	he found his family looted, looted by an enemy
wahha ugu yimi áfar nin, intas o midna an u gáranin	there came to her four men, none of whom recognised her

262. The Subjunctive mood is used in Present or Future tenses, where the relative clause refers to a group, class, sort, or purpose.

ninki shúkhul dòneyo ha yimàdo	the man that wants work let him come
gèli la ìbíneyo mid ka kahhaiso	take for yourself one of the camels that are for sale

---

[1] Pronounced **wanăksényahai**.

mindi la kàli an kibisti ku gogoiyo	bring a knife for me to cut the bread with
bìyo an 'abo i ken	bring me water to drink

263. "He who," "they who," etc., are translated by the definite pronouns, ki, kuer, etc.

ki shălei la ìbsotei wa hòg weinyahai	the one that was bought yesterday is strong
kuer sàka yímaden wa jògan	those who came this morning are here
kuer an busta lahain, iyo kuer lehyihin	those who have no blanket, and those who have

264. "That which," "something which," "what," are translated by wahh, wihhi.

wahhan ku idi yel	do what I told you
wahhad kento i tus	shew me what you bring
wahh lagu fadìsto i ken	bring me something to sit on
wihhi ad heshei i sì	give me what you found

3. *Adverbial Sentences.*

265. (a) *Temporal and Locative sentences.*

These are essentially adjectival clauses qualifying an adverb of Time or Place.

mèshi ákhalki la díseya bu fadìya	he is sitting where the house is being built.
mahhád iss tidi markad wahhas samèinesei ?	what were you thinking of when you did that ?
kolkan imáneyei libahh ban arkei	while I was coming I saw a lion
meshian 'ashodi doweida jògei ghálabka diga	unload the kit where I stopped the other day

266. The Subjunctive is required when referring to any future time, or when the sense is general or indefinite.

kolki húkumka leidin[1] shègo wahhba weidina[2]	when you are given an order, don't ask questions

[1] la idin.

[2] Negative particle ha may be omitted after negative words, as wahhba, weliga, etc.

kolku yimàdo i so sheg	when he comes, tell me
mel wanăksan-einu degno so dòn	go and find a good place for us to camp

267. "while" is translated by inti or o.

intei habásha ghódeyen, yei ka gurgúratei	while they were digging the grave, she crawled away
ísago hajki ku mághana, ya nàgtìsi dadabtei	while he was away on the pilgrimage, his wife had a dream

268. until, as far as, inti.

intan so nokhdo meshà jògsoda	wait there until I come back
fadì inti shékada damáneso	wait until the story is finished
intad so'on karto so'o	go as far as you can

269. before that, intan (inti-an).

(*Here* an *is the neg. part., and the Verb is used in the negative.*)

intanan só nokhon ha ka tégina	don't go away before I come back
inteidinan déginin, ana wa idin gàdeya	I will catch you up before you halt

270. after, kolki...dabadéd.

kolkan Badwein ka tegeí, dabadéd mahhá ka da'ei ?	after I left Badwein, what happened ? (When I left B., afterwards what happened ?)
kolkad Bèrberah timid, dabadédto wa la hélei	it was found after you came to Berberah
kolkad sidà yesho, dabadéd ákhalka gal	after you have done that, enter the house

271. (*b*) *Final sentences* : "in order that," in.

Always used with the Subjunctive.

magàlodan[1] ghobóneya inan barìs iyo tímir so dònto	I am going to Berberah to fetch rice and dates

---

[1] magàloda an.

nimanka igu yèda, inan la hádlo	call those men that I may talk to them
meshà 'ss ka dumo, inan lagu arkin	hide there that you may not be seen

272.   (c)   *Conditional Sentences.*

If, **hadi.**

A Conditional sentence consists of two parts,
    the Protasis, or Condition or Assumption, and the Apodosis,
or Conclusion.

273.   (i)   *Assumptions.*   Indicative mood in both.

hadad moskhìn tahai, mahhád u shakhéison weida ?	if you are a pauper (as you say), why do you not work ?
hadánad moskhìn ahain, mahh-ád u shakheísata ?	if you are not a pauper, why do you work ?
hadad magàloda tégesa, Sul-dànka u tag	if you are (really) going to the town, go to the Sultan
hadánu imáninin, sugi mayo	if he is not coming, I will not wait
hadad jògtei, mahhád árk-esei ?	if you were there, what did you see ?
hadánad jògin, sidad ògtahai ?	if you were not there, how do you know ?

274.   (ii)   *Future Definite Condition, or Promise.*
    Protasis—Aorist Subjunctive.
    Apodosis—Future Indicative or Imperative.

hadu yimàdo, u shègi dòna	if he comes, I am going to tell him
hadad tegi weido[1] (or hadánad tegin), wa lagu ghobóneya	if you do not go, you will be caught

275.   (iii)   *Present or Past Unfulfilled condition (Imaginary).*
    Protasis—Aorist Subjunctive.
    Apodosis—Conditional.

hadeinu Bèrberah jògno, la'agti-an ku sìn laha	if we were in Berberah, I should give you the money

[1] The verb **wah** (§ 117) is often used in Conditional sentences to translate the negative verb, in place of the particle **an** with a negative tense.

hadaneinu Bèrberah jògin, wahha badan maan ku sìyen	if we were not in Berberah, I should not give you so much
hadad shălei takto, wa u ghobón lahaid	if you had gone yesterday, you would have caught him
hadánad Àdan ollí jirin, wah-has maad gáraten	if you had not been living in Aden, you would not have understood that

276. (iv) *Future Indefinite Condition, or Suggestion.*

Protasis—Continuative Subjunctive.

Apodosis—Conditional, or Neg. Pres. Continuative.

hadannu berrì tégeno, ninki-annu ghobón lahain	if we were to go to-morrow, we should catch the man
hadanannu téginin, ghobon mayno	if we were not to go, we should not catch him

Note. In a long sentence the Conjunction, Neg. Part., and Pronoun, may be split up.

hadiad shúkhulka an dòneya anad ghóbonin, shukhul-kaiga ku má wanăksanid	if you do not do the work I wish, you are no good to me

277. Whether...or... is translated by **hadi...iyo hadi....**

hadad dòneso iyo hadanad dòninin, iss ká tag	whether you want to or not, go

or by **ama...ama,** followed by the Imperative.

ama ha samàdo ama ha hhu-màdo, yel	whether it is good or bad, do it

278. "unless," "without," may be translated by **o...mahai.**

ha só nokhon, bandukhi o heli mahái	do not return, without finding the rifle

279.   (d) *Causal sentences.*

There is no conjunction meaning "because," but **o** is used in the following way.

wa lagu takhsìrei o ádigu shúk-hulki ghobon wai	you were punished because you would not do the work
wahhan ku adàdei, o íyagu laba sa'adod ka ràgen	I was angry, because they were two hours late

280.   (*e*)   *Concessive sentences* (although).

There is no conjunction, but they may be translated as the last,
or paraphrased.

halkanad tillen, haddana daugi ma taghánin	you do not know the road, although you have lived here

281.   The conjunctions ending in -soever are Concessive.
They may be used with Subjunctive or Potential or Imperative.

wihhi kasta ad sameineso, meshà ka kàli	whatever you may be doing, come away from there

o is usually added to the Imperative.

wahh kasta makhla-o, ha so nokhónina	whatever you hear, do not come back
dal kasta ghobo-o, si so'o	however tired you are, go on
wahh kasta ha ku shègo, ha makhlin	whatever he tells you, do not listen
'id kasta ha gùrsado, wahhba u sìn mayo	whomsoever he marries, I will give him nothing

In the following the Potential Tense is used.

wahh kasta an arke, jògson mayo	whatever I may see, I will not stop
in kasta ha ahàden, wa 'erìyena	however many they may be, we will defeat them
in kasta há jirte, wa gàdeya	however far it may be, I am going to reach it
wahh kasta ad áraktide, ha jògson	whatever you may see, do not stop

4.   *Substantival Sentences.*

282.   These sentences stand in relation to a Principal sentence,
as Substantives, and may be either the subject or object of the
principal verb (or an Indefinite Pronoun or Adverbial Noun). They
are introduced by in (that), followed by the Subjunctive in Present
or Future time, by the Indicative in Past time.

283.   (*a*)   *As Subject.*

in la jèdlo ma wanáksana	it is not good to be whipped
inad hilibkas 'unto wa haràn	it is unlawful for you to eat that meat

284.   (b) *As Object.*

(i) Indirect statement, thought, wish, etc.

wahhannu dònena inad sor na sìso	we want you to give us food
wahhan dòneya inan Àdan tago, or inan Àdan tago ban dòneya	I want to go to Aden
wa ù maleineya in ròbku di'i dòno	I think the rain is going to fall
kolkasu oghàdei in răg u yimi ínanti	then he learned that men came to the girl
kolkasa wadádki dama'ei inu áraro	then the priest tried to run away

285. (ii) Simple indirect questions.

inu yimi so hubso	find out if he came
bal inei fògtahai so weidi	go and ask if it is far
inu tégeyo iyo in kăleh war [1] ma hayo	I do not know if he is coming or not
môyi inanu fùlan oghòn iyo inanu dònin	I do not know if he does not know how to ride or if he does not want to

286. (iii) Indirect questions, introduced by interrogative pronouns.

'id ú yahai so dòn	find out who he is
hadanad oghòn 'iddi goïsei, mahhán ku samèya?	if you do not know who cut them, what am I to do?
wuhhu dòneyo weidi	ask what he wants
weidi bal wahhai ka baghá- neyan	ask what they are frightened of
i sheg wahhai u shakhein wayen	tell me why they·would not work

287. (iv) Indirect questions, introduced by interrogative adverbs.

hòluhu intei yihin ma ku shègei?	did he tell you how many animals there are?

---

[1] =I have no news.

so eg inti tambukhi lèheg-yahai	go and look how big the tent is
meshas intéi jirto war ma hayo	how far that place is I do not know
mel ú jiro garan wai	I do not know where it is.
gor u si so'óneyo war ma haisa ?	do you know when he is going on ?

5. *Oratio Obliqua.*

288. In narrative there is no oratio obliqua in Somali, but after the verbs, 'say' 'tell' (**odo, sheg**), the oratio recta is repeated.

The pronouns, **wahhan**, etc., are generally used.

wuhhu yidi, "libahh ban arkei"	he said he had seen a lion
wuhhu yidi, "wa idin ka daba so so'oneya"	he said he would follow on after you
wahhad na tidi, "gèl badan beidin hélesan"	you told us we should get many camels
wahhad tidahhda, "sor ban dòneya"	tell him I want food
wahhad tidahhda, "'ss ka taga"	tell them to go away

289. In place of **wahha, wa ti** is often used with the pronouns.

watan ku idi, "só nokho"	I told you to come back
watad tidi, "'ss ka jòg"	you told me to stay
warákhdi me ? wa ti la gubei	where is the letter ? that was burned

APPENDIX I.

Seasons in Somaliland.

Jilal   January—March
(Kalil)   April
Gù   May—June (S.W. Monsoon)
Hagar   July—October (**Karif** on the coast)
Dair   November—December (N.E. Monsoon)

Names of months (corresponding to the Arabic).

Arabic.	*Somali.*
Moharram	**Dago**
Safar	**Durahh hore**
Rabia al Awal	**Durahh dambe**
Rabia al Akhir	**Rajal hore**
Jumad al Awal	**Rajal dehhe**
Jumad al Akhir	**Rajal dambe**
Rajab	**Sà buha**
Shaaban	**Wà barìs**
Ramadhan	**Sòn** (or **Soukad**)
Shawal	**Sòn fur**
Dhul Kada	**Sidatal**
Dhul Hijjah	**Arafo**

Days of the week are the same as Arabic.

Monday	**Isnin-ti**	Friday	**Jima'-i**
Tuesday	**Salasa-di**	Saturday	**Sabti-di**
Wednesday	**Rabuhh-i**	Sunday	**Ahád-di**
Thursday	**Khamis-ki**		

Times of the day and night.

The Arabic times of prayer are freely used.

a.m. 6	wà beri } arorti }	sunrise			
6—8	subahh-di				
	barghádddi hore	early grazing			
	barisáddi hore	early rice			
8—9	barghád-di	grazing time	gélinka hore		
	barisád-di	rice time			
9—10	barghádddi kúluleid	hot grazing			
10—12	marki haůki so koreisa				
p.m. 12—2	haů-ki } gàdid-ki }	noon			'asho-di
2—3.30	duhur-ki		galáb-ti,		
3.30—6	ásar-ki		gélinka		
6	makhrib-ki	sunset	dambe		
6—7	fìdki				
7—10	aweisin-ki				
10—12	sakhdi hore				
a.m. 12—2	sakhdi (dehh)		habèn-ki		
2—4	sakhdi dambe				
4—6	arorti hore } saladdi }				

The time of day, etc.

arorta	in the early morning
sà ka	this morning
galábta	this evening
manta	to-day
àwa	to-night
shălei-to	yesterday
hălei-to	last night
habèn hore	the night before last
shălei galáb	yesterday evening
dorràd-to	the day before yesterday
'ashodi hore } 'ashodi ůoweid }	the other day
berrì-to	to-morrow
berrì arorta	to-morrow morning
sà dambe	the day after to-morrow
sà kub	the day after the day after to-morrow
habèn dambe	to-morrow night

APPENDIX II.

Money.

la'ag-ti	money, silver
mushahâro-di	wages
hisab-ti	account
sarrif-ki	small change
dahab-ki	gold
rubiad-di	rupee (pl. **rubod**)
rubi-gi	$\frac{1}{2}$ rupee, 8 annas
bòlad-di	4 annas
antìn-ti	2 annas
gambo-di	anna
beisad-di	2 pies
ardi-di	1 pie

Weight.

misan-ki	weight, scales
rodol-ki	pound
nus rodol	$\frac{1}{2}$ pound
waghed-di	4 oz.

Measure.

ba'-i	"fathom" (roughly 5 ft. 10 in.) used in measuring rope
gedi-gi	a camel's march (about 9 miles)
laba gedi	a day's march
nus gedi	a half march (4 or 5 miles)

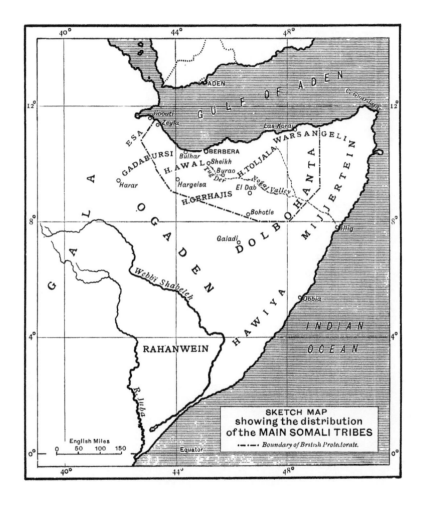

SKETCH MAP
showing the distribution
of the MAIN SOMALI TRIBES
—·—·— *Boundary of British Protectorate.*

APPENDIX III.

A knowledge of the chief tribes of Somalis is important, in order to identify individuals, as, in any official description of a man, the native custom of describing him by name and sub-tribe is adhered to. The relationships of the tribes are also most important in any dealings with the people. These are very confusing at first, as, for instance, three brothers may correctly describe themselves respectively as Abdallah Ismail, Hersi Bareh, and Rer Sugulli, at first sight three different tribes.

The following are only the better known tribes; for further details, Cox's Genealogies may be consulted.

The inhabitants of the country are divided into

ASHA, or **GOB** ....**ISHHAK**
(Noble birth)
                                DARUD
DIR.............................**ESA**
                                GADABURSI
SAB (outcast) ....**HAWIYA**
                                TOMAL
                                MIDGAN
                                YIBIR

None of these eight tribes have any known relationship with one another, within the history of Somalis as a race, except perhaps the **TOMAL,** who are said by some to be a branch of the **DARUD**; and the **DIR,** who may be a branch of the **ISHHAK**.

The **ISHHAK** are divided into four, or usually five, great divisions, called

HABR AWAL

HABR GERHAJIS {**EIDEGALLA**
                               {**HABR YUNIS**

ARAB
HABR TOLJALA

The **ARAB** are a small tribe, and, though genealogically distinct, are more or less adopted into the **HABR GERHAJIS.**

HABR means " old woman," or " wife of."

ARAB, and **EIDEGALLA** are nicknames, the other are proper names, of the sons and grandsons of Sheikh **ISHHAK.**

The **HABR AWAL** are divided into

```
          ⎧ Makahil
          ⎪ Hussein Abokr
Saad Musa ⎨ Jibril Abokr
          ⎪ Abdarahhman
          ⎩ Abdallah Saad
                                 ⎧ Musa Jibril                  ⎧ Ba Abdarahhman
               Mohammed Esa ⎨ Abokr Jibril  ⎨ Rer Wais
                                 ⎩
Esa Musa  ⎨ Abokr Esa
                                 ⎧ Damwadaga
                                 ⎪ Abdurahhman
               Adan Esa      ⎨ Rer Idleh
                                 ⎪ Rer Farah
                                 ⎩ Rer Odowa
```

The **EIDEGALLA** are divided into

```
⎧ Abokr Musa
⎪ Rer Yunis Abdurahhman
⎨ Ba Delo
⎪ Gashanbur
⎪ Damal Yera
⎩ Rer Esa
```

The **HABR YUNIS** are divided into

```
                        ⎧ Ishhak        ⎧ Abdillah Ishhak
                        ⎪                ⎩ Kassim Ishhak
                        ⎪                ⎧ Jibril Adan
                        ⎪                ⎪ Musa Adan
            ⎧ Arreh Said⎨ Musa Arreh ⎨ Mohammed Adan
            ⎪           ⎪                ⎪ Ali Adan
            ⎪           ⎪                ⎩ Hassan Musa
            ⎪           ⎪                ⎧ Saad Yunis
            ⎪           ⎩ Ismail Arreh  ⎨ Musa Ismail
            ⎨                                              ⎧ Idris
            ⎪                Abdallah Ismail ⎨ Musa Abdallah
            ⎪                                              ⎩ Omar Abdallah
            ⎩ Ali Said
```

The **Omar Abdallah** are important as the Sultan's tribe, or
Royal House, and are divided into a number of important sub-
tribes.

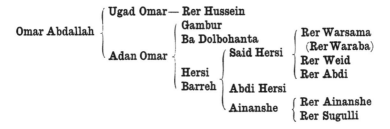

Omar Abdallah
- Ugad Omar — Rer Hussein
- Adan Omar
  - Gambur
  - Ba Dolbohanta
  - Hersi
  - Barreh
    - Said Hersi
      - Rer Warsama (Rer Waraba)
      - Rer Weid
      - Rer Abdi
    - Abdi Hersi
    - Ainanshe
      - Rer Ainanshe
      - Rer Sugulli

The **ARAB** are divided into

- Rer Othman
- Abdallah
- Rer Ali
  - Ahmed Abdallah
  - Rer Ali
  - Adan Waraba

The **HABR TOLJALA** are divided into

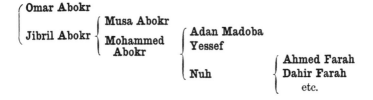

- Omar Abokr
- Jibril Abokr
  - Musa Abokr
  - Mohammed Abokr
    - Adan Madoba
    - Yessef
    - Nuh
      - Ahmed Farah
      - Dahir Farah
      - etc.

The chief divisions of the **DARUD** are

> OGADEN
> BARTIRI
> ABSGUL
> HARTI............MIJJERTEIN
>   WARSANGELI
>   DOLBOHANTA

The **DOLBOHANTA** are divided into

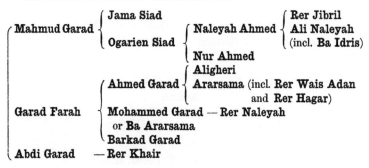

Note. Ba Idris, Rer Wais Adan, Rer Hagar, are three small sub-tribes which have intermarried with HABR YUNIS, and live with them in the district of Burao. They are included among the tribes friendly to the British Government, the other Dolbohanta having largely sided with the Mullah.

EXAMPLES OF PROSE AND VERSE.

The following stories and songs were dictated to me by Somalis of the Habr Toljala and Habr Yunis tribes[1], living at Burao.

The language used in the Prose Stories is exactly in the style of modern colloquial speech.

The sentences are very short and simple, and in ordinary conversation, especially in narrative, the speaker would hesitate after each one, in order that the listener might reply with some ejaculation expressing his attention or surprise. Such ejaculations are **Kôd, Kôdi** or **Haiye, Weiye,** meaning "Yes," "I see," "Go on"; or **Dèga, Wallahh,** meaning "Really," "By God." **Wallahh** is usually replied to again by **Ega wallahh.**

Example,

A.	**B.**
A complainant I am.	Well?
Mashtáki ban ahai.	**Weiye.**
A camel someone from me has stolen.	Yes.
Hal ba leiga hadei.	**Kôd.**
Yesterday it was lost.	Yes.
Shălei bei ka hallàdei.	**Kôd.**
There beyond, the flocks were grazing.	Yes.
Hagga ká shishei, hòlaha wa dàjeyei.	**Kôd.**
When we were returning it was stolen.	Yes.
Gorteinu ka so nokhónenei leiga hadei.	**Kôd.**

[1] I—IV were told by an educated Somali, Mohammed Jibril, of the Habr Toljala, Musa Abokr, then serving as an office clerk.

V—IX were told me by a professional poet and story-teller of Burao, Ismail of the Habr Toljala, Rer Ahmed Farah.

X was told me by an interpreter called Ali, of the Habr Yunis, Musa Arreh.

A.   **B.**

There with it went two men, on horseback—By God !
**Wahha la   tégei lába nin,   o fáras ku
    jòga.**   **Wallahh !**

and rifle carrying.   By God !
o bandukh sita.   **Wallahh !**

See by God !   Well ?
Ega Wallahh !   **Haiye.**

There it is.   (That is all.)   What do you want ?
Wa inta.   **Mahhád dònesa ?**

I want,   Yes.
Wahhan dòneya,   **Kôd.**

that one may catch those men.   Where they went ?
in la ghóbsoto nimánka.   **Haggei u ka'en ?**

They are here, in the town they stay.   Really !
Wa jògan,   magàlodai   fadìyan.   **Dèga !**

By God etc.......   this morning I saw   (them)
Wallahhi iyo Billahhi iyo Tallahhi ! sàka-an arkei.

B.

Very well.   A man soldier accompany, and shew him.
Wàyahai.   Nin sibaihh la ra', o u tus.

A.   **B.**   **A.**

All right.   Go away   now.   Very well.
Hauràrsan.   **'ss ká tag, háddaba.**   **Wàtahai.**

In the fables and narrative which follow, these exclamations are omitted, but no Somali could tell a story, nor could another listen, without introducing them.

In a native court, or **banjàd**, it is not uncommon for the counsel on one side to repeat the speech of his opponent sentence for sentence, or bit by bit, in order apparently to gain sufficient time to digest the full meaning properly. Repetitions are frequent and tedious, owing to this necessity for short, clipped sentences, and the absence of relative pronouns.

A speech or story is usually concluded by the expression **Wa sida**, or **Wa inta** There it is, That is all.

An excellent collection of some forty-five Somali tales, with German translations, is to be found in Schleicher's *Somali-Texte*.

I. HABIYO BUTIYA[1].

LAME HABIYO.

Suldàn bá jirei, ínan bu lahá[2]. Ínanka hoyodìsi ya dimatei.
A Sultan there was, a son he had.   The son his mother   died.

Kolkasa Suldànku[3] nàg bu gùrsadei. Suldànki ba hajki[4] ghobtei
Then   the Sultan a wife he married. The Sultan the pilgrimage made.

Nàgti   Suldànka[5] ya Yuhòdi la sahhèbei, ínanki Suldànka ya
The wife of the Sultan   a Jew with was friendly, the son of the Sultan

Yuhòdigi la   'ollôbei[6].   Nàgti   ya Yuhòdigi ku yidi[7], "Ínanka
the Jew   with was at enmity. The woman   the Jew   to said, "The boy

an   dilno." Kolkasei   sorti   sun   ugu dartei. Ínankuse
let us kill."   Then she the food poison with it mixed. But the boy

gènyu[8] lehyahai, wahh walba taghán[9], kolkasa gènyodi ínanki
a mare he possesses, which everything knows,   then   the mare the boy

ku tidi, " Ha 'unin sorta."   Kolki sorti lo[10] só digei, ya ínanki
to said, " Do not eat the food."   When the food was placed,   the boy

sorti   dìdei. Màlinti dambe ya Yuhòdigi u yimi[11]   nàgti
the food refused. The day following   the Jew   came to the wife

Suldànka,   wuhhu yidi, "Kolka Suldànki yimàdo, wahhad
of the Sultan,   he   said, "When the Sultan comes,   do you

---

[1] This is a good example of ordinary narrative style with its broken short sentences. It is also an excellent exercise in the uses of **ba, ya**, the adjectival clause, and the concord of plural nouns, upon which special notes are not given in many cases.

[2] **laho** means "have in possession," or "own," and is different from **hai**, have in the hand, hold.

[3] Note article **u**, for " the above-mentioned Sultan."

[4] i.e. the Mecca pilgrimage.

[5] Article **a** for possessive case.

[6] § 99.

[7] address. **ku** is the particle. Cf. **wahhad ku tidahhda** below. **yidi** is masc., and therefore the subject is **Yuhòdigi**, and not **nàgti**.

[8] **gènyo u**.

[9] From **ogho**. The Aorist is here used for Present Participle.

[10] **la u**.

[11] **u** to (a person).

K.   10

tidahhda, 'Wa buka.'   Kolku   ku   yidahhdo, 'Mahha ku dawaä[1]?'
say,   'I am sick.'   When he to you   says,   'What   you will cure?'

wahhad   tidahhda,   'Gènyoda bèrkèda.'"   Daràrti   dambe   ya
do you   say,   'The mare   her liver.'"   The day   following

Suldànku yimi, kolkasei   sàn   gogoshei,   o wahhai   hòsta ka
the Sultan came,   then she a skin laid on the bed,   and she   underneath

gélisei[2]   'àlen   beirda.   Kolkei   ku   sehhotei, ya   'àlenti
inserted   a leaf of a fig-tree.   When she on it   slept   the leaf

jababa' tidi, kolkasa Suldànki yidi, "Mahha ku haya[3]?"   Kolkasei
crackled,   then the Sultan said, "What   you   has?"   Then she

tidi, "Fèdaha hanòneya."   "Mahha ku dawaä?"   Kolkasei tidi,
said, "My ribs are hurting."   "What   you will cure?"   Then she said,

"Bèrka   gènyoda ínankàga."   Ínanki ba Suldànki u yèdei,
"The liver   of the mare of your son."   The boy   the Sultan   called,

wuhhu yidi, "Gènyodàda yan u gháleya   ayodà."   Kolkasu
he   said, "Your mare   I   will slay for your stepmother."   Then he

yidi, "Hauràrsan. E galábta-an ku   so   mermero[4]."   Galábti
said,   "All right.   This evening let me on it take a walk."   In the evening

ba ínanki gènyodi   fùlei, kolkasu   abihi   ku yidi,   "Abo,
the boy the mare mounted,   then he to his father   said, "Father,

nabad,"   o   gènyodi la tegei. Wuhhu tegei,   magàlo-u tegei.
goodbye,"   and with the mare   went.   He   went, to a town he went.

Magàloda agtèdi bu ku[5] arkei lehh gabdod o[6]   'el ku maidóneya[7].
The town   near he   saw   six   girls   a well at   washing.

Ínanti ugu yereid ya áraktei,   kolkei   ninki áraktei, bei   'elki
The girl   youngest   saw,   when she the man saw   she the well

ka   so bahhdei, ninki bei   ka   hishótei. Kolkasu gènyoda
from   came,   the man she concerning was ashamed. Then he the mare

saintéda gubei, kolkasa gènyodi   'erka taktei. Ínanki ba wuhhu
her tail   burned,   then the mare to the sky went.   The boy   he

'ss ka diga   nin   ádinla, magàloda bu galei.   Wuhhu   la
pretended to be a man crippled, the town he entered.   He   lived

---

[1].dawa, 1st conjugation. The Aorist here means, "is to," or "can."

[2] geli. Causative verb derived from gal enter, § 123.

[3] i.e. what is the matter with you?

[4] go and take a walk.   [5] at.

[6] gabdod is qualified by a numeral and therefore the relative clause is coupled by o.

[7] 3rd singular after Indef. plur., § 168.

fadìstei[1] nin. Bérigi dambe ya gabdihi Suldànka ya
as servant to a man. The time after   the daughters of the Sultan

yidi, "Wa gùrsónena." Suldànki ba durban ku diftei[2], wuhhu yidi,
said, "We will marry." The Sultan   drum   beat,   he   said,

"Gabdahaiga ya gùrsóneya." Kolkasa inámodi hòdna ya
"My daughters   will marry."   Then   the young men   rich

iss u yimi, kolkas gabdihi ba la kenei, meidanki răgu
together came, then the girls   were brought, in the plain the men

jògei. Kolkasa gabdihi la yidi, "Răga dònesan[3] ma wada
stood.   Then the girls were told, "The men you wish are they all

jògan?" Kolkas ínanti yereid ba tidi, "Ninkan dòneyei ma
here?"   Then the girl young   said, "The man I wanted is not

jògo." Adònihi răga u yèdeyei ya la yidi, "Răga
here." The slaves (who) the men were calling were told, "The men

magàloda wada jòga u yèda." Kolkasa ínanki adinkálaä[4],
(that) in the town all are call."   Then   the boy   cripple,

e Hàbiyo Butìya, yu[5] u yèdei. Kolkasa Suldànki gabdihi weidìyei,
Habiyo Butiya, they   called.   Then   the Sultan the girls   asked,

"Răgi ma wada jòga?" Kolkasei yidahhden, "Ha." Gabdihi
"The men are they all here?" Then they   said,   "Yes." The girls

ya lo dìbei lehh hábadod[6] o lìnah. Wahha la yidi, "Ínan
were handed six   oranges.   It   was said,   "Girl

walba ninkei dòneso ha ku dífato." Shanti gabdod e kăleh[7]
every the man she wants let her   strike." The five girls   other

wahhai ku diftan, shan ínan o hòdanah, ínanti yereid ya ku dífatei
they   struck, five young men rich,   the girl young   struck

Hàbiyo Butìya. Kolkasa nahhdinti-ai ka náhhen ya abahèd
Habiyo Butiya. Then with horror they were astonished her father

iyo hoyodèd indo bèlen. Ínanki ba ínanti yereid gùrsadei.
and her mother eyes lost. The boy the girl young married.

---

[1] lit. sit with. An idiom meaning "be servant to." **la jog** has the same
meaning.

[2] **difo** is used with **ku**, meaning "strike."

[3] The pronoun is omitted.

[4] **adinla** is inflected to agree with article -**kì**.

[5] ref. to **adónihì**.

[6] "articles," often used in this way with numerals.

[7] **kăleh** is the second epithet, but **o** is not used as **o kăleh** has a special
meaning, § 177.

Daràrti dambe ya la yiđi, "Suldànka iyo nàgtìsa wahha u
The day following it was said, "The Sultan and his wife there

dawaä 'ano wìyiled." Inámodi shanti gabđod gùrsadei,
cures milk of rhinoceros." The young men the five girls married,

shan fáras o wanáksan ba la sìyei, ínankina Hàbiyo Butìya dabeir
five ponies good were given, and the boy Habiyo Butiya a donkey

ba la sìyei. Kolkasa magàloda-ai ká behhen[1].
was given. Then the town they from departed.

Ínanki Hàbiyo Butìya, ya gènyodìsi sainti u gubei, gènyodi
The boy Habiyo Butiya, his mare the tail he burnt, the mare

ba u timi, kolkasu đarkìsi dahabkaäha iyo sèfti intas u
to came, then he his clothes of gold and the sword that he

gashodei[2].
put on.

Kolkasu gènyodi fùlei. Kolkasa gènyodi dùshei, 'erkas yei
Then he the mare mounted. Then the mare flew, that sky she

ghóbotei. Kolkas wuhhu taga mel wìyili ku dashei,
reached. Then he goes to where rhinoceros was born,

wìyishi yereid bu dohhei, sànti bu kala bahhai, 'o'ob bu
the rhinoceros young he skinned, the skin he stretched out, a figure he

ka samèyei. Dúhurki kolkei ahaid ya wìyishi timi,
from it made. The afternoon when it was the rhinoceros came,

ínanki Hàbiyo Butìya ya 'ss ka đigei đalkèda, 'anihi yu
the boy Habiyo Butiya pretended to be her young, the milk he

hohhdi[3] sibràr ku lissei, gudulkina sibràr ku lissei.
the first part a skin in milked, and the second a skin in (he) milked.

Wìyishi ya gèdo dònatei, kolkasa ínanki 'o'obki 'ss ka
The rhinoceros grass sought, then the boy the figure threw

tùrei, 'anihi bu ghadei, gèd bu tegei, gènyodi bu ku heđtei.
away, the milk he took, a tree he went to, the mare he to it tied.

Ísago[4] gèdka hurda, ya shanti ínan e gabđaha
While he at the tree was sleeping, the five young men who the girls

---

[1] from **bahh**.

[2] reflexive verb from **gal**. Verbs in 1 usually change 1 to **sh** in forming these derivatives.

[3] the first part that is milked, and not so rich as the second, or **gudul**.

[4] **Isaga o**, § 218.

gùrsadei u yímaden, kolkasei yidahhden, " Salàm aleikum." Hàbiyo
married to him came, then they said, "Salam aleikum." Habiyo

Butìya ku yidi, "Aleikum salàm." Kolkasu yidi, "Haggad ku
Butiya said, "Aleikum salam." Then he said, "Where do

so'otan?" Wahhai yidahhden, "'Ano wìyiled bannu dònena."
you go to?" They said, "Milk of rhinoceros we want.'

Kolkasu yidi, "'Ano wìyiled ana haya, mahha iga sìsó-
Then he said, "Milk of rhinoceros I have, what to me for it will you

nesan?" Kolkasei yidahhden, "Wahhad dònesid." Kolkasu yidi,
give?" Then they said, "What you wish." Then he said,

"Hòlo dòni mayo, ninkìnba¹ maga'aiga yan futada kaga
"Goods I do not want, each of you my name I the buttock upon

dijíneya." Kolkasei yidahhden, "Hauràrsan." Maga'ìsi yu futadi
will print." Then they said, "All right." His name he thebuttock

kaga wada² dijìyei shanti nin ba. Kolkasa 'anihi hohhdaäha³
upon all printed the five men. Then the milk the first

u sìyei, gudulkina Hàbiyo Butìya ghatei⁴.
he gave, and the second Habiyo Butiya took for himself.

Magàlodi Suldànki jògei yei tegen o 'anihi gèyen.
The town the Sultan dwelt in they went to, and the milk took.

'Anihi, shanta nin sídatei, ya Suldànki indihìsi logu shubei,
The milk, the five men carried, the Sultan his eyes was upon poured,

wahhba tari waiyen⁵. Daràr dambe ya Hàbiyo Butìya
nothing to be of use it failed. A day following Habiyo Butiya

'anihìsi nàgtìsi u si dìbei, wuhhu yidi, "Abahà iyo hoyodà
his milk to his wife he gave, he said, "Your father and your mother

yanei ku arkin, kolkad ku shúbesid." Kolkasei 'anihi
let them not you see, when you in pour." Then she the milk

geisei, kolkasei ku shubtei. Indihi Suldànka iyo indihi hoyodèd
took, then she in poured. The eyes of the Sultan and the eyes of her mother

ya u⁶ dila'ei. Kolkasei ínanti so árartei, ákhalkèdi bei timi.
opened. Then she the girl ran away, to her house she came.

¹ you men, cf. §§ 200 (iii) and 206.
² Note order of particles, § 236.
³ ah may be added to any noun used adjectivally or descriptively.
⁴ from **ghado** take to yourself.
⁵ plural agreeing with **'ano**, which is a plural noun.
⁶ i.e. by reason of it.

Kolkasa Suldànki oghàdei in Hàbiyo Butìya indihi u dila'ei.
Then   the Sultan learned that Habiyo Butiya the eyes   opened.

Suldànki ba u yèdei inámodi kăleh e gabdihìsi gùrsadei,
The Sultan   called the young men other who his daughters married,

wuhhu yidi, "Ínanki Hàbiyo Butìya e gabaddaidi yereid gùrsadei
he   said, "The boy Habiyo Butiya who my girl young   married

yan u dìbei magàlodaida hukumkèda.   Ídinkuna eidan u
I   have given my town   its government. And ye   servants to

nòkhda." Hàbiyo Butìya dabadéd Suldàn nòkhdei.
him be."   Habiyo Butiya afterwards Sultan became.

II.   INANKI MASKA DILEI.

Ínan iyo ínan wa walàlaäha. Lo' bái jiren, mel 'idlaäh bai hèr
ku ahayen. Ínankuna lo'du ra'í jirei, ínantuna ákhalka yei fadiyí
jirtei, habènki bei heroda iss ugu imán jiren. Ínanti ba ghorohh
bádatei, răg ba weidìstei, ínanki ba u dìdei in la gùrsado ínanta.
Màlin dambe ya niman ákhalki ínanti ugu yímaden. Kolkasei la
hassàwen, ínanki e walàlaähayen ínanta, ya galábti so hoidei. Kolkasu oghàdei in răg u yimi ínanti, o iss ka àmus. Màlinti dambe ya
nimanki ínanti u so nòkhden, wahhai yidahhden, "An walálka dilne,
gormu dagányahai?" Kolkasei ínanti tidi, "Kolku lo'di lisseyo."
Habènki bei yímaden, kolku lo'da lisseyei, muski bei ka so bòden.
Kolku arkei 'ollki, yu sèfti labahhai, kolkasa waláshi timaha
ghóbotei, kolkasu timihi u goiyei, muski bu ka bòdei. Ôdi bai
ghorihìsi ka goisei. Kolkasu bahhsodei, wuhhu taga magàlo agtèd,
wahha[1] ku hedna gèd ínan. Wuhhu yidi, "Na yàtahai?" Kolkasei
tidi, "Suldànki magàloda ya i dalei." Wuhhu yidi, "Mahhád ugu[2]
hedántahai mesha?" Wahhai tidi, "Mas ba lei hedei, maskas ba i
imáneya o i 'uneya." Kolkasu yidi, "Gormu yimàda?" Kolkasei
tidi, "Ásarka." "Kolku yimàdo muhhu samèineya masku?"
Wahhai tidi, "Bìyuhu[3] 'abeya marka hore, dabadédto-na ánigu[4] i
'uneya." Kolkasu yidi, "Wàtahai." Kolki maski yimi yu bìyihi
ku da'ei, kolkas ínanki sèfti labahhai o mádaha kaga diftei, kolkasa
maski dintei. Ínanti bu kahaistei, magàlodi bu gèyei. Dadki

---

[1] Note this use of **wahha**—There was tied to a tree, a girl.
[2] **mahhad u mesha ku hedántahai?**
[3] **bìyaha u.**   [4] **ániga u.**

magàlodi jògei ya ku so árarei, isago ínanti wada. Wahha la yiḍi,
"War, wá side?" Kolkasu yiḍi, "Maski ban dilei." Kolkasa
Suldanka lo gèyei, o lei yiḍi, "Ninkasa maski dilei." Kolkasa
Suldanka yiḍi, "Inantaida gùrso." Halkasa ínanki ínanti ku
gùrsadei.

III. ÍNANTI LUGAHÁLAEID.

Suldàn ba ínan laha, ínanta ghorànka lo ḍigí¹ jirei. Bérigi dambe
ya Suldànki hajki ghobtei, ínanti bu amáneyei nin wadàdah, o yiḍi,
"Ínantas ghorànka u si ḍig².'' Wadádki ba ínanti iss ka dama'ei
inu ka simeisto, ínanti ba dìdei. Daràrti dambe yei tiḍi, " Berrì i
kàli." Daràrti-ai mudeisten yei sallànki ákhalki ka ghadei, halki
wadádki ka so fùlí jirei. Abahèd yu warkhad ú direi, wuhhu ku
ghorei, "Inantàdi dilo' ei nokhotei." Suldànki ba hajki ka yimi.
Ínanti bu u aḍàdei, wuhhu u ḍìbei niman adòmaäh, wuhhu yiḍi,
"Ínantas ghorta ka so goiya." Adòmihi ya ínanti kahhayei, wahhai
gèyen mel ḍìrleh. Ínanti bei lugaha ka goiyen, kolkasei habashèdi
ghoden. Intei habáshi ghodeyen, yei ka gurgúratei, mel ḍìrleh yei
gashei, o kaga ḍùmatei. Adòmihi kolkei habáshi ghoden yei
meshiei faḍídei ka ègen³, wa ka waiyen, Kolkasei dèro dilen, digi
dèroda gharòrad ku shuben. Suldànki bei u gèyen ḍìgi, o yiḍahhden
"Ínanti dilnei." Màlin dambe ya sáfar meshi so marei, meshi
ínanti faḍídei yu degei. Dúhurki kolki sáfarku aurti rèrtei, yei
ínanti o ḍìrti faḍída arken. Ínanti ya nin so ghadei, aur bu so
sàrei. Magàlodi-ai yímaden yu kenei. Ínanti ya ninki so ghadei
akhal faḍìsìyei. Beri dambe ya ínan Suldan ḍalei ya ínanti weijigèdi
arkei, weijigèdi o wanáksan⁴ ya ínanki arkei. Ninki-ai akhalkìsa
faḍidei yu ku yiḍi, "An ínanta ka gùrsado." Ninki ba yiḍi,
"Ínanta wa lugoládahai." Kolkasa ínanki Suldànkaü yiḍi, "Ana
gùrsáneya, i si." Kolkasu yiḍi, "Hauràrsan." Ínanti ba ínanki
Suldànka gùrsadei. Laba ínan yei u ḍashei. Ìyadu ùrleh ya
ínanki yiḍi, "Hajki ban ghobóneya." Ínanki ba ínanti uga tegei

¹ teach.
² continue to teach.
³ **ka ègen.** Note the use of **ka** in these expressions, meaning, to look for in
a place, or being unable to find in a place.
⁴ The Possessive adjective suffix -**gèdi** is treated as an epithet, and therefore
the particle o is required for the second adjective **wanáksan.**

wan[1], o hajki ghobtei. Isago hajki kú maghan, ya nagtìsi ɖaɖabtei, wahhai rìyotei ìyadu labada lugod laba shimbirod kaga jògta, o lugihi u behhen, o hajki ghóbotei. Arorti kolki wàgu berìyei, ya wahhai árakta labadi shimbirod o labadi lugod kaga jòga, o lugihi u behhen. Arorti kolkei ahaid, yei labadèdi ínan iyo wanki iyo labadi shimbirod kahhaisatei, hajki bei ghóbotei. Dàr dauga dehhdèda yei taktai, wahha ugu yimi abahèd iyo walalkèd iyo wadádki iyo ninkèdi intas o midna an u gáranin. Inamodèdi yei u shekeisei, dawodi iyada heshei yei ugu shekeisei, abahèd ba makhlei iyo wadádki, kolkasa wadádki damaʻei inu áraro, kolkasa Suldànki yiɖi, "Faɖi inta shékado ɖamáneso." Suldànki, ínanta abahèd, ya wadádki ghorti ka goiyei, ínanti iyo abahèd iyo ninkèdi inti wa leiss wada raʻei. Hajki ba la tegei. Ínanti iyo abahèd halki yei iss ku girten.

IV. HÒGGI DÀRTA.

Suldàn ba ínan laha, ínanki ba yiɖi, "Wa gùrsáneya." Suldànki ba hòla badan sìyei, markabna wa sìyei. Ínanki Suldànka ya dòfei magàloü tegei. Magàlodi kolku tegei, yu nin Suldàn la sahhèbei Suldànki ba dàr sìyei, dàrti u kú jirei ínanku iyo dàrti Suldànka ya iss u dalòliyei. Nàgti Suldànkú[2] la sahhèbei. Màlinti dambe yu nàgti Suldànka ínanki ku yiɖi, "Sorti ninkàga adu saméin jirta o kàleh i samei." Suldànki ba ínanki u tegei, wuhhu yiɖi, "Àwa anad wahh i la ʻunese." Suldànki wuhhu yiɖi, "Hauràrsan." Ínanki ba nàgti Suldànka ku yiɖi, "Àwa kolka anigu iyo Suldànku annu sorta ʻuneno, wahhan dòneya inad sorta na sìsid." Nàgti ba tiɖi, "Suldànki ya i garanéya." Kolkasu yiɖi, "Ku garan mayo, ana ku oɖan wa nàgtaidi." Nàgti ba tiɖi, "Hadu i garan waiyo, adiga yan ku raʻi dòna, o nàg ku nokhon." Habènki ba Suldànki ákhalki yimi, ɖarkisi bu ghàtei, ínanka ákhalkìsi bu yimi. Nàgti ba hòggi ákhalka ka so dustei[3], ìnanka ákhalkìsi bei timi. Kolkasei Suldànki iyo ínanki sorti sìsei. Suldànki ba garteí nàgtìsi, kùrsigi bu ka kaʻei, ákhalkìsi bu u kaʻei. Intanu ákhalki gàdin yei nàgti hòggi ka dustei, gogoshèdi yei ku faɖìsatei, Suldànki ba arkei. Kolku arkei yu haɖɖana ákhalki ínanka ku so nòkhdei, hòggi bei ka

---

[1] lit. went from a ram for her, i.e. left a ram for her.
[2] **Suldànka u.**   [3] come through.

so dustei nàgti, nàgti bu haddana arkei. Ínanki, u 'úntoda la 'uneyei, ya Suldànki ku yidi, " Ma nàgtatan sorta inna sìnesa miad nàgtàdi modei ? " Ínanki ba yidi, " Nàgtu wa nàgtaidi." Suldànki ba 'ss ka fadìstei. Aròryodi dambe ya ínanki Suldànka ku yidi, "Wa dòfeya." " Hauràrsan," bu yidi. Nàgti Suldànka ya ínanki la ballàmei, o yidi, " Arorta halkas ka so dus, wa dòfeya." Nàgti ba halki ka so dustei, ínanki yei u timi, markabki bu geyei, wa la dòfei, ínanki ba nàgti Suldànka gúrsadei, kolku la báhsodei.

V. MAGÀLODI HÒLAHA DADKA KU 'UNA.

Wahh lei yidi, nin ba fáras fùlei, wuhhu[1] yimi habàr, wahhai tidi, " Haggad ku so'ota ? " Wuhu yidi, " Magàlodas an ku so'-oda." Wahhai tidi, " Magàloda dadka lagu[2] ghasha, yan lagu ghalonine, ha gelin." Wuhhu yidi, " Kulli wa géleya." Wahhai tidi, " Magàloda nin Suldànah bei lehdahai, ninka Suldànka ínan bu lehyahai, ínanta bokhorkèda wa mas, masku dadka 'una. Aurna ìsagu dadka 'una, ákhalka hortìsa yu fadìsta, halko golgol ku fadìsta." Wahhai tidi, " War, nino, hadad magàloda tégesa[3], ínanta Suldanka dalei akhalkèda órod o gal." Wuhhu yidi, " Ninki bei yidi[4], Eïga dadka 'una, iyo aurka dadka 'una, iyo maska dadka 'una, haggan ka dafi dòna ? " Ìyadi bá tidi, " Gèdaha ghado o[5], aurki yu ku 'unine, kolkad dafiso ákhalkiad ku so'oto, gèdaha afka u geli, yu ku 'unine. Eïgana 'adka ghado o, eïga agtìsi dig o, ha 'uno, yu adiga 'unine. Máskana wa kan ínanta dehhdèda ku dùban, ghoriga ghado o, maska madahìsi sar, dabadéd maska u diman dòna. Kolkad sida yesho dabadéd ákhalka gal o ínanta u tag, dabadéd ínanta gùrso." Kolkasu isagu ínanta gùrsadei.

---

[1] **wuhhu** here represents **wahha u**, in which **u** is the particle = to. It means literally therefore, There came to (him) an old woman.

[2] **la ku. ku** in, and refers to the town. **ghalonine.** The usual form is **ghalon** for the negative Imperative. This must be some Continuative form, but I have not met it elsewhere.

[3] Indicative mood, i.e. If you are (as you say) going.

[4] **bei = ba i.** Who is the man referred to is not clear. There must be some omission in the rendering of the story.

[5] The conjunction **o** is frequently used like this with the first coordinate sentence, instead of introducing the second.

VI. NASIB.

Wahh lei yiđi, nin ba đàn rèrei, đànki bu kahhayei, 'elki bu geyei, wa ka so đànshei[1]. Kolku so đànshei yu aurti 'ss ku so heđishei. Kolkiu dehhdi jògei ya lehh aur ka hađei, lehhdi kǎleh so kahhayei. Kolku mel fòg jògei yu lehhdi ka hađei wai. Kolkasu dib u so órdei. Lehhdi aur o² lehh libahh 'unesa ayu gu yimi, kolkasu iss kaga yimi. Lehhdi aur ó kǎleh o² lehh libahh ó kǎleh 'unesa ugu yimi. Kolkasu sibràr bu ka ghatei aurti, gurigòdi yu yimi, rerkòdi o² la da'ei bu arkei, o 'oll da'ei.

VII. NÀGTI WANAKSANEID.

Nin ba ínau laha. Ínanki ba yiđi, abihi ku yiđi, "Abo, wahhan dòneya, nàg an gùrsada." Kolkasu yiđi, "Wahhad so kahhaisata nàg armáli." Kolkasa armálidi so kahhaistei, kolkasu yiđi, "Gùrso." Kolkasu gùrsadei. Kolkasu yiđi, "Hađig ku heđ, kolkei ku la hádasho hađiga ka fur." Kolkasu hađiga ku heđei. Nàgti ba tiđi, "Wahhan³ maan arkí jirin, mahhád nogu⁴ sameinesa?" Kolkasu hađigi ka furei. Arorti yu abihì bu yimi, kolkasu yiđi, "Mahhai ku tiđi?" Kolkasu yiđi, "Wahhai i tiđi, 'Wahhan maan arkí jirin, wahhas mahhad nogu sameinesa?'" Kolkasu yiđi, "'ss ka 'eri." Tasu wa mid.

Ínanki ya abihi bu yiđi, "Nàg kǎleh so kahhaiso, ínan wein so kahhaiso." Kolkasu yiđi, "Awa hađig ku heđ. Kolkei ku la hádasho ka fur." Kolkasu heđei, kolkasei tiđi, "Wahhan maan u makhlí jirin, mahhád wahha nogu héđesa?" Kolkasu ka furei. Arorti abihì u yimi, kolkasu yiđi, "Wahhai tiđi, 'Wahhan maan makhlí jirin, mahhád hađiga nogu sameinesa?'" Kolkasu yiđi, "Tanna 'ss ka 'eri." Tasna wa mid.

Kolkasu yiđi, "Wahhad so kahhaisata ínan yer o wanáksan." Kolkasu so kahhaistei. Kolkasu yiđi, "Awa hađig ku heđ, kolkei ku la hádasho hađiga ka fur." Kolkasa ínanki 'ss ka sehhodei, habènki ó đan yu 'ss ka hurdei. Kolki arorti ahaid ínanti yei ínanki ke'isei, kolkasei tiđi, "Hađigi-ad igu heđtei wa iga da'ei, o igu ma heđna, hađiga igu heđ." Arortina abihì yu u shègei, "Abo, wahhai tiđi, 'Hađiga iga da'ei, o igu ma heđna, hađiga igu heđ.'" Kolkasu yiđi abihì ba yiđi, "Tas haïso, tasa ba wanáksan." Ti dabadéd yu 'ss ka gùrsadei.

---

1 from đànso, cf. § 104.   2 Adjectival sentences with o, cf. § 261.
3 This thing.   4 na u ku.

VIII. DADKU IYO WARÀBUHU.

Wahha lei yiđi, Waràbuhu hòlahá laha, Dadku wahhba má
lahain. Bérigi dambe ya Dadku hòlaha Waràbaha u ilàliyei,
Waràbahana wa shirei. Bérigi dambe aya Dadku tashàdei, wuhhu
yiđi, " An Warabaha hòlaha ka ghadno, íyaga o shirki Waràbihi ku
maghányahai." Ya Dadki hòlihi òdei. Habènki u yimi, kolki-u
yimi ya laga 'erìyei. Waràbihi ya ghailo tegei, bahalihi kăleh ugu
tegei, wuhhu yiđi, " War, lei da'ei." Kolkasei yiđahhen, " An
dùlno." Mel bei so maren, balli bìyo kú jiran yei yímaden. Sakàro
lab aya yiđi " Balli hadeidinan i dein, ka 'abi maysán." " War, wa
ka 'abena, naga tag," yei yiđahhen. Bìyihi yu 'idi ku shubei,
kolkas bìyihi idlàden, kolkas haràd u bakhtìyen, kolkei bìyo waiyen.

IX. HASHU IYO HÒLAHEDA.

Wahha lei yiđi, Hal wahh wada laha, mas iyo hhas, iyo dab,
iyo dàd, iyo libahh, iyo ghaiyàno, iyo àmin, wa todòbodas ya hashi
ka dahhaisei. 'Ashodi dambe ya ghaiyànodi tiđi, " Libahha hasho
wein inna ka ghadne, an libahha dillo." Kui kăleh ya yiđi, " Side
u dilla ? " Kolkasei tiđi, " Maska libahha ha ghànino. Kolkad
ghàninto, hhaska gal." Kolkasa yo[1] ghàninei, kolkasu hhaski galei.
Kolkasei tiđi, " Dabka O, hhaski iyo maska gub lábada ba." Kolkas
hhaski iyo maski dabki ya gubei. Kolkasei tiđi, " Dabku iya maska
iyo hhaska bakhtìyei, dàdkuna dabka ha bakhtìyo." Kolkasei àminta
tiđi, " Dàdku bùrta ma maro, dehhda un bu mara, an innagu hasha
bùrta la marro." Kolkasei bùrti la maren. Kolkasei tiđi ghaiyànodi,
" An hasha ghalono." Kolkasei ghashen, kolkasei 'adka bisleisaten,
'adki bei lukhoten. 'Adki mahai wahh kăleh ka ma 'unin, 'adki ya
ku mergadei, 'ad wein bu aha, afkina u mari wai. Kolkasei
bakhtiyen.

X. NINKI INDAHALAÄ.

Meshà răg badan ya wada hádleyei. Laba nin, midna wa
indálayahai midna ma indalaä. Ninki indahálaha[2] aya yiđi,
" Mahhad nin indála kala hádlesan ? Wahhba arki mayo." Ki
indahálaä[3] ba yiđi, " Ya nin indála u[4] taghánin ? " Inti kălehto ya

---

[1] ya u.
[2] Note inflexion of adjective. **nin indáleh** a man with eyes, but **ninki
indahálaha** the man with eyes.
[3] **nin indala, ninki indahalaä.**
[4] By what do you know a blind man?

tiḍi, "Wahhannu ninki indahalaä u naghán, ninki an wahhba arkenin." Markasu ki indahalaä yiḍi, "Wahha indála, ninki an oghòn lahain, ya indala."

XI.

The following is an example of the pure narrative style, being an account of Col. Swayne's expeditions against the Mullah, from the raising of the levy in November 1900 to the battle of Erigo in October 1902. It was taken down by me from the mouth of a Somali native officer with the force, Nur Jama, Habr Awal.

Note the use of **iyanna, iyu,** etc. for the pronouns **yannu, yu,** etc. The Present tense is freely used for the Past.

The raising of the Levies.

Kolkas "Swayne" ba imáneya, askàrr badan bu ghoríneya (enlist). Kolkas "Swayne" so bahhai, Harrar bu nogu yimid. Kolkasu yiḍi, "Askàrr ban dòneya." Markas Oskar Garad, "Imisad dònesa?" bu yiḍi. Markasu yiḍi, "Boghol fardòleh ban dòneya." Markasu yiḍi, "Bogholki lagu sìneya." Bogholki aya la sìyei. Kolki la sìyei, iyannu so so'ona. Adadleh iyannu nimid. Sidèd kumbani (company) iyannu nokhonei. Kolkas iyannu ayarsina (drill), bil keliah iyannu faḍinei. Kolkasu 'ollki "Swayne" no yimi, Burao-na ka so so'onei, Bèr bannu tagnei.

"Col. Swayne" iyo "Col. Phillips" lábadas u sarrèyen (were in command). Wadádku wuhhu yal Olesan. Kolkas iyannu nimid Uduwein. Ilàlo la direi, wadádki, so ego[1] la yidi. Dabaded wahha lei yiḍi, wadádki bahhsei[2]. Uduwein iyannu ka gùrrei (started). Dabaded wahhannu tagnei Olesan. Wadádki wuhhu jirei Nogàl. Olesan bannu ka gùrrei, dabadédto Wadámagô ilàlo iyannu ka dirrei. Ilàlodi iyei rèro so áraktei, hal iyo aur iyei so heshei. Fáraski iyo Rakùbki iyannu ka dùlinei (sent to attack), dabadéd 'ollki kolku dùlei iyannu ka daba gùrrei. Kolkas laba daràrod iyannu so'onei, kolkas Haridig (Sanala) bannu degnei. Rakùbki iyo Fáraski sidèd kun o gèlah[3] iyei kenei. Kolkas "Swayne" iyu yiḍi; "Laba kumbani iyei halkan faḍìyesa, gèlina halkas iyei laga ka tegi" (will be left). Kolkas kumbanayága u so haḍei, iyo gèli. Kolkasa 'ollki "Swayne" u tegei.

---

[1] in la so ego. [2] cf. § 104, note.

[3] After **sidèd kun o, gèl** is made adjectival by the termination **ah.**

MacNeill's zariba (Sanala).

"Capt. MacNeill" iyo "Murray" iyei héroda laga ka tegei.
Kolkas ilàlodi wadádka iyannu áragnei. Màlinti lábada sa'adod
(2 o'clock) 'ollkisu no yimid. Kolkannu 'ollki áragnei, iya sirkálku,
"Zarìbada so gala," bu yidi, dabadédna iyannu wérerrei (fought),
kolkas iyannu iss leïnei (slew each other), dabadédna áfar sa'adod
(for 4 hours) iyannu dagàlla (fought). Lehhdi sa'adod (6 o'clock)
iyannu ka 'érinei (chased) kolka dabadéd zarìbada gudahi iyannu iss
ku fadìsona. Kolkasu dabadédto todòbadi sa'adod habènki iyannu
wérerrei, lába sa'adod bannu dagálla, kolkasa sagalki sa'adod iyannu
'érinei. Haddana kôdi bei so nokhden, haddana sa'ad keliah iyannu
dagàlla. Kolkas iyága iyannu leïna, dabadédna wa áraren (they
ran away). Kolkas wàga iyo beri (in the early morning) todòbadi
sa'adod iyei so nokhden, kolkasannu iss leïna, kolkasannu derewishti
iyannu wada leïna.

Intanei so dowànin (Before they came close) gidligànki (the
Maxim gun) iyu leï. Kolkei so dowàden askàrrti banadúkhdi iyei
ku dishei. (Gidligánki wa wanàksányahai, wa bahal, wa shaitan).
Kolki nimanki fogèyen iya gidligánki lagu si dayei, kolkas ràg badan
ka lai (died), kolkas dabadéd haggi zarìbada iyei ku so ya'ei (fled).
Áfar nin o askàri wadád[1] wáranki iyu ku dilei. Kolkas iyannu
'érinei, afárton nin iyannu ghóbonei.

"Capt. MacNeill" iyu ániga u yèdei, wuhhu yidi, "Inti wadádka
laga dilei so tiri." Wahhan kahhaistei tòban askàri, wahhannu ka
dignei áfar bóghol iyo lehhdon inti dimatei. Annaga lábadi
kumbani sagàl nin iyei ka dilen. Kolkas "MacNeill" ba yidi,
wuhhu yidi, "Ràgi derewishki dintei mel iss u gei." Kolkas iyannu
mel keliah so kennei. Kolkasa 'ollki "Swayne" iyu no yimid,
wadádki wahhba ísagu ka ma helin.

Ferdiddin.

'Ollki o dan iyu Bòhotle iss ugu yimid. Dabadédna ilálo iyannu
ka dirrei. Kùrmis iyei gèl badan ku so áraktei. Ilàlodi ba so
nokhotei, gèl badan iyannu áragnei, 'ollki o dan iya gùrei, dabadèdna
Kurmis iyannu tagnei. Allegheri gèl badan laga so ghadei. Shan
iyo tòban 'asho iyannu fadínei. Dadki hòlahálaha ba no yimid.
Dadki iyu "Colonel"-ki u yímaden. Wuhhu yidahhei, "Edinkannu
idin ra'ena, adigi iya lo 'elin" (will be recovered). Kolkasu yidi,
"Hadeidin ra'esán adigi iyan idin ku 'elíneya. Rèraha o dan so
rèra o agtèda kena." Kolkasi Allegheri na ra'ei. Kolkasu yidi,

[1] **wadád** here used for a Mullah's man.

" Wadádki bannu idin la dònena." Dabadéd iyannu gùrrei. Bòhotle iyannu nimid. Rägi buka o askàrrtaäha iya Bòhotle lagu rèbei (were left behind), dabadédna Bòhotle iyannu ka gùrrei. Wahhannu degnei Wudwud, dabadéd ilàlo Wudwud iyannu ka dirrei. Wahhai yiḍahhen, "Wadádku wa fògyahai." Kolkasannu ka gùrrei, shan habèn iyo shan daràrod so so'onei. Daràrti dambe iyannu 'ollki wadádka iss hellei (met). Dabadéd iyannu dirirrei. Wahhai kaga dilen shan iyo tòban askàri iyo sirkálki af-Arabed (i.e. Capt. Friedrichs). "Dickinson" sahib rasàs ba ku da'dei, bòdodi kaga da'dei. Shan iyo labàton askàri iyei rasàsti ku da'dei, an dimanin (without being killed). Kolkas iyannu bìyo wehna (could not find) o so nokhonei. Wahhannu ka so baghanei, askàrrti hadanei bìyo haïson, wa bakhtìyesa. Shan iyo tòban 'asho iyannu Berberah u so dahhnei. Kolkannu halkan nimid, askàrrti gèl badan la sìyei, hawildàrki sadehh halod iya la sìyei, ninki jemadàrkaäha áfar ba la sìyei. Askàrrti fasahh, nin ba bil fasahh iyu helei. "Force"-kan halkas iyu ku ḍamadei.

Las Idleh raids.

'Ollki labad iyu Burao wa so yimi. Burao-na dabadéd áfar bìlod faḍína, kolkas ilàlo laga direi. Ilàlodi Ali Naleyah iyei u taktei, wahhai tiḍi, "Hòlo badan iyannu so áragnei." Afar kumbani iyo "Col. Cobbe" iyo "Col. Swayne" iyannu ku so'onei, wahhannu tagnei Las Idleh. Las Idlehna fáras badan nogu yimid. Kolkas iyannu ilàlo dirrei. Ilàlodi iyei tiḍi, "Hòlo badan iyannu so áragnei." Kolkasannu Las Idleh ka gùrrei, kòbyo-tòban habèn u si so'onei. Jid Ali iyannu Ali Naleyah u tagnei, kolkasu kumbani waliba mel marei. "Col. Swayne" iyo kumbani baḍki iyannu mel kaga tagnei. Kolkas iyannu Ali Naleyah wérerrei, habènki iyo daràrti wa hòlihi ka da'nei. Kolkas hòlihi iyannu zarìbadi i so kennei, wihhi-annu räg áragnei iyannu leïnei. Kolkasannu ka so gùrrei. Wahhannu tagnei, Las Idleh shan iyo tòban habèn iyannu u so dahhnei. Kolkas askàrrti ba aḍi la sìyei, ninki askàri aha lábyo-tòban aḍi la sìyei, ninki hawildàrka iyo naikka labàton la sìyei, jemadarki iyo "color-havildar"-ki soddon ba la sìyei. "Col. Cobbe" iyo "Col. Swayne" Berberah ku nokhden. "Maj. Petrie" iyo áfar kumbani Burao-annu so nokhonei, kolka bil faḍínei Burao. Kolkasa "Col. Swayne" iya no yimid. Wuhhu yiḍi, "Force"-ku wa bahhàya, wadádka iyannu dònena. Reidka Somàlida gèl maawinah i kena," bu yiḍi. Kolkasi Habr Awal iyo Habr Yunis gholi walba sidèd boghol o halod iya lo kena, Habr Toljàla lehh boghol o halod lo kena.

The Nogal Campaign.

Kolkas 'ollki iyu dakhàghei. Kumbanayága sidèd daràrod naga dambèyei. Kolkasu Rakùbki iyo Fáraski Berberah ka yímaden, o Burao nogu yímaden. Wahha u sarrèyei "Capt. Osborne." Kolkas annu 'ollki ka daba tagnei. Shan daràrod dabadéd Bohotle iyannu ghobonei. Kolkannu Bohotle ghobonei, "Col. Swayne" iyo 'ollki iyannu u tagnei. Kolkasa ilàlo laga direi, ilàlodi iya tòban habèn iyei naga mághana. Ilàlodi wa so nokhotei, wahhai yidahhen, "Wadádki maannu árag." Kolkasa "Colonel"-ku ba yidi, "Wa dùlena." Nogàl iyannu ku dùllei. Kolkas iyannu tagnei Gerowei. Hòlo badan iyannu Mohammed Garad ka ghadnei. Gerowei labàton habèn bannu fadínei. Ilàlo iya la direi. Ilàlodi wadádki iyei Mudug ugu taktei (went to Mudug for the Mullah). Ilàlodi ba no timid, ilàlodi ba tidi, "Wa omániaha, o bìyo heli mayno." Kolkas iyannu Bari ghóbonei. Halin bannu ghóbonei. Naleyah Ahhmed hòlo badan iyannu ka so ghadnei. Kolkasa sirkálku yidi, "Wa nokhonena." Lábyo-tòban 'asho bannu so so'onei, kolkasannu Gaulo nimid, kolkas "Colonel"-ku yidi, "Laba nin o sirakil, iyo wáranlaha iyo hòlaha ha nokhdan." Kolkasa hòlihi iyo waranlihi iyo laba sirkal iyei nokhden. Sádehh kun o gèli iyu "Colonel"-ku so rèbei.

Erigo (Oct. 6, 1902).

Kolkas ilàlo la direi, wahhai taktei, wadádki iyei u taktei. Kolkasei tidi, "Wadádku Mudug bu fadìya." Kolkasannu ku gùrrei, kolkasu shan habèn bannu dahhnei, 'ashodi lehhad arorti Erigo derewishti iyannu iss ku hellei. Kolkasu mel bannu fadìsona, kolkasa dabadédto derewishti iyei nagu so dakhághdei. "Mile" kolki no só jirei, sirkálku yidi, "Inna la díriri mayan, aurta rèra, inna dakhàghna." Kolkasannu ku dakhàghnei. Mesha wa mel aïnah. Kolkas kumbani walba "extend" ba lo dakhàjìyei, sidaannu so'onei o kol keliah íyagu "fire" nogu ridei. Kolkasa bèrka iyannu dulka digna, kolkas iyannu dirirrei. Áfar kumbani wa teg, iyei haggà ka bághatei, o árarei. Sadehh kumbani iyannu dagàllei, inti kàleh wa bághatei. Kumbanayága iyo lába kàleh sádehhda kumbani ba dagàlen.

Zaribadi iyannu so gallei, kolkas derewishti iyei timid. Sadehh kumbani iyei dibadda u bahhdei o 'éridei. Dabadéd Bohotle iyannu nimid.

TRANSLATIONS OF THE STORIES.
I–XI.

I.   HABIYO BUTIYA (LAME HABIYO).

There once was a Sultan who had a son, whose mother was dead.   But
the Sultan married another wife, and went on a pilgrimage.   Now a certain
Jew was a friend of the Sultan's wife, but the Sultan's son and the Jew
were enemies.   The Jew said to the woman, "Let us kill the boy."   So she
mixed some poison in his food.   But the boy had a mare, who knew everything, and the mare said to the boy, "Don't eat the food"; and when the
food was put before him, the boy refused it.   The next day the Jew came
to the Sultan's wife and said, "When the Sultan comes back, say you are
sick, and when he asks what will cure you, tell him the liver of the mare."
The next day the Sultan came.   Then she laid a skin on the bed and
placed under it some fig leaves, and when she lay down the leaves crackled.
Then the Sultan said, "What is the matter with you?" and she said, "I have
a pain in my ribs."   "What will cure you?" he said; and she answered,
"The liver of your son's mare."   The Sultan called the boy and said, "I
intend to kill your mare for your stepmother."   And the boy said, "Very
well, but let me take a ride on her this evening."   In the evening the boy
rode the mare, and said to his father, "Good-bye, Father," and departed
with the mare.   He went to a town, and near the town he saw six girls
washing at a well.   The youngest of the girls saw him; and when she saw
the man, she ran away from the well, being ashamed before the man.   Then
he singed the tail of the mare, who went up into the sky.   The young man
then pretended to be a cripple, and went into the town, and there became a
servant.

Later the daughters of the Sultan said, "We wish to marry."   The
Sultan beat his drum, and announced, "My daughters wish to marry."
Then the rich young men came together, and the girls were brought, and
the people stood in the plain.   Then the girls were asked, "Are the men
you want all here?"   And the young girl said, "The man I wanted is not
here."   The slave girls who were summoning the men were told to call all
the men in the town, so they called the young cripple, Lame Habiyo.   Then
the Sultan asked the girls, "Are the men all here?" and they said, "Yes."

The girls were given six oranges, and they were told, " Let each girl hit the man she wants." The five other girls hit five rich young men, the young girl hit Lame Habiyo. Then her father and mother were so struck with horror, that they lost their sight ; and the young man married the girl. On the next day they were told, " That which will cure the Sultan and his wife is rhinoceros' milk." And the young men who married the five girls were given five good horses, and Lame Habiyo was given a donkey, and they left the town. There came to Lame Habiyo the mare, whose tail he had burned, and he put on his gold dress and sword and mounted the mare. The mare flew up and reached the sky. Then he went to a place where rhinoceroses are born. A young rhinoceros he cut open, and opened out the skin and made a figure from it. In the afternoon the mother rhinoceros came, and Lame Habiyo pretended to be the young one. The first portion of milk he milked into one skin and the second portion he milked into another skin. Then the rhinoceros went to graze. Then the young man threw away the figure, and took the milk. He went to a tree and tied his mare to it. While he slept under the tree the five young men who married the other girls came to him, and said, " Salam Aleikum " ; and Lame Habiyo said, "Aleikum Salam." Then he said, " Where are you going ? " And they said, " We are looking for rhinoceros' milk." Then he said, " I have some rhinoceros' milk. What will you give for it ? " And they said, " Whatever you wish." Then he said, " Wealth do I not want, but I will brand my name on the buttocks of each of you." Then they said, " Agreed." So he branded his name on the buttocks of all five. Then he gave them the first milk, and the second milk Lame Habiyo took for himself. They went to the town where the Sultan lived, and took the milk. The five young men carried the milk, and it was poured on the eyes of the Sultan, but was of no use. Another day Lame Habiyo gave his milk to his wife and said, "Let not your father and mother see you, when you pour it in." Then she took the milk and she poured it in. And the eyes of the Sultan and her mother were opened. Then the girl came running away and came to her house. Then the Sultan learned that Lame Habiyo had opened his eyes, and the Sultan called the other young men that married his daughters, and he said, " To the young man Lame Habiyo, who married my young daughter, have I given authority over my town, and you, be his servants." Afterwards Lame Habiyo became Sultan.

II. "THE DRAGON-KILLER."

(*A variant of the story of Perseus and Andromeda.*)

There were a brother and sister who kept a cow. They dwelt in a deserted place, and the brother used to go with the cow, while the sister used to sit in the house, and at night they met in the zariba. The sister was of great beauty, and men asked for her, but her brother refused to let the girl be married. One day some men came into the house for the girl,

K. 11

and they conversed; and the brother came in in the evening and found that men had come for his sister, but he said nothing. The next day the men returned to the girl and said, "We think of killing your brother; when is he engaged?" And the girl said, "When he is milking the cow." In the evening they came as he was milking the cow and leaped in over the fence. When he saw the enemy, he drew his sword. His sister seized his hair, but he cut it off, and jumped over the fence, which cut off his genitals; and he escaped. He went near a town where there was a girl tied to a tree, and he said, "Who are you, girl?" And she said, "My father is the Sultan of the town." And he said, "Why are you tied up here?" And she said, "I am tied up for a dragon, which will come and eat me." Then he said, "When does it come?" And she said, "In the evening." And he said, "When the dragon comes, what will it do?" And she said, "First it will drink the water, and afterwards eat me." And he replied, "Very well." When the dragon came, it went down to the water, but the young man drew his sword and struck it on the head, and it died. Then he led away the girl, and brought her to the town, and the people of the town came running to him, as he led the girl, and they said, "What is this?" And he said, "I have killed the dragon." Then he was brought to the Sultan, and they said, "This man has killed the dragon." And the Sultan bade him marry his daughter. So thereupon the man married her.

III. THE GIRL WITHOUT LEGS.

A Sultan had a daughter, and the daughter used to be taught the Koran. One day the Sultan went on a pilgrimage, and entrusted his daughter to a priest, and said, "Continue to teach that girl the Koran." The priest coveted the girl, wishing to lie with her, but the girl refused. One day she said, "Come to me to-morrow." On the day arranged she removed from the house the ladder by which the priest used to ascend. He then sent a letter to her father, and he wrote, "Your daughter has become a harlot." The Sultan returned from the pilgrimage, and he was angry with the girl, and he handed her over to some slaves, and he said, "Cut that girl's throat." Then the slaves took the girl, and they brought her to a wooded place, and they cut off her legs, while they dug her grave. While they were digging the grave she crawled away, and went into some trees and hid. When the slaves had dug the grave they looked in the place where she had lain and could not find her. Then they slew a gazelle, and the gazelle's blood they poured into a bottle, and brought the blood to the Sultan, and said, "We have slain the girl." One day later a caravan passed by the place, and camped where the girl lay. In the afternoon as the party were loading up the camels, they saw the girl sitting under a tree. A man took the girl, and put her on a camel, and brought her to the town they came to. The man who took the girl put her to live in a house. Later on the son of the Sultan saw the girl's face, and the young man saw that her face was beautiful, and he said to the man whose house she dwelt in, "Let me marry that girl from you." And the man said, "The girl has no legs." Then the Sultan's son said, "I will marry her, give her to me." And so the man said, "Well and good." And the Sultan's son married her. She bore two children, and while she was with child the young man said, "I am going on a pilgrimage," and he left her a ram, and went on the pilgrimage. While he was away on the pilgrimage his wife had a dream, and she dreamed that two birds sat upon her two legs, and her legs had grown out, and that she made the pilgrimage. In the morning at break of day she saw the two birds sitting upon her two legs, and the legs had grown out. After daylight she took her two children and the ram and the two birds, and went on the pilgrimage. She came to a building at the half-way, and there came to her her father and her brother and the priest and her husband, none of whom knew her. She told stories to her children, and she related all that had happened to her, and her father heard, and the priest. Then the priest tried to run away, but the Sultan said, "Sit down until the story is finished." Then the Sultan, the girl's father, cut the priest's throat, and the girl with her father and husband went on and made the pilgrimage. And so the girl and her father were reconciled.

IV. THE HOLE IN THE WALL.

There was a Sultan who had a son, and his son said, "I want to marry." So the Sultan gave him many presents, and also a ship. The Sultan's son set sail and came to a town, and when he arrived at the town he became friendly with a Sultan, and the Sultan gave him a house. The young man made a hole between the house he was in and the Sultan's house, and he became friendly with the Sultan's wife. One day the young man said to the Sultan's wife, "Make some food for me just as you are accustomed to make it for your husband." And he went to the Sultan, and said, "To-night will you take food with me?" And the Sultan said, "Well and good." And the young man said to the Sultan's wife, "To-night when I and the Sultan are having our food, I want you to serve us with the food." And the woman said, "The Sultan will know me." Then he said, "He will not know you, I will say you are my wife." And she said, "If he does not know me, I will go with you and be your wife." At night the Sultan came home and dressed himself, and came to the young man's house. And his wife passed through the hole in the wall, and came to the young man's house. Then she served the food to the Sultan and the young man. The Sultan recognised his wife, and got off his chair, and went to his house. Before he reached his house, the woman passed through the hole and sat upon her bed, and the Sultan saw her. When he saw her he straightway came back to the house of the young man, while the woman came through the hole, and still

11—2

he saw her. The young man, who was dining with him, said to the Sultan, "Did you think this woman who is serving our food was your wife? The woman is my wife," he said, and the Sultan sat down. The next morning the young man said, "I am sailing." "Very good," he answered. And the young man arranged with the Sultan's wife and said, "In the morning come through that place, I am sailing." So the woman passed through and came to the young man, and he took her to the ship, and sailed. And the young man having run away with the Sultan's wife married her.

V. THE TOWN OF MAN-EATERS.

There is a story that a man was riding a horse, and there came to him an old woman, who said, "Where are you going?" And he said, "I am going to that town." And she said, "In that town people are slain and eaten; do not go in, lest they slay you." And he answered, "Still I am going in." Then she said, "The town has a Sultan, and the Sultan has a daughter, and the daughter's sash is a snake, and the snake eats the people. And there is a camel who eats the people, he sits in front of the house, over there upon a bed." And she said, "See, my man, if you are going to the house, run and enter the house of the Sultan's daughter." And he said, "The man told me, The dog eats the people, and the camel eats the people, and the snake eats the people. How am I going to pass them?" And the woman said, "Take this grass, and let not the camel eat you, but when you pass the house you are going to, put the grass in at the door, lest it eat you. And for the dog, take this piece of meat, and put it near the dog, and let him eat it and not you. And for the snake, which is tied round the girl's waist, take this stick, and place it on the snake's head, and then the snake will die. After you have done this enter the house and go to the girl, and then marry her." So he married the girl.

VI. MISFORTUNES.

There is a story that a man once loaded his water-camels and took them to the well, and went to draw water. When he went to draw water he tied his camels together. When he was in the nullah he left six camels behind while he led the other six. When he was some distance off, the six camels that were left behind were not to be seen. So he ran back, and came up to find six lions eating the six camels. Then he left them, and returned to the other six camels, and found six other lions eating these. Then he took a waterskin from the camels, and came to his home, to find his family looted by an enemy.

VII. HOW TO CHOOSE A WIFE.

A man had a son, and the son said to his father, " Father, I want to marry a wife." Then his father said, "Do you take a widow." So he took a widow, and his father said, " Marry her." So he married her. Then his father said, "Tie her with a rope, and when she speaks to you, untie the rope." So he tied her with a rope, and the woman said, "This is not what I have been accustomed to see. What are you doing with me ? " Thereupon he untied the rope. In the morning his father came and said, " What did she say?" And he answered, "She said to me, This is not what I have been accustomed to see. Why are you doing that to me ?" Then his father said, " Send her away." That was one.

The father said to his son, " Take another wife, take a grown girl." Then he said, " To-night tie her with a rope, and when she speaks to you, untie it." So he tied her, and she said, " This is not what I have been accustomed to hear, why are you tying me with that ? " So he untied her. In the morning he came to his father, and he said, " She said, This is not what I have been accustomed to hear, what are you doing to me with the rope ? " Then his father said, " Send her away too." And that was another.

Then his father said, " Do you go and take a nice, young girl." So he took one, and he said, " To-night tie her with a rope, and when she speaks to you untie it." So the young man did so, and went to sleep, and was asleep all night. In the early morning the girl woke him up, and said, " The rope with which you tied me is fallen off and is not tied to me, tie it upon me." And in the morning he told his father, " Father, she said, The rope has fallen off, and is not tied to me, tie it upon me." Then his father said, " Keep that one, she is the right one." So she was the one he afterwards married.

VIII. MAN AND HYAENA.

It is said that the Hyaena owned flocks and Man had none. One day Man was looking after the Hyaena's flocks, and the Hyaena went to the Council. After this Man thought, and he said, " Let us steal the Hyaena's flocks, while he is away at the council." So Man put the flocks in a zariba, and night came, and when it was night, they were driven off. The Hyaena howled, and went to the other animals, and he said, " See, I have been looted." Then they said, " Let us attack." They came along, and arrived at a pool of water, and the male Dikdik said, " If you do not let me come to the pool, you shall not drink." " Sir, we will drink, leave us," they said. Then he scratched sand into it, until the water was gone, and they died of thirst, when they found no water.

IX. CAMEL AND HER FOLLOWERS.

It is said that a Camel possessed altogether a Snake, a Zariba, a Fire, a Flood, and a Lion, and Deceit, and Honesty. Those seven the Camel owned. One day Deceit said, "We might steal the Lion from that big Camel, let us kill the Lion." The others said, "How are we to kill him?" Then she said, "Let the Snake bite the Lion, and when you have bitten him, go into the Zariba." So he bit him and went into the Zariba. Then she said, "O Fire, burn up both the Zariba and Snake." So the Fire burned both Zariba and Snake. Then she said, "The Fire has killed the Snake and the Fence, let the Flood too put out the Fire." After this Honesty said, "The Flood does not travel on the mountain, but only in the nullah, let us travel on the mountain with the Camel." So they travelled on the mountain, and then Deceit said, "Let us slay the Camel." So they slew her, and cooked the steak, and gulped down the steak, and except the steak nothing else of the Camel did they eat. And the meat stuck in their throats, for it was a big piece, and could not pass through their mouths. So they died.

X. THE BLIND MAN.

In a certain place many men were talking, and there were two men, one of whom was blind and the other was not blind. The man with sight said, "Why do you talk with a blind man? He can see nothing." And the blind man said, "How do you know a blind man?" The other one said, "We know a blind man, he is a man who sees nothing." Then the blind man said, "He that is blind is the man who knows nothing, he is blind."

XI.

Then Swayne came and began to enlist many askaris. Then Swayne left and came to us at Harrar. Then he said, "I want askaris." Then Oscar Gerard said, "How many do you want?" Then he said, "I want a hundred horsemen." Then he said, "The hundred shall be given you." The hundred were given. When they were given we marched and came to Adadleh. We made eight companies. Then we drilled, and we stayed for one month only. Then Swayne's force came to us, and we left Burao and went to Ber.

Col. Swayne and Col. Phillips were in command. The Mullah lived at Olesan. Then we came to Uduwein. An illalo was sent and told to look for the Mullah. Afterwards it was said to me, the Mullah had fled. We left Uduwein. Afterwards we went to Olesan. The Mullah was in the Nogal. We left Olesan, and afterwards at Wadamago we sent out illalos.

The illalos found some *karias*, and captured camels, female and male. We sent the horsemen and camel corps to attack. Afterwards when the force attacked we loaded up and followed. Then we marched for two days, and then halted at Haridig. The Camel Corps and horsemen brought in 8000 camels. Then Swayne said, "Two companies will stay here, and the camels will be left there." Then my company was left with the camels. Then Swayne's force went.

Capt. MacNeill and Murray were left at the zariba. Then we saw the Mullah's illalos. At 2 o'clock in the day his force came to us. When we saw the enemy the Sirkal said, "Come inside the zariba," and afterwards we attacked and then we slew each other and fought for four hours afterwards. At 6 o'clock we chased them away. After that we sat down together inside the zariba. Then later on, at 7 o'clock at night, we attacked and fought for two hours, and at 9 o'clock drove them away. Now at 1 o'clock they returned and this time we fought for one hour only. Then we slew those men, and afterwards they ran away. Then the next day at 7 o'clock they came back, and then we fired at each other, and then during the day we shot all the dervishes.

Until they came close the maxim shot them, when they came close the askaris shot them with their rifles. (The maxim is a fine thing, a wild beast or devil.)

When the people went further off and the maxim was let off at them, then many people perished. After that they fled up to the zariba. A Mullah man killed four askaris with his spear. Then we chased them and caught 40 men.

Capt. MacNeill sent for me and said, "Count for me all the Mullah men that are hit." I collected 10 askaris, and we counted 460 dead. Of our two companies they killed 9 men. Then MacNeill said, "Put the dervish dead men together somewhere." Then we brought them to one place. Then Swayne's force came to us, it had got nothing from the Mullah.

The whole force came together to Bohotle. And afterwards we sent out illalos, and they found many camels at Kurmis. The illalos came back and we saw many camels; the whole force loaded up, and we went to Kurmis. The Allegheri were looted of many camels. We stayed fifteen days. The owners of the animals came to us. The people went to the Colonel and said, "We will follow you, and the sheep will be brought back." Then he said, "If you follow I will get you back your sheep, load up all your *karias* and bring them close in." Then the Allegheri followed us. Then they said, "We will look for the Mullah with you. Afterwards we loaded up and came to Bohotle. The askaris who were sick were left behind at Bohotle, and then we left Bohotle. We halted at Wudwud and afterwards sent out illalos from Wudwud. They said, "The Mullah is far off." Then we started and marched for five nights and five days. On the next day we met the Mullah's force. Then we fought, 15 askaris were killed, and the Sirkal who talks Arabic. Dickinson sahib was struck with a bullet, he was struck in the thigh. Twenty-five askaris were struck with bullets, but not killed. Then we found no water and came back. We were afraid, if the askaris have no water they will die. We spent fifteen days marching to Berbera. When we came here the askaris were given many camels. Every havildar was given 3, every jemadar 4, milk camels. The askaris received a month's leave.

There was the end of this force.

The second force came to Burao, and we stayed at Burao for four months afterwards. Then illalos were sent out and they went to the Ali Naleyah. They said, "We have found many animals." We marched there, four companies under Col. Cobbe and Col. Swayne. We went to Las Idleh, and at Las Idleh many horses came to us. Then we sent illalos, and the illalos said, "We have seen many animals." Then we left Las Idleh and marched on for eleven nights. We went to Jid Ali, to the Ali Naleyah. Then each company went its own way. We left Col. Swayne and half a company. Then we attacked the Ali Naleyah, and during the night and day looted the flocks. Then we brought the animals into the zariba. Any men we saw we slew. Then we left. We reached Las Idleh in fifteen nights. Then the askaris were given sheep, each askari was given 12, a havildar or naik 20, jemadar or colour-havildar 30. Col. Cobbe and Col. Swayne went back to Berbera. Maj. Petrie and our four companies came back to Burao. Then we halted for a month at Burao. Then Col. Swayne joined us. He said, "The Force will go out; we will look for the Mullah. Let the Somali people bring camels to help," he said. Then the Habr Awal and Habr Yunis each brought with them 800 head of cattle, the Habr Toljala 600. Then the force moved. My company remained behind for eight days. Then the Camel Corps and horsemen came from Berbera to Burao under the command of Capt. Osborne. Then we followed after the force. In five days we reached Bohotle. Then we joined Col. Swayne and the force at Bohotle. Then illalos were sent out. The illalos were away for ten nights. The illalos came back, and they said, "We have not seen the Mullah." Then the Colonel said, "We will advance." We advanced into the Nogal. Then we went to Gerowei. We looted many animals from the Mohd. Gerad. We stayed at Gerowei twenty nights. Illalos were sent out, they went to the Mullah at Mudug. The illalos came back to us and said, "It is a dry place, and we shall get no water." Then we made east and reached Halin. We looted many animals from the Naleyah Ahmed. Then the Sirkal said, "We will go back." For twelve days we marched and then came to Gaulo. Then the Colonel said, "Let two officers with the spearmen and animals go back." Then the animals and spearmen and two British officers went back. The Colonel left 3000 camels behind. Then illalos were sent. They went to the Mullah, and then said, "The Mullah is staying at Mudug." Then we loaded up and marched for five nights. On the sixth day in the early morning we met the dervishes at Erigo. Then we halted somewhere. After that the dervishes made a move towards us. When there was a mile between us, the Colonel said, "They will not fight with us, load up the camels and move." Then we moved. The country was thick with trees. Then every company was extended ; thus we moved, and all at once they sent a volley into us. Then we lay our bellies on the ground, and we fought. Four companies departed. They were frightened and ran away. We three companies fought, the rest ran away. The three companies that fought were mine and two others. We came into the zariba, then the dervishes came. Three companies went out and drove them away.

Afterwards we came to Bohotle.

SONGS.

In the songs a distinctly poetical style is noticeable, also a number of words, not found in colloquial Somali, many of which are absolutely unintelligible by themselves to an unpoetical native. Many of these words are coined by the author, but many are probably old words handed down from generation to generation. It is necessary therefore in many passages for the author himself, or a fellow poet (of whom there are many, both professional and amateur), to explain the real meaning. Several of those which I collected I have not published here, as I could get no satisfactory rendering or explanation even from interpreters.

Those translations which I have given are necessarily free in many places and by no means literal. They are interesting as examples of style, rather than of grammar.

Songs are divided into three classes, known as

Gerar, Gabei, and Hes[1].

The **Gerar** is sung on horseback, and usually relates to raiding and fighting.

The **Gabei** is a chant of a more peaceful nature, and is often a love song. It is usually sung round the fire in the evening.

The **Hes** is the Dancing-song, and always accompanies a dance. It is often in parts for men and women, and is usually of an amorous nature.

---

[1] Paulitschke (II. Cap. 2) describes six kinds of songs, and gives numerous examples.

All three seem to have a somewhat similar rhythm, which runs as follows :

Hălnă wă | īgă să|lān,
Hălnă wă | īgă să|'abghād,
Hălnă wă | īgă sŭ|āl.

Hăl wā | ī să'ăb|ghād,
wă | ī sūl|dănkă ă|māntī,
sīrād|kī Bĕrbĕr|ād,
ïyŏ | wā hăl|dă sŭbăhh | jōgā,

The length of the whole line may vary considerably. An essential point is the alliteration of one letter throughout the song, each line of which must contain a word which contains that letter. Thus one song may have g, another d, and so on ; in a " g " song this letter occurs in some word in every line. The songs usually consist of solo and chorus, often sung in parts. Besides these, there are certain well-known chants which are sung while watering or grazing animals, marching, loading or unloading. Many of these are very old indeed. The watering chants vary for the different animals ; camels, horses, and sheep have each their special chants sung to them, which again vary in different tribes, and are adapted to the nature of the well in order to suit the action of drawing the water.

I. GERAR, in *s*.

Greeting to Sultan Nur on his visit to the Habr Toljala. ? 1885.

Somali.	*English.*
Halna[1] wa ìga[2] salàn[3],	First we salute thee,
Halna wa ìga sa'ábghad,	then we shake thy hands,
Halna wa ìga suàl.	then we ask a question.
Hal wa i sa'abghád,	First is our handshake,
wa i Suldànka amànti,	is praise to our Sultan,
siradki Berberád,	the light of Berberah,
iyo wá haldá subahh jòga,	who is as an ostrich standing in the morning,

[1] A poetical word meaning "one thing," "item," similar to **kodi** in prose.
[2] from me. The sing. pronoun is used for the plural.
[3] salaam.

bàlashi kala saide[1],	shaking out his wings,
wahh la sìsto la wáh[2].	beyond compare.

. . .   . . .

Halna wa ìga salàn.	Again we salute thee.
Gèla, Sènyo[3] iyo Làn[3],	The camels, Senyo and Lan,
sangayásha gharéistei,	(and) the stallions have become fat,
gabdaha súrta la mòda[4],	the young girls are like straight sticks,
iyo seyahháinu ku jìfna.	and we lie in the dew.
Sàdadà nabad bá leh.	The tribute is one of peace.

. . .   . . .

Halna wa ìga sual.	And again we have a question.
Suldànki bokhronàdo,	The Sultan who reigns,
hor mahhau so'otén,	why hast thou come forth,
sèdka ainu 'úneno[5] ?	that we should eat the sinews ?
Ràbi ya inna sìyei,	God granted to us,
sadehhdèni Ishhàk[6],	us three (sons of) Ishhak,
hadanán ku salùghin,	if we do not make trouble with thee,
ádiga O Suldàno,	thee, O Sultan,
sàlo yanna ka yèdin[7].	that thou shouldst not bring complaint against us.

II. GERAR, in g.

The singer's tribe has been severely looted, and he demands justice.

Somali.	*English.*
Ma[8] sidi gelòga,	Like the bustard,
o guluf mel ku darèmei,	who has seen an enemy somewhere,
yan gam'i wai habèn.	I cannot sleep at night.
Sidi àrka iyo gòsha,	Like the lion and lioness,

---

[1] The Potential tense is often used in songs for the Indicative.

[2] This literally means, "nothing can be found to be given for it," i.e. no price.

[3] names for camels.

[4] lit. "is thought," an idiom meaning "is like." Cf. **la bida** in Yibir, q.v.

[5] i.e. have the poor parts of the animal to eat.

[6] i.e. Habr Gerhajis, Habr Awal, Habr Toljala, the three Ishhak tribes.

[7] for **inanad sàlo naga yèdin.**

[8] appears to be frequently used in songs without necessarily asking a question, especially in introducing similes.

o gábnihi laga làyei,
gurhan ma igu bôte.

    .   .   .

Sidi Gòdir irmán,
o élmihi ka ghálen,
garti mau ulule.

    .   .   .

Sidi gànleh shishèyei,
tollkei ma iss ugu géftei.

    .   .   .

Ma sidi nin gabôbei,
o nàgu, gunyo ka dìbei,

ku geshiyèya hhumàtei,
yan ugu hantamèya.

    .   .   .

Wehher gèrida jòga,
ma gèl annu lahain,
e gúdub nogu mághana,
O hághi so gudbìya[1].

    .   .   .

Nabsì[2] wa ma ghabôbei,
herna[3] wa ma gúdan,
Gùli wa wáhh ma môgi,
gòbina[4] wa wárranta.

    .   .   .

Gèlan manta haïno,
hènya godonkòda,
iyo wagérki wádana,
hádano gudídin
lábadiba an góine,
mia no gáraten[5]?

whose young have been slain,
I would make much clamour.

    .   .   .

Like Godir, when with milk,
whose young have been slaughtered,
I would groan for justice.

    .   .   .

Like enemies apart,
my tribe is divided among itself.

    .   .   .

Like an old man,
whose wives, for whom he paid much,
have grown bad and lazy,
I am angry at it.

    .   .   .

For the lives that were taken,
camels that were ours,
whose fine has not been paid us,
O bring out the "diya."

    .   .   .

Fortune has not grown old,
and law is everlasting,
God is all-knowing,
and the high-born have the news.

    .   .   .

Let us have the camels to-day,
their genitals,
and heart,
?
let us cut both,
do you decide for us?

---

[1] The price of a man's life is 100 camels, whether it takes place in a tribal fight, or raid, or in a private affair: this is the Arabic "diya," or Somali "hagh."

[2] Nasib.   [3] Somali custom.

[4] gentry, or well born, opposed to tribes of doubtful origin, Esa, Gadabursi, Hawiya, and outcasts.

[5] The general meaning of this stanza is clear, but l. 27 I cannot translate.

III. GERAR, in *gh* and *g*.

To my Bay Pony.

Somali.	*English.*
Hamar O, ghorohhdàdo !	O Hamar, your beauty !
Hamar O, garadàdo !	O Hamar, your strength !
Hamar O, guwidàdo !	O Hamar, your size !
Hamar O, ghofalkàgo !	O Hamar, your obedience !
Hamar O, gadankàgo !	O Hamar, your price !

Hamar O, ghorohhdàdo !	O Hamar, your beauty !
ghaili¹ dòf laga kénei,	a cloth brought from over the sea,
iyo ghánfirka Híndi,	and Indian raiment,
gh labkan ku árkei,	things which I look at,
gésuhugu dínta².	(and) die of astonishment.

Hamar O, guwidàdo !	O Hamar, your size !
ghàridi Mílmilad³	⎫ as a camel which has grown very fat
rati⁴ ghaib ugu nàhhai	⎭ on the sand of Milmil,
ghorigi Berberád	⎫ as a ship at the pier of Berberah,
markab, ghaid u sugaya,	⎭ waiting for orders,
ghun u jòga, miya⁵.	stands fast.

Hamar O, garadàdo !	O Hamar, your strength !
ghalimali libahh,	as a black-maned lion,
iyo saryen ghortu u ba'dei,	and a bull oryx with broad neck,
iyo wìyil ghorah, miya.	and a bull rhinoceros.

Hamar O, ghofalkàgo !	O Hamar, your obedience !
suryadan kaga ràbto,	the path which I desire
ghálbigu ka gárta,	your heart understands,
gelafdìdka hàwen,	as a dutiful wife,
iyo wàyel haj u ghóbtei,	and an elder gone on a pilgrimage,
an iss ku ghónsan, miya.	without grumbling.

Hamar O, gadankàgu !	O Hamar, your price !

---

¹ a bright tartan cloth, most worn by Dolbohantas.
² for **gesaha ugu dinta**, lit. I die of astonishment at the thing I look at.
³ Milmil, in S.W. Somaliland.
⁴ Dolbohanta for "camel."
⁵ This word like **ma** is often used in similes. Perhaps it is only " eh ? "

gholidán la halèlo	(from) the tribe I fight with,
marna gás ka ma hóio[1].	never can enemy take (you) away.
Ma gasànad Sirkálku[2]	Can the Sirkal !
ghaib u só ballàgha ?	who scatters his money so lavishly?

IV. GERAR, in d.

The singer tries to persuade two tribes to make peace.

Somali.	*English.*
Wa innagi dán wadágta[3],	We are all of one salt,
iyo iss ku dôlad ahain,	and under one government,
jini yu ídin dúfsan.	a spirit entices you to evil.
War, tollo, inna[4] daya!	Ye tribes, desist !
. . .	. . .
Mel e ghailo dalúntei,	The place you raised your shout,
ma nàgo urleh la dòhhai[5],	like women with child ripped up,
o gùriïhi dab la rùbei,	whose homes are burned with fire,
an dùnyo so dakhdaghàghin,	who have no property to move,
bal dugèda hissàba[6],	O think how old it is,
wahh ku daida halkàsa.	consider somewhat there.
War, tollo, inna daya !	Ye tribes, desist !
. . .	. . .
Wayelka ya dad aslahha,	The elders settle the affairs of a people,
dalintàse ka dìda.	but the young men disobey.
Bal da'danahai, dai,	See then, how old am I,
bal dórkan talináyo,	how fairly I will decide,
iyo dawodèda hissàbo,	and weigh the case,
wahh ku daida hálkana.	consider somewhat here too.
O war, tollo, inna daya !	O ye tribes, desist !
. . .	. . .

[1] Among the Somalis, a mare, a well and a woman belong to the tribe, and cannot be parted with without the consent of the tribe. Hence the singer here says "No one can take you from our tribe."

[2] refers to British Officer.

[3] **la wadago** take meat together. The 3rd sing. is used, just as the 3rd sing. of a verb is used after a pronoun with **ba**, e.g. **idinka ba shakheineya.**

[4] or **naga**, is often used in such expressions, without necessarily referring to "us."

[5] A custom fairly common among the Somalis until recently. The Mullah has often practised it on his raids against the Ishhak.

[6] i.e. it is so long since it occurred.

Matàni la dagùghei¹,
iyo fardi ghad ku dulbèlei,
iyo dèbilihi la kahhàyei,
gàshan kun² la darèyei,
ma dimòne wahhas,
o tollimòno ka dòrne,
o sàmir bannu³ dèdallei,
wahh ku ɖaida halkasna.
O war, tollo, naga daya !

The wells are shut down,
and the horses are sore-backed,
and the camels are driven off,
milk is drawn on to shields,
we must not forget that,
and must choose to be of one tribe,
and wish for peace,
consider somewhat there too.
O ye tribes, desist !

Hadi tána la dìdo,
o laga dórto 'olládda,
ánnana² wa dírirra,
'ollo, ha inna dùlin !

If this is refused,
and enmity preferred,
we too must fight,
ye armies, do not attack us !

V. GERAR, in *g*.

To my Pony.

Somali.

Nefka gàdada wèinleh
amàntis garan màyo
Ma Haud⁴ gèdaleh ba?
'Erku o gálab hore
gabdankìsa, miya ?
Libahh mel fòg ka gùhha
gabnihìsi, miya ?
Gèla, Gèdo⁵ iyo Làn⁵
gànihisu, miya ?
Ana, Gèd⁶ iyo Hohhad⁷,
gerarkeigu, miya ?
Áfartìsi gundod
dulka ugu gára'a,
ma sidi gábaɖ wein,
o geyankèda⁸ la sìyei,

English.

My broad-chested beast,
how to praise him I know not.
Like grass-covered Haud ?
⎫ Like the pattering
⎭ rain from last evening's sky ?
⎫ Like the cubs of a
⎭ lion roaring afar ?
⎫ Like the foals of the
⎭ camels, Gedo and Lan ?
⎫ Like my own song
⎭ of Ged and Hohhad ?
His four hoofs
clatter over the ground,
like a grown girl,
who has been given her husband,

---

¹ lit. covered with stones. Wells out of use are shut up by their owners, by covering them with wood and stones.

² upon. This means that there is only enough to fill the hollow of a shield.

³ refers to "we, the singer's people," and not to the others. The pronoun **innagi** in line 1 includes the people addressed.

⁴ The district S.W. of the Nogal Valley.

⁵ Names of camels.   ⁶ The spring winds. (Hagar.)

⁷ The summer wind. (Karif.)   ⁸ means the "betrothed."

Somali	English
o gùyo¹ wein lagu dìbei,	and has received great flocks,
darka ti gana'leh,	who, with most costly robe,
iyo gárbasárka harìdah,	and silken raiment,
iyo gàshali huwàtei,	and dress, has clothed herself,
o gor gadidka hadkèda,	and at the time of mid-day shadows,
ninkiyo gamà'san,	to her sleeping husband,
gàsinka u sita	brings his food,
o kabihi gadda lo'ada²,	as with the shoes of cow's hide
gara'ésa miya?	she clatters?

VI. GERAR, in s.

To my Pony.

Somali.	English.
Faraskeigu soyan,	My fine horse,
midabkàgu ma sô kan 'ád ba?	your colour, is it not white?
Sifahàgu guyédna	Your manners and age
ma sagàl gù jir ba?	are they not nine years?
Ma sidi nin sirkàlah?	Are you not like a gentleman?
Intan ku salàhho,	As I groom you,
sankarkàga tùra,	I throw away the dirt,
golahan salèbeya,	I clean the stable,
o sahárka ka idlèya,	and remove the dung,
an gèdo kugu saya.	while I put down grass for you.
Halki sènyo ku sófto,	Where camels graze,
ádigo wáhh ku sèma³,	with you I must attack,
o sèma iga ríd mahai,	and until I get my share,
sunka ká de'b'in mayo.	I will not loosen girths.
Wahhba ha i la sula'an,	Do not prance with me,
o salogiga ghunyar⁴.	and neigh softly.

VII. GERAR, in b.

A Raiding Song.

Somali.	English.
Idinku baneyál⁵,	Have ye, over plains and plains,
banan idinku baneyál,	over (countless) plains,

¹ i.e. the dowry.

² The women's shoes are not fastened by a strap at the heel, and, being just as heavy as the men's, make a great clatter in walking. The best shoes are of cow's hide.

³ touch, but here the meaning is "loot."

⁴ This is the meaning given me by the author, but I cannot explain it.

⁵ An intensive form of the plural.

Somali	English
Illahh bèididi haïsta,	whose richness belongs to God,
dùlan mau bùlaten ?	gone out to war ?
Barbar ma iss ka gúrten?	Have ye assembled the young men ?
Badô¹ mau ghóbsoten?	Have ye caught Bado ?
Bustihi² iyo shalka³ ma Badô huwisen ?	Have ye put on Bado the blanket and trappings ?
Rakábka birtaah sulka mau barkisen⁴ ?	Have ye put the toe in the stirrup iron ?
Yassin⁵ maugu bahhden ?	Have ye made your prayers ?
Butìyihi 'ollku jehhai,	Where the enemy cut the ground,
iyo búdulki ma héshen ?	have ye found the tracks ?
Ísago ka balawaya,	While he is talking,
banán maugu takten ?	have ye taken to the plain ?
Wìlal, Ebba badbádshei,	Boys, enriched by God,
dabka mau bilbíshen ?	have ye prepared the fire ?
Sibràr 'anaha bokha⁶,	A skin of curdled milk,
iyo habènkana barùrta,	and fat for to-night,
ma barùra 'unten ?	have ye eaten fat ?

VIII. GERAR, in b.
On the Raising of the Tribal Horse, 1903⁷.

Somali.	English.
Gerar wa bogholal,	Songs are in hundreds,
wa badwein iyo môjad,	like the great sea and waves,
wa babùrki sidìsa.	like the ships.
Ninki an badinahain	The man who is not full of them,
bèrka wa ka ghálaha.	his bowels are cut out.
Babìr mai mákhashen ?	Do ye hear my song ?
Hadi gàso lo bilàbo,	If companies are collected,
o Burao lagu tontòmo⁸,	and hailed to Burao,

¹ Name of a horse.
² is the hairy skin placed over the saddle.
³ is the woollen trappings on headstall and breast-plate (sita‘).
⁴ With the Somalis, as with other African horsemen, the stirrup iron is small, and only the big toe is inserted.
⁵ The Prophet.
⁶ Curdled milk and melted sheep's tail fat are the usual supplies taken by a Somali on a raid.
⁷ This and the next two were made by my sais, or groom, on the occasion of the raising of mounted native levies for the operations against the Mullah, 1902–4.
⁸ from "tomtom" drum.

wilal bèrka Ishhàkah,	sons of Ishhak's loins,
adunkòda badna,	of great wealth,
an ku berkadsádahain[1],	who are not weak-hearted,
ayan Sirkál Basha ka ra'i.	I will follow the Sirkal Pasha.

IX. GERAR, in *b*.

Leaving Burao before Jidballi.

Somali.	*English.*
Innagu Burao jògna,	We wait at Burao,
ma jawábta illàlo[2]?	has the scout brought answer?
War, bulàli[3] jadèr, O,	Lo, wiry dun,
so'od beinnaga[4] jòga.	the time to march is upon us.
Jiryal affeyei,	I have sharpened spears,
iyo sun b'e'id laga jehhai[5],	and cut a thong from an oryx,
aya iss ku jìdei bilàwa.	I have tied on a dagger.
Wa jehhád[6] tégeya,	I go on a crusade,
aya jìd aròryo,	and start in the early morning,
illa[7] jidáneya.	in order to hasten.
Anna 'ss ku jàd[8] nókhona.	We are of the same mettle.

X. GERAR, in *b*.

The Object of Fighting is Loot[9].

Somali.	*English.*
In kastàda bareiso,	However many you kill,
o ghasirádi bokhosho,	and cut their pay,
la'agteidi bakshìshleh,	my bakshish money,
iyo hadan bùr[10] na la sìnin,	if it is not given us in heaps,
ama gèla Badwein bada leigu	or the camels at Badwein if they are
'erìyin,	not looted for me,

[1] I do not know the derivation or correct form of the word in this line, but the meaning was explained as I have given it.
[2] scout, spy. [3] dun-coloured pony. [4] **ba innaga.**
[5] Oryx hide is the strongest in Somaliland.
[6] Being an ignorant man, he did not realise the meaning of this word, or he would not have used it in referring to a campaign against fellow Mohammedans.
[7] **in la.** [8] is the Hindustani word.
[9] The Somalis, even our so-called friendly and protected tribes, have no compunction in saying that they will not join our army unless we promise them loot, in the shape of camels. It is also implied here that money is of little consequence compared to camels—an important fact to remember in dealing with these people.
[10] mountain. Here equals "piles of money."

inan forska[1] u bòdo,	that I join the force,
wa hal an bihhihainin,	is a thing of no value,
Sirkal bèrka u sheg.	let the Sirkal remember in his heart.

XI. GABEI[2], in *d*.

Lament on the Invasion and Raids of the Mullah,
Mohammed Abdallah, 1900—1904.

Da'da[3] gabeiga watan[4] beriaha dába'ei digéya,
Forget the holy song I formerly laid down,

Hadba anigu o dayei ya dári tídahhai,
Now I myself too have ceased from what people sang,

An dubeyo wa ki beriaha igu dahhsonei.
And from what came to me to sing before.

An ku d'odo, Somàli yan hádalka deínahain,
Let me speak out, and if Somalis cease not their chatter,

Dabòlki an ku rido, hedoda an dáboka gud sàro.
Let me put on the lid, and cover up the dish.

Digti hälei dahhdiga ka ma gam'in, dá'kirka an ka'ei,
All last night my heart could not sleep, in the morning I arose,

Derewíshtu wa ti ka tími degalodoïyo,
There were the Dervishes come from their homes,

Darùdki[5] wàgi hore yei dabin oghòlen,
Darud first had laid his snare,

Dabadedna wa ti lei yími dágahhan Idòro[6],
And afterwards he was come to the land of Idoro,

Daregháda[7] iyo wa ti guben, dìnti Nébiga dab ku shiden,
There were the priests' schools burned, the faith of the Prophet set fire to,

[1] Adopted from the English.

[2] I have given as literal a translation of these "Gabeis" as I can, but in some cases where I am not able to explain how the meaning is arrived at, I have given the meaning derived from a colloquial paraphrase by the author.

[3] 1—5. Old songs do not suit the present days of strife,
        Now keep quiet unless you wish me to stop.

[4] And later l. 7, **wa ti**, cf. § 289.

[5] Name of the Somali tribes, including Dolbohanta, Ogaden, etc., i.e. the tribes of the Mullah.

[6] A name for Ishhak.

[7] **Daregho** is a school where young men learn their religion, or are trained for priesthood. The chief schools are at u. Sheikh, Hargeisa; the u. Sheikh one is that referred to here.

Dabuna da'ei iyo dùnida nafòdei,
And he carried off loot and laid waste the earth,

Dadku da'ei, agònti dulmiya[1], derisádu layei,
He robbed the people, injured the orphan, slew the neighbours.

Dubki[2] iyo shaládki, arladdi lagu doàfei,
Their headcovering and chant, as they tramp over the ground,

Sidi dánab ku da'ei, rèrihi digoda lo rèbei.
Fell like lightning and thunder, our homes were left as dung.

Ebbo, adi ya dayènah, an duri ku moghène,
O Father, thou art everlasting, and all knowing,

Dalki adaha laba nin[3] ya dàsaddu tùnei,
Two sides have clamoured for portions of the land,

Rabo, kala dabál eida madhar leiss la dòneya.
O God, separate the armies which seek one another.

XII.   GABEI, in *m*.

My future Wife.

An malèyo tan[4] màge wa madahhàda Gulèdo.
It is in my mind that she whom I would marry is the (daughter of) the head of the Guleds.

Marrin[5] 'as weiyei, o ga'amo wa majèno ròbah,
She is pink, and her hands are like drops of rain,

Kub malàsan ba lehdahai, márodi wa sòhhei,
Her ankles are round, her skirt is pleated,

Taláboda màgug o ma rídei, wa miyìrisei.
Her steps are not those of a fool, she walks daintily.

Malaëk sameis an farsámo, lagu ma nàgin[6].
She is after the fashion of an angel, a virgin full of skill,

[7]Wèli melod jogtana maärag, ku maana moghène.
Never yet have I seen the place of your abode, nor have I any knowledge of you.

---

1 Orphans are ordered to be specially protected by the Koran.
2 The white cloth they tie over their heads as a badge.
3 The Mullah's people and the British Government.
4 **ti an.**
5 pink colour, or light copper, the favourite colour among Somalis.
6 From **nàg** woman.
7 The singer now addresses the lady.

Halun[1] ba mirtídaha ghálbigu ka muradsidei,
Last night, for half the night, in my heart I dreamed of you.

Marrwein hoyoda wahhannu sìn Mur[2] ai rèrato[3],
We will give your aged mother a loading camel,

Walálkana hámar maiđan ban màlin ho odáne[4].
And to your brother one day I may present a pure bay pony.

Mos ban u jebin ábaha, Mùra[5] iyo Hèmaleh[5],
I will divide a host of camels with your father.

An majàlis wada ghadónne, midayóda kàli.
Let us all take our places, come to my people.

XIII. GABEI, in *d*.

To Dahab.

Dirahh hórte, Guban[6] o lei dilei, dúkha la hayàmei.
In the spring time, Guban is dead, the people have taken the road.

Ninki đàno kahhàyo banan dauga so ghóbeya,
He who leads water-camels, takes the road to the plain.

Dukhan[5] iyo Ogaz[5] ó đalei, derig la danshòdo,
Dukhan and Ogaz have foaled, and are proud with repletion.

Wa derèjo labadèni o ghollad 'ss kú đarei,
Here is honour for both of us, who meet in one room,

Unsiga ad nagu dadisida. Dàhab O, no kàli!
While you sprinkle scent over us. O Dahab, come!

Wahhad dònto wa laga héleya, Dàhab O, no kàli!
Whatever you wish will be given you, O Dahab, come!

Dùd[7] annu nahai la ma horèyo, Dàhab O, no kàli!
Our tribe is second to none, O Dahab, come!

Ákhal dòrah mod leiss kú đarei, galmo daba jòga,
Our goods are laid together in a beautiful house, the camels wait behind,

Durba hòlaha naga ghobo, Dàhab O, no kàli!
Now take our flocks, O Dahab, come!

---

[1] **Halei un.** [2] Name of a camel.
[3] That she may load. [4] **Ho** take, hold. **Ođo** say.
[5] Names of camels.
[6] The maritime plain from which the tribes wander into the more fertile **Ogo**, or southern slopes of the Golis range, at this time of year.
[7] Forest. Here used for tribe.

Wan lei dilei, barùr laga dala'ei,
A ram is slaughtered, fat is cooked,

Aulaláda diran, manfa'an wada dònonne, Dàhab O, no kàli!
The ribs are ready, let us all find food, O Dahab, come!

Sar dabòlan[1], hes[2] danoneiyo, wèso darandèra,
Put on the shield-cloth, hang up spear and white flask,

Tusbah dòrah, iyo wátahhan[3] hore u si dadsha.
Lovely rosary and prayer-mat lay in front.

Kabo dàlinka leisska diga e malmo lagu dàlo,
In weariness one lays aside shoes in which one toils by day,

Iyo ga'anta ka ma dèin karo jèdal dubandábeyo.
And the whip which the hand cannot cease from flicking.

Daf hadan, la so yidi gogolaha darah gogoshùwa,
Enter now then, the beds are ready spread,

Dalaghdalagh[4] u so'odkad hubki dib u lo lafiyotei[5].
? ? ? ?

XIV. Hes, in g.

Dumar O, kunka kabaha, kulliga damánta,
Ye women, the thousand generations, all and everyone,

Sikakaäga ákhal gudi u garáne.
Of your ancestors within the house we may know.

Illahed goïsi u garane. Ràga gèlìsi u garáne.
The partitions of a room we may know. We may know the men's camels.

Gàshan ma ghàdan, ma ku gàban taghánin?
Do you carry a shield, do you know how to lower it?

Marka răg iss u só galo, ma gangàni taghánin?
When men compete, do you know how to draw a bow?

Gáranka afki u badan iyo gojoda lugtaah môyi.
The great clamour from your lips, and the dancing of your feet, I know not.

Gembi kăleh ma gáratan?
Is there any other art you understand?

---

[1] Somalis keep their shields white and new by covering them with a white cloth.

[2] Name of a particular kind of spear.

[3] **Watahh** is the tree from which the bark is taken for tanning leather.

[4] Wagging of the head. [5] Walk.

THE DIALECTS OF THE OUTCAST TRIBES, YIBIR AND MIDGAN.

1. ACCOUNT OF THE TWO TRIBES.

These two tribes are called by Somalis *Sab*, or outcast, being considered of low origin and not descended from *Darùd* or *Ishhak* (cf. Appendix III). For this reason Somalis will not mix with them or intermarry.

The *Yibirs* are said to be sorcerers, and to have prophetic powers and the power of cursing. They live by begging, but especially by the levy of a tax on Somalis, at a marriage or the birth of a child, according to an old tradition told in a story which is given here in *Yibir* dialect.

The *Midgans* are by nature hunters or trappers, and live largely by the meat of game they can kill in the jungle. They are also employed by Somalis to work for them, in return for which they receive occasional payment, in food or otherwise, and protection, from their employer. This work consists in fetching wood, drawing water, and digging and cleaning wells.

Both tribes also work in leather, tanning hides, and making leather ornaments, saddles, shoes, etc.

They profess to be Mohammedans like pure Somalis, but the *Midgans* are very lax in their religion, being unclean in the matter of the meat they eat. Many, however, are comparatively civilised and are strict on this point.

Neither Yibir nor Midgan have any definite tract of land, like the numerous tribes of Somali. They are scattered as wanderers over the whole country, the Midgans either attaching themselves to some Somali tribe as *abban*, or living upon them as robbers and thieves.

Each tribe has its own dialect, which has hitherto been kept as a solemn secret from the rest of the world. They still insist upon secrecy from Somalis, and made me promise not to divulge to their hereditary enemies what they were quite willing to explain to the white man.

I, therefore, rely upon any who may read this not to disclose to any Somali what I have been allowed to write down for the benefit of the *Sirkal*, but if any other officer of an enquiring disposition wishes to pursue the subject, he should be acquainted with the Somali language, which all the *Sab* know, and discuss these things with one of them.

2. OBSERVATIONS ON THE DIALECTS.

(Quoted by kind permission of the Editor of the *Journal of the African Society*[1].)

Yibirs and Midgans are both very jealous of their languages, and keep them a secret from other Somalis, although all speak the common language of the country, namely Somali. There are, I believe, no Somalis who know anything of either dialect, and while I was having my interviews with these people, they were very particular not to allow any Somali within hearing, our conversations having to be carried on in the latter's language.

Here let me repeat that I was put on my word by both peoples not to divulge anything to a Somali, but was allowed to write it down for the use of British officers, their vanity being evidently touched by the idea of a white man wanting to study their language.

Therefore I must ask any who may read this and who may sojourn in the country, *not to repeat what I give here to any Somali, not of Yibir or Midgan birth.*

A. W. Schleicher is the only author who refers to an unknown language (*Die Somali-Sprache*, p. x) :

"Unter den Somali leben mehrere Helotenvölker, von denen die Midgan, Tomal und Yibber die bekanntesten sind. Nur die Yibber scheinen eine eigene Sprache zu besitzen, die sie unter sich sprechen."

"Bestimmte Angaben darüber konnte ich nicht erhalten, dem Somali sind die Yibber ein Greuel. Nach Hussein versteht kein Somali ihre Sprache, doch verstehen die Yibber alle das Somali."

[1] *Journal of the African Society*, No. XIII., October, 1904.

The construction of the languages, I find, is the same as that of the Somali tongue, as spoken all over the country, and by all tribes ; that is to say, they are identical in, and the same rules apply in

(1) Syntax,
(2) Conjugation of Verbs,
(3) Inflexions of Nouns and Adjectives,
(4) Methods of forming Derivative Verbs, etc.

In the matter of Vocabulary, the following parts of speech are practically altogether different from Somali and from one another, though a very few roots are common to all three :

(1) Nouns,
(2) Adjectives,
(3) Verbs,

and consequently,

(4) Adverbs,
(5) Conjunctions,
(6) Prepositions.

On the other hand such parts of speech as,

(1) Definite Article,
(2) Demonstrative Pronoun,
(3) Possessive Pronoun,
(4) all Particles,

are common to all three, and have the same forms and constructions.

The Yibir vocabulary is fairly complete, though poorer than Somali. The Midgan, on the other hand, is extremely deficient. A large number of words have therefore to do duty for several meanings each, according to the context.

Examples,

Yibir.

dalanga	any animal or bird (an appropriate epithet or description being required for each individual kind).
agar	thing, stuff, food, etc.
à	" rer," family, home, flocks, belongings, baggage, property.
awas	any vegetable, tree, grass, wood.
iftin	light, sun (fem.), moon (masc.), star, rupee, silver, money (as adjective = bright or white).

ilahh	fire, gun (as adjective = hot).
mid	exist, be, stop, stand.
tomàla	anything hard, hill, stone (adjective = hard).
lawo	water, rain, river, year.

Midgan.

hangagùri	any wild beast (carnivore).
nas	thing, place, time, town, person, self.
ghoribirro	wood, and anything made of wood, tree, bow, shaft of spear, thorn.
gôsad	iron, knife, any iron tool.
iftimowa	sun, light, day.
gomosímo	water, rain, river.
ghan	*good*, large, heavy, far, white, hot, full.
neghatal	*bad*, small, light, near, black, cold, empty.
makabùr	stone, hill, money, rupee (as adjective = hard).

I could not find any other native words to translate the various meanings given opposite each of the above.

Where special definition is required, some paraphrase is used. Yibirs have no special names for animals, but use such expressions as the following :

dálangihi khábarki ghandìdsan	hyaena (lit. the animal with plenty of noise).
dálangihi walahúmo ku dashìya	oryx (lit. the animal having spears).

Midgans describe the lion and leopard as, **hangagùri ghan**, and **hangagùri neghatal**, respectively.

The following are good examples of other paraphrases required by the languages :

my father	(Mid.)	**alowihi i so finfinshei.**
	(Yib.)	**goriedki i jagh'idei**, literally, the man who begat me.
yesterday	(Mid.)	**iftimowihi tegèdei.**
	(Yib.)	**iftinti tegèdei**, literally, the light that has gone.
to-morrow	(Mid.)	**iftimowihi so tegèdeya**, literally, the light that is coming.

I am hungry (Mid.) **guratáda wa neghatal,** literally, my belly is small (or thin).

look at   (Mid.) **indókholaha ku yef.**

              (Yib.) **ainta ku yef,** literally, turn your eyes to.

pray   (Mid.) **gomosímo 'ss ku dahhdahhbi,** literally, buy yourself with water.

     (N.B.   Does this refer to the Mohammedan ablutions before praying, or has it any connexion with Christian baptism ?)

evening   (Mid.) **iftimowihi neghatála himirki so 'idbeya,** literally, the small light, as night comes on.

Notice that these phrases are similar in each language. A number of words too are common to both :

Examples,

tegèd	go
shan	go
bakhrin	head
gànad	hand
yal	foot
rùf, rôf	dead
yef	turn
ku dashi	have

On perusing a grammar of Galla, I found that no special connexion exists, as I had expected, between that language and either of these dialects. Where any similarity occurs, it pervades the Somali as well.

Many Somali roots are found in these dialects, with additional syllables.

Somali.	*Yibir.*	*Midgan.*	*English.*
if	iftin	iftimowa	light
indo (plur.)	ain	indókhol	eye
makhal	makhalei	makhashimei	hear
ghori		ghoribirro	wood
af		afjaghin	mouth
san		saneg	nose
kol	kulhi		time
laf	lafìl	lafeiti	bone
lugh (voice)	laghdan (tongue)	laghowa (throat)	
	lagh (talk)		

The inflexions of Yibir and Midgan are the same as those of the Somali, and not of the Galla language, as, for instance, agreement of Adjectives, inflexions of Verbs, plurals of Nouns, and the Definite articles.

Derivative words are formed in the same way as in Somali ;

Examples,

'idib ⎱ go.
shan ⎰

so 'idib ⎱ come.
so shan ⎰

'idbi ⎱ take.
shamei ⎰

so 'idbi ⎱ bring.
so shamei ⎰

fed (Y) wish. ⎱
fedo look for. ⎰

kul (M) give. ⎱
kusho eat, or drink. ⎰

'id (Y) give.
'ido eat, or drink.

indókhol (M) ⎱ eye.
ain (Y) ⎰

indókholei ⎱ see.
aimei ⎰

indokoleísi ⎱ shew.
aimeisi ⎰

makhali (Y) ⎱ ear.
makhashin (M) ⎰

makhalei ⎱ hear.
makhashimeí ⎰

makhaleido ⎱ listen
makhashimeíso ⎰ to.

ghàn (M) ⎱ good.
yifan (Y) ⎰

ghàmi ⎱ make good.
yifnei ⎰

ghàmo ⎱ be good.
yifno ⎰

The following Midgan root **ragh**, or **raghahh**, is interesting as regards its various derivatives and constructions, which are all purely Somali.

raghahh	act, do, fix
raghahhi mayo	I will not do it
'ss ka raghahh	sit down (set yourself)
so raghahh	wait
ku raghahh	catch, hold
faras ku raghahh	ride a horse
raghahhi	set, place, make
gôsad ku raghahhi	cut (with a knife)
raghahho	take to yourself, marry
raghahhsan	be, exist, lie, live
ku raghahhsan	wish, have
raghahhsanei	give
raghahhsano	look for
ku raghahhsano	like, love

In an account, given me by a Midgan, of the traditional origin of his tribe, it was suggested that this language was invented by the Midgans' ancestors in the jungle as a secret code. This may possibly be the case, judging from the following examples :

Midgan.

hand	farolaháto	from Somali	{ faro laho	fingers possess
arrow	degoyir	,,	{ dego yir	ears small
breast	fèdolaháto	,,	fèdo	ribs
Clarke's gazelle (Dibatag)	diboder	,,	{ dibo der	tail long
oryx	gesoder	,,	geso	horns
sheep	yiryiro	,,	{ yeryer plur. form of yer small	
skin	gadlaháto	,,	gad	beard
liver	madôbiyo	,,	{ madô biyo	black water

3. EXAMPLES OF SENTENCES AND CONVERSATION IN YIBIR AND MIDGAN.

Midgan.	*English.*
higge ka so 'idibtei ?	where have you come from ?
alowa ba so 'idbeya.	a Midgan is coming.
naskas i kul.	give me that.
goriedki ghànsana.	the good man.
àwinti ghànsaneid.	the good woman.
higgan so duhur.	come here.
'ss ka sir.	go away.
higga 'ss ka raghahhsano.	stay there.
gararàti shar bannu dagnei.	we saw many horses.
gedgharomed ma ku raghahhsana ?	are there trees there ?
raghahhi mayo.	I will not do it.
jalmihi gomosímodi u 'idbi.	take the camels to water.
hajìaha gôsad ku raghahhi.	cut the rope.
bulalki so shanshamei.	light the fire.
gomosímo ma raghahhsanid.	there is no water.
makabùrta u sharei.	give more money.
ma dukhanta ?	are you sick ?
ma sharodei ?	are you well ?
ghoribirro ghàn i kul.	give me a big stick.
baghdankini i dagsi.	teach me your language.
nasina i kulin.	give me nothing.
guratáda wa neghatal.	my stomach is empty.
wahhan kushodo i kul.	give me something to eat.
iftimòwihi tegèdei alowihi i so finfinshei la rùfìyei.	yesterday my father was killed.
iftimòwihi neghatála bodowyashi higgar u shamei.	in the evening take the burden camels over there.

Midgan.	*English.*
iftimòwaha ban Àji sukhodin ku dukhei.	to-day I shot a Somali with a bow.
àwintaida yagòlka raghahhsanta.	my wife is at home.
moyodi higga erifogad iss dukhesa wa shar.	the people fighting over there are many.
wa mahai naskas bakhrinka ku raghahhsan?	what is that on your head?
yagòlkaigi makabùrta ghàn ku raghahhsana.	my house is by the big hill.
naskakan hangagùri shar ku midsha, hajìa bannu ku raghahhadna.	here are many animals, we catch them in traps.
hadad hangagùri ghàn i indokholeisíneso, makabùr shar ban ku kuleya.	if you shew me a lion, I will give you much money.
himirki jalmahaiga laga la sirei.	in the night my camels were looted.
iftimòwihi tegèdeya, kulhidi moyodi jalmihi higga erifogad u shameineso, an rùfino moyoda, o jalmihi la sirno.	to-morrow, when the people take the camels over there, let us kill the people, and go off with the camels.

Yibir.	*English.*
ma yafántahai?	are you well?
ma yáfnan ba? so yáfnan miya?	is it peace?
higge u bidbideínesa?	where are you going?
higga dugageìgu wa tegèdeya.	I myself am going there.
mahhad fédesa?	what do you want?
wahhan ka fédeya inad kalwein i 'ida.	I want you to give me a tobe.
humággi mahhad 'ídatan?	what do you eat at night?
gòdibki ma 'ídatan?	do you drink milk?
dugagàgu wèli ma awèlisatei?	are you married yet?
wèli ma awèlisan.	I am not married yet.
dérigas mahhad ku awèlein?	what are you going to do with that?

Yibir.	*English.*
jalmo ma ku dashisa ?	have you any camels ?
ku ma dashìyo.	I have none.
alkhailahàgu wa inhíma ?	how many are your horses ?
wa ghàndiḍ.	they are many.
áwaski yafneisíya, dálanga wa so bidbideìneya.	make the zariba strong, a wild beast will come.
anghagi ad yiftimeisei ma so ganiden ?	have you caught the Mullah you were fighting ?
góriedkas ain ba rùfsan.	that man is one-eyed.
derigi lagu angháksodo "huwad" ba la biḍa.	the thing one prays on is a "huwad."
khabar ghàndiḍ ba lagu biḍa.	you are good at the language.
mahha bakhreíneya ? ma lawo ?	what is that noise ? rain ?
agarma ku midesa ?	what is in there ?
agar ku ma mideso.	nothing is there.
kulhímad bidbideinesa ?	when are you going ?
higge ka so tegèḍei ?	where have you come from ?
alkhail ku tegèḍeya.	I am riding a horse.
mahhad u tegèḍi weida ?	why don't you go ?
goriedki ma mideya ?	is the man here ?
higgà darsad 'ss ka midi.	sit down at the back there.
ainta igu so yef.	look this way.
godib i so shimi.	bring me some milk.
jalamada so shimìya.	bring the camels here.
dálangaha bakhreìneya ágarma u fèḍeya ?	what does the animal making that noise want ?
áda higgan midsìya.	put the things down here.
jalamada kabàrta ku midsìya.	load up the camels.
agartàda la tegèḍ.	take your things away.
higgìsa ha mideyo.	(leave it alone.) let it be.
khabarma awèleinesa ?	what are you doing ? (abstract.)
wa lei rùfìyei.	I am killed.
difadki iga bilehh.	cut the rope from me.
kalweìnti hümáksaneid yáfnan iss ugu shimí.	fold up the blanket well.
ágarma aimeisei ?	what did you see ?
khabarma makhaleidanesei ?	what did you hear ?
dérigas ma ku duhùresa ?	do you understand that ?
ku ma duhùro.	I do not understand.

Yibir.	*English.*
kulhída góriedka so tegèda, i so lagh.	when the man comes, tell me.
khabarkas 'ss ka ládishei.	never mind that. leave it alone.
ágarteìdi wa ku mìdesa.	my things are there.
sáddehhi kúlhiod wa ku laghei.	I have told you three times.
wátahhadi darsad galabídi so tegèda.	come back to-morrow evening.
wátahho walba kulhídi iftinti so godista wa so tegèdena.	we will come every day at sunrise.
àni, yahaínyahh ba la bida.	it is big, small.
gamàghdà, gamaghdis ba la bida.	you are right, he is right.
hegha yu lakheya.	he is telling a lie.
khabar lagu awèleya, ma ku duhùresa?	do you understand what is said to you?
gorieddi yiftimeisa khabar yafan ma ka so tegèdeya?	is there good news from the army?
higgà wa lagu orèmei.	he was killed there.
khabarkas urshèn ba la bida.	that is bad news.
gorieddi almanki fèdatei ágar ma aimeisei? ágar ghàndid bei aimeisei.	has the force found some stock? they have found plenty.
higgi lo gùrei, almanki ma la ga baghèyei?	was the force frightened away from where they went to?
aïhi darsad, awas ba aimeina yafan.	at the next village we find good grass.
ghorimada yafan dugagìna awèleyei, lawihi laga tegedo, deriïhi urshèna ma awelin.	your people made the good boats to cross the sea on, the bad ones they didn't make.
igu makhaleido, khabar an ku laghi.	listen to me, I will tell you a story.
wa ku makhaleidaneya, khabarkas i lagh.	I am listening, tell me that story.
higgas ugu orensanyahai.	it is torn there.
goried yafan ba lagu bida, khabarkagi i lagh, bidbidsin mayo.	you are a good man, say your say, I will not go against it.
ha bidin.	no. it is not.
wafèrka katowa ku ma dashìyo.	that knife is blunt.
hilaghamaha hadeidinan agar ka 'idin, ma yafna khabarkas.	if you do not give anything for the wives, it is not good.

Yibir.	*English.*
fil iftin wa so doïyoneya.	I am going to buy some rice.
dérigan asuwan bu ku dashíya.	this one has a wife.
lawihi darsad yu awèlisaneya.	he will marry next year.
derigi asuwanti jagh'idei daḍo yu u 'ida iyo iftimo.	to the girl's father he gives sheep and money.
altob yafan, tobánihi íftimod, iyo límihi gánadod o dàḍo yu u 'idei, kulhídan ya ka feḍeya.	he gave a good shield, 10 rupees and 20 sheep, now he is engaged.
jalmahaiga derigo ya ka almàmei.	that man looted my camels.
jalanka inhíman kaga doïyoda?	how much do I pay for a camel?
hosi u bidbidei.	put it down below.
Abiryaha walahumo awèleya.	the Tomals make spears.
kabàrti horyadèdi kulhídi ad midesen, ya'unki ku la khabreyei iyo dugagàgu deri yafan ba la biḍa.	the old man who spoke with you, when you went to the front of the house, and yourself are great men.
dugagisu u yafan.	he is the senior.
tomàlaha aniga àdayada u shantei, lawo iyo awas yu u fèḍatei.	my "rer" has gone to that hill, for water and grazing.
dugageigu u shámeya, hadanan rùfin.	I am going myself, in order not to die.
goriedki jalmihi iyo daḍodi fèdtei, ma so tegèḍeya?	is the man coming who fetched the camels and sheep?
deriïhi anghàga ka daras tegèdei.	those who followed after the Mullah.
goried difada ya la gu biḍa.	you are a gentleman.
shanihi kulhiod wa anghaksona, saddehhi kulhiod wa humaggi, limihhi wa watahhádi.	we pray five times, three times at night, and twice by day.
dífadki jálanki u lagu aweleín jira.	the rope with which the camel is tied.
dantashi seyadki lagu shimín jira.	the vessel one puts ghi into.
deriihi yabar yifno o Anasioda 'idin jirta, Hanfili ka so godisa.	Hanfili leaves alone people who give plenty to the Yibirs.
Anas ain rufsanei kulhina ma ku so godisei?	has a blind Yibir ever come to you?
wafèrti humaksana lugu tegèjiyo.	the knife to cut the hair with.

A CONVERSATION, IN YIBIR.

Ánaski ya'ùnkaaha dàdodisi inhíde rùftei ?

How many of the old man's sheep died ?

Aferi ganadod iyo limihi ganadod ya rùfei, huwadisi inhida aha.

Thirty have died, that number of skins there were.

Khabarma u laghei ?

What did he say ?

Kalweinaleh bu u shimìyei.

He took them to Berbera.

Iftimo yu ka fedtei, jalankisi ànigaaha yu la tegèdei.

He wants to sell them, he went with his big camel.

Inhima ku so shansáneyei ?

How much was he carrying ?

Ya'un fila iyo ya'un asèra, limihi kalweinod, iyo mado kushan iyo difad asuwanta kalweinta ku shansoto, yu ku so shansodei.

One man's (?) rice and dates, two tobes, and an anna, and a sash to tie his wife's dress, he took.

Asuwantàdi inhide iftimo u 'idei ?

How much money did he give your wife ?

Aferi iftimod iyo aferi gànadod inhidas u 'idei. Kulhidiu 'idei bu i laghei, "higgàga midi, hadan iftimo darsad aimeisto wa ku so 'idahaya."

Twenty-four rupees he gave. When he gave it, he said she was to stay where she was, and if he got more money, he would give it.

Kulhidas dugagèda na laghdei, "Gamàgh."

Then she said to us, "All right."

Anasko hadi asuwantadi u inhidas o iftimo u 'idei, asuwanteidi inhide ad u 'idei ?

If that man gave that money to your wife, how much did you give mine ?

Limihi gànadod iyo limihi iftimod ban u 'idei.

I gave her twelve rupees.

Hadad inhidas u 'idei, miad inhi ghandidah u 'idei ?

If you gave that, did you give much ?

Inhida o iftimo an ku dashiyei, inhi kelemad hadan ku dashiyo, ban u 'idi laha.

So much I had, if I had had more, I would have given it.

Iftimo mad u maghùrtei ?

Did you borrow money ?

Maghùrti aimein wai.

I could get no loan.

An iftimo u maghùre, ma u shimínesa ?

I may lend you some money, will you take it ?

U shimin mayo, higgeigannu midinena.

I will not take it, we are staying where we are.

MOHAMMED HANIF (Ancestor of the Yibirs).

Kulhídi horimad anghàg ba lagu biḍei[1]. Hig bu mìdsha[2],
The time before a priest there was. Where he lives

goried la ma midín jirin. Deriïhìni[3] horimad, iyo deriïhi
people with not to live used. Your people before, and the people

angháksodei dehhdodi u mìdshei, limihi ya yíftimeyei. Deri
(who) prayed (who) among them lived, both fought. A man

yabar ghandìdsan ya la biḍei. Deriïhìni horimad ya u so
of property plenty he was. Your people before to (him)

godisei. "Awas no 'idbi," yei laghen. "Khábarke ku feḍesan[4]?"
came. "A herb to us bring," they said. "What reason for do you want (it)?"

yu laghei. Kulhídas yu laghei, "Deriahan angháksoda yannu ku
he said. Then they said, "These people (who) pray we with (it)

rùfinena." Kulhídas yu laghei, "Wa iftimo ghandiḍah, idinku
will kill." Then he said, "It is money plenty you

i 'idi mahai[5], awaskeiga idin 'idin mayo." Kulhídas yu
to me give without, my herb to you give (I) will not." Then they

goḍerówi iftimo iyo goḍerówi jalmo inhídas àwaski yei kaga
a hundred rupees and a hundred camels so much the herb they for

doïyòden. Kulhídas yu àwaski u sara 'idei[6]. Kulhídas ya deriïhi
bought. Then he the herb to (them) gave. Then the people

anghaksóneyei alman so feḍten[7]. Kulhídasa yei deriïhìni horimad
(who) prayed a raid went for. Then they your people before

yei alman u so feḍten. Kulhídas limihi goḍerówi o lawod[8] yei
they a raid on (them) went for. Then for two hundred years they

hig midshei, o higgiu tegèdei ya aimein waiyen. Kulhidasa
a place lived, and where they went (they) find could not. Then

---

[1] Think. **la bida** it is thought. This is used for "is" (Somali **wa**).

[2] Aorist, from **midso**.

[3] Plur. **dério**. Here the narrator refers to the people of the person he was addressing (i.e. myself), whom he considers to be the same as the Gala. **deriïhi angʻhaksodei** means Moslems.

[4] Somali: **mahhad ku dònesan?**

[5] Somali: **idinku i sìn mahai** unless you give me.

[6] Hand over. Somali **dib**.

[7] Look for. (wan **feùta**.) Somali **dòno**. **alman feðo**, Somali **dùl**.

[8] Water, rains, i.e. year.

deriïhi   anghaksóneyei higga ku rùfen.   Kulhídas yei anghàgi
the people   (who) prayed   there   died,   Then   they the priest

yabar   yifmeíyen[1] anghàgi bu rùfei.   Àdìsi ya la alman.   Weled
property   fought   the priest he died.   His home   was looted.   A boy

yahaínyahh   u u   jagh'ídei, ya higgi ka so godisei, weledki iyo
small   (whom) he   begat,   there from   came,   the boy and

aferi kelemad hig midín jirei.   Weledki Mohammed Hanif ba
four   others a place live used to.   The boy   Mohammed Hanif

la bidei.   Weledku kulhídas yu anghàg nokhdei, asuwàno yu
was.   The boy   then   he a priest   became,   women   he

difadín[2] jirei.   Dugagìsu[3] higga midsha o asuwàno difadsha[2],
used to.   (while) He   there   lives   and women   ,

anghàgi yifna ya u só shamei, Au-Bakhardli bu nokhdei.   Kulhídas
the priest great   to (him) came,   Au-Bakhardli he was.   Then

yu u laghei, "Khábarma higgo u   mìdesa,   o anghàg lagugu bida?"
he   said,   "What   there for do you live, and a priest   for   are?"

Kulhídas bu laghei, "Dugagàgu   ma   iga   anghaksántahai?"
Then   he said,   "Yourself (are you) me than   (more) holy?"

Kulhidasu laghei,   "Ka anghàksanahai."   Kulhídas yu u laghei,
Then he   said,   "More holy I am."   Then   he   said,

"Khabarka ad   iga   anghaksántahai igu aimidsi."   Kulhídasu
"The reason you me than (more) holy are me to shew."   Then he

laghei, "Higgas an ka[4] godisaya,   ka   godis dugagàgu."   Kulhídasu
said,   "There   I will penetrate, through go   yourself."   Then

tomàlaha ànigah yu hosidìsi   ka godisei.   Kulhídas ka godisei,
that hill   great   he beneath it through went.   Then (he) went through,

o   higgo u ku godisei, yu u laghei Au-Bakhardli, "Tomàlaha O,
and there he in   went,   he to him said Au-Bakhardli,   "O Hill,

gan'id."   Kulhídas tomàlihi 'ss ku godisei, kulhídas yu   hig u
seize."   Then   the hill together went,   then   he where he

ka so godiso aimein wai.   Tomàlaha dehhdìsi yu ku rùfei
out may come see   could not.   The hill   in it   he   died

---

[1] This is not correctly given, but the sense is "They fought over the dead priest's property."

[2] Whether this means "marry," or "rape" is not clear. **difad** rope. There is one story that Mohammed Hanif was expelled by Sheik Ishhak because of his immorality.

[3] Self, person. **dugagaiga** I myself.

[4] Through, across.

anghàgi.   Anghàgi aïháyaga higgas u ku rùfei.   Kulhídas ya
the priest.   The priest of our tribe there he   died.   Then

weldihi[1] u jagh'idei yu u laghei, "Augayo ada rùfìyei,   agar
the boys he begat they   said, "Our father you have killed, something

no-ga[2] 'id."   Anghàgi ba   ku   laghei, khabarkan kulhídasu
to us for it give."   The priest   to (them) said,   this word   then he

u laghei, "Ma   watahhádan goderówi jalmo idin 'ida, mase
said,   "(Am I) to-day   a hundred camels to you to give,   or

weledki goried u jagh'ido yan ilbir idin   ka   sara 'ida? Sara-
the son a Somali begets I a ewe to you for (him) am I to give?   The

doshíski mian iftin idin ka sara 'ida?" Kulhídas ya weldihi
marriage am I money to you for to give?"   Then   the boys

laghen, "Weledka ilbir   noga sara 'id,   saradoshíska iftin,
said,   "The boy a ewe to us for (him) give, the marriage money,

wéldahana[3] ilbir. Inhídi ka   darseisa   inhída khabarka
and the boys a ewe. That (which) follows (hereafter) so much for that

yannu ágarta   ku   'idónena."   Khabarkas yannu ágar ku
we   as the price for will receive." For that reason we   a price

shansonna, Anàsyodáyadu. Kulhídi iftinta   iyo   ilbirta   na lo
take,   we Yibirs.   When the money and the ewe to us is

'ido, àwasyo yahaínyahh yannu u   'idna. Wannu u   yabarónna.
given, sticks small   we to them give. We thus earn our living.

Àwas kelemad o ghandìdah wa ku duhùrna.   Derigi   rùfrùfeya
Herbs other   many   (we) understood. The man (who) is sick

iyo derigi alman   fedóneya,   iyo derigi lagheya,   "an
and the man (who) is going on a raid, and the man (who) says, "let me

derigas ka   ur behhénsanàdo," inhídas àwas lo   'ido   yannu
than that man   be better,"   for that a herb to be given we

ku duhùrna.   Deriga,   annu u 'idna, iftimo ghandìdah yu,
know.   That man, (to whom) we give, money plenty   he,

kulhída u   yifnàdo,   no sara 'ida.
when   he is successful, to us hands.

---

[1] Plur. **weldo-hi.**
[2] **na u ka.** Cf. **ka siso** pay for.
[3] And.

YIBIR-ENGLISH and MIDGAN-ENGLISH VOCABULARY.

The following is a list of Yibir and Midgan words not used by other Somalis.

Words, such as Pronouns, Particles, etc., are not given, being common to all three dialects.

Nouns are recognised by the Definite Article which follows each noun, separated by a hyphen.

Examples,

ain-ti	eye	**bulal-ki**	fire

In these examples, **ain** equals an eye, **bulal** equals a fire; "the eye," "the fire," would be, **ainti, bulalki.**

The suffixes, **-ki, -gi, -hi,** are masculine, **-ti, -di,** are feminine.

Abbreviations :

(Y)	Yibir dialect.
(M)	Midgan dialect.
(Y), (M)	common to both dialects.
v.i.	intransitive verb.
v.t.	transitive verb.
a.	adjective.

The Arabic letter ain (ع) is represented by ', ghain is represented by **gh, kh.**

đ represents the "cerebral d," which at the beginning or end of a word sounds like *d*, but in the middle of a word is more like *r.*

This letter in Yibir is pronounced usually like **dh.**

à-di (pl. **àö-hi**) (Y), family, "rer," possessions

abàbo-di (M), Plateau Gazelle, "dero"

Àbir-ki (Y), Tomal (an outcast tribe that work in iron)

adeisímo-di (M), milk

áferi-hi (Y), four

afjaghin-ti (M), mouth

ágar-ti (Y), thing, any concrete object ; *agarma ku midesa ?* what is there ?

aghtul v.t. (M), strike, hit

aimei v.t. (Y), see, find, understand

aimeisi v.t. (Y), shew, teach

ain-ti (Y), eye ; *ainta ku yef,* turn your eye (i.e. look)

aintoli-hi (Y), lie, untruth

Aiyifan-ti (Y), Gala

Àji-gi (M), Somali

albákhar-ti (Y), cow

alèliso-di (M), bird, bustard

alkhail-ki, -shi (Y), horse

alman v.t. (Y), rob, loot

alman-ki (Y), army, enemy

alówa-hi (M), man (esp. ref. to Midgan man), not used in referring to a Somali; *alowihi i so finfinshei*, my father

altob-ki (Y), shield

amèdo-di (Y), goats

anaduhr-ki (M), elephant

Anas-ki (Y), Yibir

Anasnimeiso v.i., collect the " samanyo "

Anasnímo-di, the " samanyo " paid to Yibirs

anghàg-gi (Y), priest, "mullah "

anghakso v.i. (Y), pray

àni-gi (Y), largeness; *ani ba la bida*, it is large

àniah a. (Y), great

ànisan a. (Y), complete, correct, new

asahan-ti (M), woman

'asèr-ti (Y), (M), dates (*'asèro-hi*)

'asèrah a. (Y), red (sometimes *asè-raäh* is used)

'asèro-hi (Y), blood

'asówa-hi (M), blood

'assi (M), lynx

asuwan-ti (Y) wife

au-gi (Y), ancestor

Awashona-hi (Y), God

áwas-ki (Y), vegetable, grass, tree, bush, zariba, grass mat; *awaski aldibo*, the sacred tree of the Yibirs, used as a charm.

aweilei v.t. (Y), do, make, construct, cause

aweiliso v.t. (Y). do for yourself, marry

àwin-ti (M), woman

babàto-di (M), cloth, dress

baghdan, v.i. (M), talk, tell, say; *nasker bad baghdamesa?* what are you saying ?

baghdan-ki (M), talk, speech, language

bagh v. (Y), (M), be in fear

baghei v.t. (Y), (M), frighten

bagho v.i. (Y), (M), be afraid; *ka bagho*, be afraid of

bakhar-ti (M), cow

bakhrei v.i. (Y), make a noise (? inverted "khabrei")

bakhrin-ki (Y), (M), head

balkhalo-hi (M), lesser bustard

baneisin-ki (M), in front, before

behhensan a. (Y), useful

bid v.t. (Y), think; *khabarma bidesa?* what do you think ?

The Passive, formed by "la," is used for the verb " be "—

lei bida, I am ; *lagu bida*, thou art ; he, she is ; you, they are ; *la na bida*, we are—

e.g. *derigas ba la bida*, that is ; *Anas ba lei bida*, I am a Yibir ; *ha bidin* (don't think) it is not. No

bidbidei v. (Y), go

bidbidsei v.t. (Y), make to go, send away, throw away

bikho-di (M), "Dik-dik"

bilehh v.t. (Y), cut

bi'yuso v.t. (Y), like, be pleased

boba'un v.t. (M), gulp down

bodówa-hi (M), camel

bùf-ki (M), donkey

bulal-ki (M), fire, smoke, fire-arm

bulalyei, v.t. (M), burn, heat, forge

bulbul-ki (Y), stick

bulbul-shi (Y), whip

buskulohh-i (Y), butter

dabo-'ad (M), Haartebeest

dado-di (Y), sheep

dag v.t. (M), see, understand

dahir-ki (M), fat, ghi

dahhbi v.t. (M), buy

dalanga-hi (Y), animal

damòmei v.t. (M), dig, excavate

damomya-hi (M), inside

dangharei v.t. (Y), refuse

dáras-ti (Y), behind, tail; *ka dáras tegèd*, follow behind

d'arowa-hi (Y), breast, udder

darsád (Y), afterwards, subsequent ; *watahhádi darsád*, to-morrow

darsei v.i. (Y), be behind, be left ; *kulhídi ka darseisa*, afterwards

dashi v.t. (Y) (M), have, possess (always used with "ku"); *inhima ku dashisa?* how many have you ?

degayir (M), arrow

degíg-gi (M), donkey

deri- -gi, -di (Y), finger ; one person ; *derigas*, that one ; *deri ba ku mideya*, there is one

derigab (Y), loins

diboder (M), Clarke's Gazelle

dibyalin-ki (M), behind, after, back, tail (of an animal); *dibyalin u raghahh*, stand back ; *dibyalin-keigi*, behind me

dífad-ki (Y), rope, snare

dikhràrin-ki (M), hide (of game), prayer-mat

dilin-ti (M), " Dero "

doïyo v.t. (Y), buy

dubadyo-hi (Y), jugular vessels

dugag-gi (Y), person, people, self ; *dugaggeigu*, I myself

duhur v.i. (M), travel, go

ku duhur v.t. (Y), understand; *ku duhuri mayo*, I don't understand

dujo v.t. (M), leave ; *'ss ka dujo*, let be, never mind

duk v.t. (M), strike, kill

dukhan v.i. (M), be sick, be afraid ; be empty, be broken

dukhumei v. (M), ? fear

dul-shi (Y), end of backbone

dusàr-ki (M), elephant

dussi (M), leopard

erifogád-ki (M), distance, in time or space, year, country ; *higgar erifogád*, away over there ; *erifogádkini*, your country; *erifogádki tegèdei*, last year

falèd-di (M), rupee

fardaho-hi (?M), finger

farolaháto-hi (M), hand, arm

fed v.t. (Y), wish, want, mean ; *mahhad fedesa?* what do you want ?

fedo v.t. (Y), look for

fèdolahato-di (M), breast

fidsin-ki (Y), camel's hump

fíl-shi (Y), grain ; *f. tomàlaah*, jowaree; *f. iftin*, rice

fin, or **finfin** v.t. (M), give birth to, beget

finso v.i. (M), be born

ga'alo v.t. (M), like

gabar-ti (M), water-flask

gabis-ki (M), shield

gadlaháto-di (M), camel-skin, shield

galabí-di (Y), evening

gamágh-i (Y), truth. Yes. All right

gamàgho v.i. (Y), be right, correct, true

gànad-di (Y), (M), hand

In counting, "gànad" refers to the five fingers and means five : *limihi gànadod*, ten ; *saddehhi gànadod*, fifteen ; *aferi gànadod*, twenty

gànaddi yafneid, right hand ; *g. yahainyahheid*, left hand

gana'id v.t. (Y), catch

gararàti-gi (M), horse

gedgharoméd-ki (M), tree

geryal-ki (M), Waller's Gazelle

gesoder-ki ⎱ (M), Oryx
gesolahato-di ⎰

gir-ki (M), ostrich

godanahh-i (M), chest

goḍerowi-gi (Y), rosary, hundred

godib-ki (Y), milk

godis v.i. (Y), come, arise, come up, begin ; *kulhiddi iftinti so godista*, at sunrise ; *humaggi wa godisa*, the night is coming on

golof-ti (M), woman

gomosímo-di (M), water, river, rain

gonya-hi (M), inside, within

gorád-ki (M), cup

gorbei v.t. (Y), pray for, beg

goried-di (Y), (M) (plur. of *goriedki*), people, men

goried-ki (Y), (M), man, person

gôsad-di (M), iron, metal, any metal article, knife ; *gôsad ku raghahhi*, cut (with a knife)

gosin-ki (M), " Aoul," Soemering's Gazelle

gujin-ki (Y), meat

gurató-di (M), stomach, belly ; *guratádi wa neghatal*, I am hungry

ghàmi v.t. (M), make good, improve

ghàmo v.i. (M), be good

ghàn a. (M), large, long, good (far, fat, hot, white)

ghàndiḍ-ki (Y), plenty

ghàndìḍah a. (Y), many; *jalmihi ghandidkaäh*, the many camels.

ghàndiḍei v.t. (Y), increase

ghànsan a. (M), good

ghodahh-di (Y), tin for ghi

ghoribírro-di (M), wood, bush, thorn, branch of a tree, any article of wood, bow

ghorin-ki (Y), plate, dish, ship

hajìa-hi (M), rope, string, trap

haman-ti (Y), bird

Hanan-ki (M), Yibir

Handud-ki (M), Tomal

Hanfíli (Y), Hanfili, the Yibirs' ancestress, spirit

hangagùri-gi (M), animal, any wild animal

hainyalisan a. (Y), mad

halyokho-di (Y), iron

hawar-ti (Y), backbone

hedig-gi (M), ostrich

hekho-di (Y), lie, untruth

hig-gi (Y), (M), place ; *higgan*, here; *higgà*, there; *higge? higma?* where?

hilghan-ki (Y), see *'ilaghan*

himir-ki (M), night

horimad (Y), before, (time)

horyad-di (Y), before, in front, (place)

horyalin-ki (M), before, in front

hosyad-di (Y), below, beneath

hosyalin-ki (M), beneath, below

humag-gi (Y), night

humaksan a. (Y), black; *humaksano bakhrinka*, hair

humbur-ki (M), fox

hur-ki (M), quïver (of arrows)

huwad-ki (Y), prayer-mat

huwìya-hi (M), sheep-skin

'id v.t. (Y) (M), give

'idbi v.t. (M), make to go, take, lead ; *so 'idbi*, bring

'idib v.i. (M), go ; *so 'idib*, come

'ido v.t. (Y) (M), eat, drink

idon v.i. (M), go away, run away

iftimo-hi (Y), money (plur. of *iftin*)

iftimówa-hi (M), light, sun, day ; *iftimówaha*, to-day; *i. tegèdei*, yesterday ; *i. so tegèdeya*, to-morrow ; *i. neghatal*, twilight; *i. n. himirki so'idbeya*, evening

iftin a. (Y), white, bright

iftin-ki (Y), moon

iftin-ti (Y), sun, light, rupee

'flaghan-ti or -ki (Y), child, daughter, or son

ilahh-hi (Y), fire, fire-arm ; *ilahh awèlei*, light the fire

ilan-ti (Y), leg

ilbir-ki (M), limb
ilbir-ti (Y), ewe
ildighán-ti (Y), bow
ilowa-hi (Y), ram
imil-ki (Y), male camel
imitirahh-i (M), wing
indóholeisi v.t. (M), point out, shew
indókhol-shi (M), eye; *indókholaha u yef*, look
indókholeí v.t. (M), look at
inhí-di (Y), (M), quantity: *inhídas*, so much; *inhíma?* how much? how many?
irso v.i. (M), remain still

jagaflaho-di (M), shoe, sandal (plur. *jagaflahöin-ki*)
jagh'id v.t. (Y), give birth to, beget; *goriedki i jagh'idei*, my father
jagha-hi (Y), child
jalan-ti (Y), (M), she-camel (plur. *jalmo-hi*)
jankho-hi (Y), kid, young goat
jehhar-ki (M), buck-Aoul
jimikh-hi (M), caracal-cat
jindar-ki (Y), ox, bull

kabár-ti (Y), house, loading-mat, load of a camel
kalahed-ki (Y), half
kalwein-ti (Y), cloth, clothing; *k. humaksan*, blanket
kalweinaleh-di (Y), town, Berberah
katowa-hi (Y), mouth, edge; *waférka katowa ku ma dashiyo*, that knife has no edge
kelemad a. (Y), other
khabar v.i. (Y), talk, speak
khabar-ki (Y), speech, talk, language, news; *khabarkas 'ss ka ladishei*, stop that talk; *khabarkas*, like that; *khabarmad fedesa?* what do you want?
khabrei v.i. (Y), talk, speak
kub'en-ti (Y), tail, tail-fat.
kul v.t. (M), give

kul-ki (M), half
kulhi-di (Y), time; *kulhídan*, now; *kulhídas*, then; *kulhíma?* when? *saddehhi kulhiod*, three times; *kulhídi horyad*, before
kulun, v.i. (M), be sick
kunoli-hi (Y), heart
kushan-ki (Y), ring
kusho, v.t. (M), eat, drink

labodin-ki (Y), (M), body, belly
ladishei (Y), leave; *'ss ka ladishei*, cease, let be
lafeiti-di (M), bone
lafil-shi (Y), breastbone
lagh v.i. (Y), speak, tell, say
laghdam-ki (Y), tongue
laghowa-hi (M), tongue, throat
lamdi (see *limdi*)
langharoméd-ki (M), rice
lawo-hi (Y), water, rain, river, year; *lawihi darsad*, next year
lawodaur-ki (Y), water-bottle
(lawo-hi (M), milk)
lig-gi (M), buck-Gerenuk
limdi v.i. (Y), (M), sleep, lie down; (infin. *limdiyi*)
limi-hi (Y), two
ludub-ki (M), penis

madôbiyo-hi (M), liver
madôkushan-ki (Y), anna
madôla-hi (M), tortoise
maghùr v.t. (Y), lend
makabùr a. (M), hard
makabùr-ti (M), hill, stone, pebble, money
makabur-ti (Y), tortoise
makhalei v.t. (Y), hear
makhaleido v.t. (Y), listen
makhali-di (Y), ear
makhashin-ti (M), ear
makhashimei v.t. (M), hear
makhashimeiso v.i. (M), listen
manahho-di (Y), food
marùbo-hi (M), plate, dish

mid v.i. (Y), be, exist, be present, remain, be alive; *agarma ku midesa?* what is there?

mid (Y), (M), go; *'ss ka mid,* go away; *so mid,* come; *la mid,* go with, accompany

midsan v.i. (M), sit down

midsi v.t. (Y), bring

midso v.i. (Y), remain, live; *ya'unki ku jagh'idei ma midsha?* is your father alive?

mirdolo-hi (Y), penis

mirgin-ki (M), plant, vegetable

moyo-di (M), people

mukhtaren-ki (Y), needle, bodkin

nafèl-ki (Y), hunger

nafèlo v.i. (Y), be hungry

nàni-gi (Y), bag, satchel carried by Yibirs

nas-ki (M), thing, place, time, self

neghatal a. (M), small, bad, few (thin, near, black, light)

nirokh-i (Y), loins

omas-ki (M), bird

oran-ki (M), guinea-fowl

orèmi v.t. (M), kill

orèn v.i. (M), die

orènsan v.i. (M), be sick; (Y), be spoilt, torn

raghahh v.i. (M), act, do, catch; *raghahhi mayo,* I will not do it; *'ss ka raghahh,* sit down; *so raghahh,* come here, wait here; *ku raghahh,* catch, hold; *gararàti ku raghahh,* ride a horse

raghahhi v.t. (M), set, place, make; *gôsad ku raghahhi,* cut (with a knife); *'ss ka raghahhi,* put it down there

raghahho v.t. (M), take for yourself, marry

raghahhsán v.i. (M), be, exist, lie, live, think; *ku raghahhsán,* have, want

raghahhsánei v.t. (M), give

raghahhsáno v.t. (M), look for; *ku raghahsáno,* like

rèmi v.t. (M), hit, strike

rer-ki (M), feather

rihin-ki (M), meat

rìsh-ki (M), ostrich-feather

robsahan-ki (Y), (M), loins

rôf v.i. (M), die

rôf-ki (M), corpse

rùf v.i. (Y), die

rùfi v.t. (Y), (M), kill

rùfsan v.i. (M), be sick, be poor

saddehh-hi (Y), three

sakhsakh v.t. (Y), slay, cut the throat

saneg-gi (Y), nose

salôlad-ki, -di (M), goat

saradoshis-ki (Y), bridegroom, wedding

sareyagh-i (M), ostrich

saryen-ki (M), bull-Oryx

seɖah-hi (M), legs of ostrich

seyad-di (Y), (M), oil, ghi

shamei v.t. (Y), (M), take, lead; *so shamei,* bring

shan v.i. (Y), (M), go; *so shan,* come

shani-hi (Y), five

shanshamei v.t. (M), kindle (a fire)

shanso v.t. (Y), take for yourself, keep, put in, carry

shar a. (M), many, plenty

sharei v.t. (M), increase

sharo v.i. (M) be well

shàshin-ki (M), things, property, belongings

shimi v.t. (M), take; *u shimi,* put in

shirfei-di (Y), small quantity

siftihh a. (Y), fat

siftihh-di (Y), fat

silsil-ki (M), hair (usu. plur. *sil-silodi*)

simokh-i (Y), leg

sìr v.i. (M), go

so'oto-di (M), foot, track

sukhodin-ti (M), bow

tabantab v.i. (M), walk, pass, wander

tàgi v.t. (Y), fasten

tahab v.i. (M), move, go; *mahhad u so tahabtei*? what have you come for?

takhalámo-di (Y), song

tegèd v.i. (Y), (M), go; *so tegèd*, come; *alkhail ku tegèd*, ride a horse; *ka tegèd*, cross

tegèji v.t. (Y), send

tingir-ki (M), Waller's Gazelle

tiro-gi (Y), liver

tobani-hi (Y), ten

tomàla a. (Y), hard

tomàla-hi (Y), stone, hill

ukub-ki (M), ram

ulud-di (M), upper arm

'unimadô- (M), cheetah

'unukh-hi (Y), throat

uro-di or ur-ti (Y), stomach

'urshèn a. (Y), bad

'urshèn v.i. (M), smell

'urshèn-ti (M), nose

'urshèni v.t. (M), smell

'urshèni-gi v.t. (M), anything that smells, dung, etc.

uskin-ki (M), leg

wafèr-ki (M), spear

„ (Y), knife, tooth

walahun-ki (Y), spear

Waran-ti (Y), Midgan

watahhó-di (Y), day; *watahhádan*, to-day; *watahhádi darsad*, to-morrow

wawa'li-gi (M), dog

weled-ki (Y), boy

yabar-ki (Y), goods, wealth, property

yabaro v.i. (Y), make your living, earn your living

Yadur-ki (Y), Midgan

yafán or yifan a. (Y), good, right hand

yafnan-ti (Y), goodness, health, Peace

yafneisi v.t. (Y), make good

yafneisiso v.t. (Y), arrange for yourself

yafno v.i. (Y), be good

yagól-ki (M), "herio," camel-mat, hut

yahaínyahh a. (Y), small, bad

yahan-ti (Y), two annas

yahhab-ti (M), herd of Oryx

yal-shi (Y), (M), leg

yaliyifo-hi (Y), shoes

ya'un-ki, -ti (Y), old man, woman; *ya'unti jagh'idei*, mother

yef v.t (Y), (M), turn

yiftimei v.i. (Y), fight

yihan-ki, ti (M), man, woman

yiryiro-hi (M), sheep and goats

COMPARATIVE VOCABULARY OF SOMALI, YIBIR, AND MIDGAN.

English	Somali	Yibir	Midgan
after	dambe	darsad	dibyalin
amulet	ghordas-ki	godahhed-ki	
animal	báhal-ki	dálanga-hi	hangagùri-gi
anna	gambo-di	madôkushan-ki	
2 annas	antìn-ti	yahan-ti	
arm	ga'an-ti	gànad-di	farolahàto-di
army	'oll-ki	alman-ki	moyo-di
arrow	fallàd-di	wafèro yahainyahh	degoyir
backbone	adahh-hi	hawar-ti	
bad	hhun	'urshèn	neghatal
be	aho	la bid (be thought)	
bear (beget)	dal	jagh'id	finfin
before	hor	horyad	horyalin
beg	bari	gorbei	
belly	leg-gi	labodin-ki	labodin-ki
beneath	hòs	hosyad	hosyalin
bird	shimbir-ti	haman-ti	alèliso-di
black	madô	humáksan	neghatal
blood	dìg-gi	'asèro-hi	'asowa-hi
bone	laf-ti	lafil-shi	lafeiti-di
bow	ghànso-di	ildighan-ti	sukhodin-ti
boy	wil-ki	weled-ki	janakh-i
bradawl	muda'-i	mukhtaren-ki	
breast	lab-ti	d'arowa-hi	fèdolahàto-di
bring	{ la kàli	so shimi	so shamei
	{ so kahhai		so 'idbi
burden (of camel)	ákhal-ki	kabàr-ti	yagòl-ki
bush	{ gèd-ki	awas-ki	ghoribirro-di
	{ dir-ti		
buy	ìbso	doïyo	dahhbi
butter	bur'ad-di	buskulohh-i	

English	Somali	Yibir	Midgan
camel (female)	hal-shi	jalan-ti	jalan-ti
„ (male)	aur-ki	{ imil-ki { jalan-ki	bodowa-hi
carry	sido	shanso	raghahho
catch	ghobo	gana'ido	ku raghahho
chest	sakàr-ki		godanahh-i
child	ínan	ilaghan	janakh
cloth	maro-di	kalwein-ti	babàto-di
come	{ imo { kàli	so tegèd (etc.) godis	si idib (etc.)
corpse	miyid-di	rùf-ki	rôf-ki
country	bilád-ki	hig-gi	erifogàd-ki
cow	{ lo'-di { sa'-i	albakhar-ti	bakhar-ti
cup	dàsad-di		gorad-di
cut	goi	bilehh	gôsad ku raghahh
dates	timir-ti	'aser-ti	{ 'assi-di { nahhad-ki
day	màlin-ti	watahho-di	iftimowa-hi
die	bakhti	rùf	rôf
dig	ghod		damòmei
do	{ fal { ghobo { samei	aweilei	raghahh
dog	eï-gi		wawa'li-gi
donkey	dabeir-ki	himár-ki	{ buf-ki { degig-gi
drink	'ab	'ido	kusho
dung	hàr-ki		'urshèni-gi
ear	ḍeg-ti	makhali-di	makhashin-ti
eat	'un	'ido	kusho
evening	galáb-ti	galabi-di	iftimowihi negh-atala
ewe	sabein-ti	ilbir-ti	
eye	il-shi (pl. indo)	ain-ti	indókhol-shi
far	fòg		erifogàd-ki
fat (n.)	haid-di	{ sahol-shi { siftihh-di	dahir-ki
tail-fat	baḍi-di	kubi'in-ti	
fear	bagho	bagho	dukhun
feather	bàl-ki		rèr-ki

English	Somali	Yibir	Midgan
fight	dirir	yiftimei	iss duk
finger	far-ti	deri-gi	
fire (and fire-arm)	dab-ki	ilohh-i	bulal-ki
flask	weiso-di	lawodaur-ki	gabar-ti
food	sor-ti	manaho-di	
foot	ag-ti	ilan-ti	so'oto-di
forge (v.)	tun	awèlei	bulalyei
frighten	baji	baghi	dukhumei
Gala	Gàlo-hi	Aiyifan-ti	
ghi	subukh-i	seyad-di	dahir-ki
girl	gabad-di	ilaghan-ti	janakh-di
give	sì	'id	kul
go	{ tag { so'o	{ tegèd { shan { bidbidei	{ tegèd { shan { 'idib { tahab { sir
goat (female)	ri-di	amèd-di	salôlad-di
„ (male)	orgi-gi	yahan-ki	salôlad-ki
God	Ilahh	Awashona	
good	wanáksan	yafan, yifan	ghànsan
goodness		yifnan-ti	
be good	samo	yifno	ghàmo
make good	(samei = make)	yifneisi	ghàmi
grass	aus-ki	awas-ki	aus-ki
great	wein	àniah	ghàn
greatness	weinan-ti	àni-gi	
gulp	lukho		boba'un
hair	timo-hi	humáksano-hi	silsilo-di
half	bad-ki	kalahed-ki	kul-ki
hand	ga'an-ti	gànad-di	{ gànad-di { farolahàto-di
hard	adag	tomàlaäh	makabùr
have	{ haï { laho	ku dashì	ku dashì ku raghahhsan
head	madah-hi	bakhrin-ki	bakhrin-ki
hear	makhal	makhalei	makhashimei
heart	wadna-hi	kunòli-hi	
hill	bùr-ti	tomàla-hi	makabùr-ti
horse	fáras-ki	alkhail-ki	{ gararàti-gi { fùf-ki
house	ákhal-ki	kabàr-ti	yagòl-ki

K.   14

English	Somali	Yibir	Midgan
how many ?	ìmisa ?	inhíma ?	inhíma ?
hot	kulul	ilohh	
hump (of camel)	kurus-ki	fidsìn-ki	
hunger	gajo-di	nafèl-ki	
be hungry	gajo	nafèlo	guratádi wa negh-atál
improve	wanaji	yifneisi	ghàmi
increase	{ badi kordi	ghandìdei	sharei
iron	bir-ti	halyokho-di	gôsad-di
jowaree	harùd-ki	fil tomàlah	
jugular vessels	tuman-ki	dubadyo-hi	
kid	makhal-shi	jagho-di	janakh-di
kill	dil	rùfi	{ rôfi orèmi
kindle (fire)	shid	aweilei	shanshamei
knife	bilawa-hi	wafèr-ki	gôsad-di
language	{ af-ki hádal-ki	khabar-ki	afjaghin-ki baghdan-ki
leave	da	ladishei	dujo
leg	lug-ti	yal-shi	{ yal-shi uskin-ki
lend	amahho	maghùr	
lie (untruth)	bein-ti	{ hekho-di aintoli-di	
lie down	jìf	midi	limdi
light (n.)	if-ki	iftin-ki	iftimòwa-hi
like (v.)	ja'alaho	ku bi'yuso	ku raghahhsano
limb	lahhad-ki		ilbir-ki
listen	degeiso	makhaleido	makhashimeiso
liver	bèr-ki	tiro-gi	madôbiyo-hi
loins	sarar-ki	{ robsahan-ki nirokh-i	robsahan-ki
long	der	der	ghàn
look	eg	ainta ku yef	indokholei
look for	dòno	fedo	raghahhsano
loot	{ da' la tag	alman	la sir
mad	wallan	hainyalisan	
madness	wallo-di	hainyali-di	
make	samei	aweilei	raghhah
man	nin-ki	goried-ki	goried-ki

English	Somali	Yibir	Midgan
old man	odei-gi	ya'un-ki	yahan-ki
many	badan	ghandìdah	shar
marriage	aros-ki	saradoshis-ki	
marry	gùrso	aweiliso	raghahho
mat (prayer-mat)	masàla-hi	huwad-ki	dikhràrin-ki
meat	hilib-ki	gujin-ki	rihin-ki
Midgan	Midgàn-ki	{ Yadur-ki Waran-ti	Alowa-hi
milk	'ano-hi	gòdib-ki	adeisímo-di
money	la'ag-ti	iftimo-hi	makabùr-ti
moon	dayah-hi	iftin-ki	iftimowihi himirka
mouth	af-ki	katowa-hi	afjaghin-ti
near	ag-ti		gonia-hi
new	'usub	ànisan	
news	war-ki	khabar-ki	baghdan-ki
night	habèn-ki	humag-gi	himir-ki
no	maaha, maya	ha bidin	
nose	san-ki	saneg-gi	'urshèn-ti
other	kăleh	kelemad	
ox	dibi-gi	jindar-ki	
peace	nabad	yifnan-ti	
people	{ dad-ki răg-i	moyo-di goried-di	moyo-di
person	ghof-ki	deri-gi	
penis	gus-ki	mirdolo-hi	ludub-ki
place	hag-gi	hig-gi	{ hig-gi nas-ki
plant (n.)	beir-ti	awas-ki	mirgin-ki
plate	hedo-di	ghorin-ki	maruba-hi
plenty	in badan	ghandìd-ki	shar
pluck	rif		rug
pray	tuko	anghakso	
put down	dig	midsi	raghahhi
put in	rid	shanso	
quantity	in-ti	inhi-di	inhi-di
quiver	gaboyo-di		hur-ki
rain	ròb-ki	lawo-hi	gomosímo-di
ram	wan-ki	ilowa-hi	ukub-ki
red	'as	'asèrah	
refuse	dìd	dangharei	
remain	jòg	midi	raghahhsan
"rer" (family)	rèr-ki	à-di (pl. ayo-hi)	yagòl-ki

English	Somali	Yibir	Midgan
rice	barìs-ki	fil iftin	langharomed-ki
right hand	midig-ti	yifan	
ring	katun-ki	kushan-ki	
rope	haďig-gi	difad-ki	hajìa-hi
rosary	tusbah-hi	goďerowi-gi	alel-ki
run	orod	bidbid	
rupee	rubiad	iftin-ti	falèď-di
sandal	kab-ti	yaliyifo-hi	jagaflaho-di
satchel	ghandi-gi	nàni-gi	
say	oďo	(see "speak")	
see	arag	aimei	dag
send	dir kahhai	shimi tegèji bidbidsei	shamei
sheep	aďi-gi	daďo-di	yeryero-hi
shew	tus	aimidsi	indokholeisi dagsi
shield	gashan-ki	altob-ki	gabis-ki gaďlahàto-di
sheep skin	harag-gi		huwìya-hi
ship	markab-ki	ghorin-ki	
skin	sàn-ti	huwad-ki	gaďlahàto-di
slaughter	ghal	sakhsakh	
sleep	sehho	limdi	alemdi
small	yer	yahainyahh	neghatál
smell (v. t.)	ʿurso		ʿurshèni
smell (v. i.)	ʿur		ʿurshèn
Somali	Somàli-di	Goried-ki	Àji-gi
song	gabei-gi	takalámo-di	
speak	hadal	khabrei lagh	baghdan
stick	ùl-shi	bulbul-shi	ghoribirro-di
still (be)	jògso		irso
stomach	alòl-shi	ùro-di	gurato-di
stone	dagahh-i	tomàla-hi	makabùr-ti
strike	ku dufo		aghtul duk
sun	ghorahh-di	iftin-ti	iftimowa-hi
tail	dibo-di	daras-ti	dibyalin-ki
take	ghad	shimi	shamei
take to yourself	ghado	shanso	shanso
then	kolkas	kulhidas	naskas
there	haggà	higgà	higgà naskà

English	Somali	Yibir	Midgan
thigh	bôdo-di	derighab-ki	
thing	wahh-i	deri-gi (indef.)	nas-ki
		agar-ti (concrete)	
		khabar-ki (abstract)	
(possessions)	ghalab-ki	à-di	shàshin-ki
think	mòd	bìd	
throat	hungùri-gi	unukh-i	lakhowa-hi
time	kol-ki (etc.)	kulhi-di	nas-ki (?)
tobacco	bùri-gi	madô-di	
to-day	manta	watahhádan	iftimowaha
Tomal	Tomàl-ki	Àbir-ki	Handud-ki
to-morrow	berrì	watahhádi darsad	iftimowihi so tegè-deya
tongue	arab-ti	laghdam-ki	laghowa-hi
tooth	ilig-gi	wafèr-ki	
town	magàlo-di	kalweinaleh-di	nas-ki (?)
track	ràd-ki		so'oto-di
trap	dabin-ti		hajìa-hi
tree	gèd-ki	awas-ki	gèdgharoméd-ki
truth	run-ti	ghamagh-di	ghàn
turn	rug	yef	yef
under	hos	hosyad	hosyalin
understand	garo	ku duhur	dag
useful	fi'an	behhensan	
water	bìyo-hi	lawo-hi	gomosímo-di
when	kolki	kulhídi	
when ?	gorma ?	kulhíma ?	
where	haggi	higgi	higgi
where ?	hagge ?	higge ? / higma ?	higge ? / higma ?
white	'ad	iftin	
whip	jèdal-ki	bulbul-ki	ghorin-ki
wing	bàl-ki		imitirahh-i
wish	dòn	fed	ku raghahhsan
woman	nàg-ti	asuwan-ti	awin-ti / asahan-ti
	habàr-ti	ya'un-ti	yihan-ti / golof-ti
wood	ghori-gi		ghoribirro-di
word	erei-gi	deri-gi	
year	gù-gi	lawo-hi	erifogad-ki
yesterday	shălei	watahhádi horyad	iftimowihi tegèdei
Yibir	Yibir-ki	Anas-ki	Hanan-ki

NUMBERS.

English	Somali	Yibir	Midgan
one	mid	deri (=finger)	
two	laba	limihi	
three	sadehh	sadehhi	
four	afar	aferi	
five	shan	gànad (=hand)	
six	lehh	gànad iyo deri	
ten	toban	limihi gànadod, or tobanihi	
fifteen	shanyo-toban	sadehhi gànadod	
hundred	boghol	goɖerowi-gi (=rosary of 100 beads)	
thousand	kun	tobanihi goɖerowiyod	

The Midgans use the Yibir numbers up to ten.

NAMES OR DESCRIPTIONS OF WILD ANIMALS.

Caracal	jambèl		jimikh
Cheetah	harimad		'unimadô
Dikdik	sagàro	d.* yahainyahha awaski ka godisa	bikho
Elephant	maròdi		dusár
Fox	da'wo	d. daɖo 'ita	humbur
Gazelle, Clarke's	dibotag	d. darasti tegèja	diboɖèr
„ Soemmering's	'aul	d. darasti iftimaleh	gosinki (buck) jehhar
„ Speke's	dèro	d. amèɖo la hega	abàbo
„ Waller's	gerenùk	d. la bilehhoda	tingir geryal (buck) lig
Guinea-fowl	digirin		oran
Haartebeest	sig	d. albakharki	dabo'ad
Hyaena	waràba	d. khábarki ghandiɖsanleh	furat
Koodoo	aderyo		goɖir
Leopard	shabèl	d. amèɖo 'ita	dussi
Lion	libahh	d. jalmo 'ita	hangagùri ghàn
Oryx	b'e'id	d. walahumo ku dashìya	{ gesoder, gesolahato (buck) saryen
herd of Oryx			yahhab-ki
Ostrich	gorei, halɖa		{ hedig, gir, sareyagh
O. feather	bàl		rish
Rhinoceros	wìyil		amadur
Tortoise	din	makabùr	madôla

* Note. ɖ (in Yibir) represents **dálanga** animal.

INDEX.

The numbers refer to the sections.

CAMBRIDGE: PRINTED BY JOHN CLAY, M.A. AT THE UNIVERSITY PRESS.

For EU product safety concerns, contact us at Calle de José Abascal, 56–1°, 28003 Madrid, Spain or eugpsr@cambridge.org.

www.ingramcontent.com/pod-product-compliance
Ingram Content Group UK Ltd.
Pitfield, Milton Keynes, MK11 3LW, UK
UKHW010337140625
459647UK00010B/661